Authors Inc.

Authors Inc.

Literary Celebrity in the
Modern United States, 1880–1980

Loren Glass

NEW YORK UNIVERSITY PRESS

New York and London

NEW YORK UNIVERSITY PRESS
New York and London
www.nyupress.org

Gertrude Stein signature is printed courtesy of the Yale Collection of
American Literature, Beinecke Rare Book and Manuscript Library.

Jack London signature is printed courtesy of the Huntington Library,
San Marino, California.

Library of Congress Cataloging-in-Publication Data
Glass, Loren Daniel.
Authors Inc. : literary celebrity in the modern United States,
1880–1980 / Loren Daniel Glass.
p. cm.
Includes bibliographical references and index.
ISBN 0–8147–3159–7 (cloth : alk. paper) —
ISBN 0–8147–3160–0 (pbk. : alk. paper)
 1. Authorship—Social aspects—United States—History—
20th century.   2. American literature—20th century—History
and criticism—Theory, etc.   3. Literature—Appreciation—United
States—History—20th century.   4. Celebrities—United States—
Biography—History and criticism.   5. Literature and society—
United States—History—20th century.   6. Authors and readers—
United States—History—20th century.   7. Authors, American—
Biography—History and criticism.   8. Canon (Literature)
9. Autobiography.   I. Title.
PS221.G55   2004
810.9'005—dc22   2004002301

New York University Press books are printed on acid-free paper,
and their binding materials are chosen for strength and durability.

Manufactured in the United States of America

c 10 9 8 7 6 5 4 3 2 1
p 10 9 8 7 6 5 4 3 2 1

For my father

In America everybody is
but some are more than others.

—Gertrude Stein

Contents

Acknowledgments

The long process of writing this book felt like a solitary affair, but now that *Authors Inc.* is completed, I realize that there are many people to thank. Although the final project bears little resemblance to the dissertation from which it emerged, it still bears the marks of my original committee: Janice Radway, Fredric Jameson, Jane Gaines, Cathy Davidson, and Tom Ferraro. Jan Radway, in particular, as chair, has been and remains a model of professional integrity and methodological rigor in the study of American popular culture. Borislav Knezevic and Helen Thompson, my friends and fellow graduate students at Duke University, also supplied invaluable support at all stages of this project. Much of the early revision occurred during my year as an external fellow at the Oregon State University Center for the Humanities; I would like to thank the late Peter Copek, professor of English and director of the Humanities Center, for providing me with that valuable fellowship. I would also like to thank Ralph Rodriguez and Shawn Smith for their insight and support during my stay at the Humanities Center. I was materially supported in my research for this project by an Archie Research Fellowship from Wake Forest University, which enabled me to spend time with the Jack London Collection at the Huntington Library, and a research grant from the JFK Library at Boston University, where the Hemingway Collection is housed. I also owe a debt of gratitude to Louis Suarez-Potts, who provided invaluable assistance for my research in the Mark Twain Papers at the Bancroft Library of the University of California, Berkeley. David Bergman, Jennifer Ballengee, and Don-John Dugas, at Towson University, and Simon During, at Johns Hopkins University, offered useful suggestions during the later stages of revision. I want to express grateful acknowledgment to *American Literary History*, where an earlier version of chapter 2, "Trademark Twain," appeared in vol. 13:4, December 2001; grateful acknowledgment is also given to *American Literature*, where an earlier version of chapter 3, "Legitimating London," appeared in vol. 71:3, September 1999. I would also like to thank the two anonymous readers at New York University Press, whose comments were extremely helpful.

Introduction

Authorial Personality in the
American Field of Cultural Production

Gertrude Stein rarely doubted herself or the value of her work. Though she was frustrated by her inability to get published in the 1910s and 1920s, she maintained a stubborn confidence, supported by a small coterie of friends and confidantes, that she was the most important writer of the twentieth century, a modern literary genius. When, however, after the publication of the phenomenally successful *Autobiography of Alice B. Toklas* in 1933 and her triumphant tour of the United States in 1934 and 1935, she finally achieved the recognition she always knew she deserved, Stein suffered from both an identity crisis and writer's block. *Everybody's Autobiography*, published in 1937, was her reflection on these uncomfortable consequences of success in the United States. Stein claims:

> It is funny about money. It is funny about identity. You are you because your little dog knows you, but when your public knows you and does not want to pay for you and when your public knows you and does want to pay for you, you are not the same you.[1]

The transformation of the literary value of a text in turn transforms the identity of the author who wrote it. Now that Stein was the world-famous writer she had always known she would become, she felt strangely as if she had become someone other than who she had been before.

Stein had, in short, become a celebrity. Her triumphant return to the United States was announced on the front page of most of the urban dailies; her name appeared in neon lights on Broadway; she was flocked by interviewers and autograph seekers. Suddenly, Stein saw her name everywhere, and strangers recognized her on the street. She had earlier alleged, "I write for myself and strangers," but this self recognized by strangers felt different than the one for whom she originally wrote.[2] Her celebrity had oddly conflated "myself and strangers" into a new public subject irreducible to either author or audience.

Celebrity Theory and Authorial Autobiography

Authors Inc. tracks the developments in American cultural and literary history that enabled Stein, an author whose writing few Americans would even attempt to read, to become for a time one of the most celebrated literary figures in the United States. Stein entered into an already-established authorial star system in which the marketable "personalities" of authors were frequently as important as the quality of their literary production. Authorial celebrities from Jack London and Edith Wharton to F. Scott Fitzgerald and Anita Loos had become loosely integrated into the larger market in "personalities," and famous authors had become part of the public "society" about which gossip and information circulated in popular newspapers and magazines. Although many high modernist authors dismissed the American culture of celebrity, Stein's fame confirmed that the modernist "genius" could easily become a star.

This modernist dismissal of U.S. mass culture has caused literary and cultural critics, until recently, to neglect the central role of celebrity in the careers of many classic American authors. The seemingly unbridgeable divide between literature and mass culture mandated that such apparently ephemeral and trivial phenomena be relegated to the "minor" genres of biography and literary gossip. Despite all evidence to the contrary, authors and the critics who canonize them have traditionally worked under the assumption that great literature is somehow beyond or outside the logic of the market.

This assumption has been challenged by more recent scholarship. Marshaling the formidable critical arsenal established by two decades of theoretical and methodological transformation in the humanities, scholars such as Daniel Borus, Amy Kaplan, Thomas Strychacz, Jennifer Wicke, and Christopher Wilson have revealed the degree to which canonical American authors have been engaged by and implicated in the U.S. mass marketplace.[3] Nevertheless, no book-length study has emerged that considers the central role of celebrity in this relationship. *Authors Inc.* is meant to prove that such a consideration is crucial to our understanding of literary authorship in the twentieth century.

If the significance of celebrity authorship has been somewhat neglected in recent cultural studies, the role of celebrity itself has suffered from no such neglect. In fact, it could legitimately be labeled a growth industry. P. David Marshall's *Celebrity and Power* is one of the more useful and stimulating studies to emerge in this new field. Marshall effectively emplots the historical imbrication of capitalism and democracy that has given rise to the contemporary culture of celebrity, and summarizes the theoretical methodologies that have proven helpful for its analysis. He settles on a semiotic understanding of the culture of celebrity in which "the celebrity sheds its own subjectivity and individuality and becomes an organizing structure for conventionalized meaning."[4] Consequently, "the denotative level of meaning of the celebrity is the empty structure of the material reality of the actual person."[5] This bracketing of the "material reality of the actual person" in turn becomes central to Marshall's methodological approach to the analysis of the celebrity text.

Marshall's study represents an important methodological and historical synthesis in celebrity criticism, a subfield of cultural studies established by the publication of Richard Dyer's groundbreaking *Stars*.[6] Like Dyer, Marshall both documents the historical rise of modern celebrity and summarizes the various approaches that have been developed for its academic analysis. Both books reveal the degree to which the academic study of celebrity has emerged as a dialectical response to the popular obsession with the "material reality of the actual person" that Marshall brackets as fundamentally "empty." Thus, Marshall opens his work by essentially dismissing "popular studies of celebrity," including celebrity autobiographies, as ideologically mystified attempts to "uncover the 'real' person behind the public persona."[7] His book then proceeds to illustrate how celebrity criticism can work to demystify the rhetoric of individualism that informs these more popular celebrity discourses.

Marshall's work shows how the opposition between high and low persists as a ballast for critical authority. It is not surprising, then, that neither Dyer nor Marshall deal extensively with literary or intellectual celebrity. Rather, they focus on the modern culture industries of film, music, and television, in which the individual agency behind the celebrity persona is clearly vitiated, if not irrelevant. The enormous scale and scope of the corporate culture industries in relation to any discrete individual makes it easy to conceive of the "celebrity" as the product of an impersonal system that responds to the needs of an equally vast and amorphous audience. Writers, on the other hand, have sustained an ethos of individual creative production over and against the rise of these culture industries in which they nevertheless have had to participate. The individual authorial consciousness as elaborated by the practice of modernist authorship stubbornly persists as something more than an empty structure, complicating the easy dismissal of the celebrity's subjectivity in so much recent celebrity theory.

Marshall claims that "the 'celebrity function' is as important as Foucault's 'author-function' in its power to organize the legitimate and illegitimate domains of the personal and individual within the social."[8] Marshall's reference to Michel Foucault is as significant here as his correlation between authorship and celebrity since Foucault—along with Roland Barthes, Jacques Derrida, and a host of other French theorists—has, in essence, enacted a peculiar modulation between these two functions in the American academic public sphere. This highly ironic oscillation between pop celebrity and authorial genius retrospectively illuminates the intimate relations between modernist modes of authorial self-fashioning and mass cultural models of fame. Foucault and Barthes, in particular, have come to be associated with the "death of the author," and the replacement of the authorial consciousness by the freer play of the "text." And yet, both theorists, unwittingly or not, found themselves objects of intense cults of personality that seemed to contradict their own theories of textuality.

Both Foucault, in "What Is an Author?" and Barthes, in "The Death of the Author," posit authorship as a historically variable belief about the source of texts—a belief whose centrality to literary production was challenged by the rise of modernism. Hence, Barthes contends that while "the image of literature to be found in ordinary culture is tyrannically centred on the author, his person, his life," it was Stéphane Mallarmé who began to see "the necessity to substitute language itself for the person who until then had been supposed to be its owner." Similarly, Foucault, mobilizing Gustave Flaubert, Marcel Proust, and Franz Kafka as signal examples, maintains that "writing has freed itself from the dimensions of expression. Referring only to itself, but without being restricted to the confines of its interiority, writing is identified with its own unfolded exteriority." Despite their differences, both essays affirm and celebrate the liberation of the text from the author as opening up a new terrain of linguistic indeterminacy and free play. It would be difficult to underestimate the influence they have had on an entire generation of literary and cultural critics in U.S. universities.[9]

I would argue, however, that they have had a paradoxical effect. On the one hand, if they have precipitated an enormously enriched understanding of the historically variable functions of the author, they have also ironically elevated figures such as Foucault and Barthes to almost legendary status as authors and writers themselves. They have become famous authors precisely by announcing the death of the author. As Seán Burke confirms in his study of *The Death and Return of the Author*:

> They have been accorded all the privileges traditionally bestowed upon the great author. No contemporary author can lay claim to anything approaching the authority that their texts have enjoyed over the last twenty years or so. Indeed, were we in search of the most flagrant abuses of critical *auteurism* in recent times then we need look no further than the secondary literature on Barthes, Foucault, and Derrida, which is for the most part given over to scrupulously faithful and almost timorous reconstitutions of their thought.[10]

This apparent contradiction strikingly resembles the careers of the modernist authors to whose work they recur.[11] Few things are more striking about the primary spokespeople for modernism than the contrast between their stated theories of self-effacement and their actual practice and literary-historical destiny of self-aggrandizement and even shameless self-promotion. T. S. Eliot no sooner claimed that poetry should be an "escape from personality" than he became the object of an international personality cult, eventually appearing on the cover of *Time*.[12] James Joyce could affirm that the author sat invisible, "paring his fingernails" behind the text; but he nevertheless became at least as well known as he was well read, particularly after the censorship of *Ulysses*.[13] In fact, the entire modernist "lost generation" was absorbed into American mainstream culture through a bombardment of gossipy memoirs that affirmed the mass cultural cachet of the personalities behind these persistent assertions of "impersonality."[14]

This tension between impersonality and personality was not only an expression of the modernist resistance to mass cultural commodification; as Eliot's famous dictum reveals, it was also internal to modernist understandings of the relation between author and text. Poetry may be an escape from personality and emotion, but "only those who have personality and emotions know what it means to want to escape from these things."[15] For Eliot, the exceptional personality is the necessary condition for the escape from personality. The personal biography of the literary artist may, as the new critics insisted, be "extrinsic" to the meaning of the work of art, but it remains significant for the exclusive social world of "those who have personality and emotions" in which the work of art circulates. For modernist artists, personality in the biographical sense tended to be sublimated into the concept of "style," which as Barthes affirms, "has its roots in the depths of the author's personal and secret mythology."[16] Personality continued to function as a factor in the literary field, even if one of the interpretive tenets of that field was to bracket it from the successful work of art. Certainly Eliot's own gaunt, vampiric pose and high-priestly charisma became tightly associated with his critical and poetic style as his fame and influence increased. This new critical take on authorial personality embodies a contradiction not unlike what Pierre Bourdieu identifies as the literary "interest in disinterestedness."[17] Much as modernist artists were interested in appearing disinterested, their personality tended to inhere in their ability to escape personality through rendering it as style. This contradiction would become particularly acute in the modern United States due to the highly unstable relations between what Bourdieu calls "the field of restricted production," in which writers and artists produce for a small public of each other, and the "field of large-scale production," in which writers and artists produce for the "general public."[18] In the modern European field of cultural production from which Bourdieu draws his examples, the split between the avant-garde and bourgeois was concretely undergirded by well-established cultural hierarchies and institutionally separated markets for art and literature. In the modern United States—with a much-less-established tradition of high culture and a far-more-developed mass cultural public sphere—many authors whose self-understanding was based in European models of restricted production found themselves having to adapt to the marketing strategies and audience sensibilities of large-scale production. In fact, the volatile passage from the restricted elite audience of urban bohemia and "little magazines" to the mass audience of the U.S. middlebrow became a signature career arc for American modernist writers. Along this arc, the model of the author as a solitary creative genius whose work goes unrecognized by the mainstream collides with the model of the author as part of a corporate publisher's marketing strategy. It is in the tensions between these two fields that the contradictions of modern American authorial celebrity emerge.

In order to unpack these contradictions, I turn to the very genre that Marshall excludes: the autobiography. Autobiographies of celebrated authors explicitly dwell on the tension between private creation and public appropriation, and reveal how the two emerge in dialectical relation. As Mutlu Konuk Blasing affirms, authorial autobiography

> represents a self-examination that is at the same time private and public, for the interaction of personality and collective life that autobiography embodies is reflected in the author's personal appropriation of the language of the times. Since autobiography thus bridges public and private life, the hero of autobiography is the paradoxical private-person-as-public-hero.[19]

This "paradoxical private-person-as-public-hero" can be seen as the textual location where the modernist creative consciousness comes up against the public personality. In authorial autobiographies, we witness the author explicitly attempting to reappropriate the public discourse that determines the authorial career.

Blasing quite broadly defines autobiography as "works in which the hero, narrator, and author can be identified by the same name"—a definition that has been codified by Philippe Lejeune as "the autobiographical pact," wherein the name on the cover confirms for the reader that "the author, the narrator, and the protagonist" are identical.[20] Lejeune's notion of the autobiographical pact has been enormously useful for scholars of autobiography in its apparent resolution of both autobiography's generic ambiguity and its problematic claims for reference. As John Paul Eakin contends,

> The beauty of the emphasis on the identity of the proper name is that it seems to locate the problem of generic definition safely in the text, free from any messy extratextual involvement with the ethic of sincerity that has bedeviled the poetics of autobiography since Rousseau. The importance of the autobiographical pact in the text, nevertheless, resides in the fact that it is willy-nilly the sign of an intention.[21]

For Eakin, the genre of autobiography challenges both new critical and poststructuralist erasures of authorial intention and control. In fact, the introductory discussion in Eakin's important study focuses on the "autobiography" of Barthes. Eakin brilliantly reads Barthes's claim that "in the field of the subject, there is no referent," over and against Barthes's late-career fascination with the referential possibilities of photography, arguing that in the end, "autobiography is nothing if not a referential art, and the self or subject is its principal referent."[22] And Eakin concludes that by reproducing his own handwriting on the flyleaf of the French edition of *Roland Barthes*, Barthes betrays "in the signature the very affiliation with the world of reference that the words purport to deny."[23]

This stubborn fascination with the possibility that the name, in the end, must somehow mandate a referential relation between the private consciousness from which writing emerges and the public sphere in which it circulates undergirds the culture of authorial celebrity. In this study, I have deliberately selected protomodernist and modernist texts that challenge or pressure the autobiographical pact in order to document the degree to which celebrity troubled many American authors' sense of their relation to their texts and audiences. Celebrity challenged deeply held convictions about authorial inspiration and property in texts by appearing to cede creative agency and control to the mass audience and literary marketplace. It is my argument that in the collision between private interiority and public exteriority that these texts document, we can see emerging the intimate dialectical relation between modernist authorship and mass cultural celebrity that deeply informed the field of cultural production in the twentieth-century United States.

Literary Property and the Right to Privacy

Any study that deals with the emergence of a modern culture of celebrity in the United States must engage the work of Warren Susman, whose essay "'Personality' and the Making of Twentieth-Century Culture" established the shift from nineteenth-century moral character to twentieth-century performative personality as a foundational interpretative paradigm for any cultural history of the U.S. self during this era. Susman's observation that "character . . . is either good or bad; personality, famous or infamous," economically indicates the pertinence of his paradigm for the emergence of modern celebrity.[24] Susman himself notes that the "new consciousness of personality . . . leads . . . to a new profession—that of being a movie star or a celebrity."[25]

This easy contrast between character and personality, and the apparently obvious correlation between personality and celebrity, however, risks obscuring the complications and contradictions of this new "modal type of person."[26] The emergence of "personality" has become virtually axiomatic as an interpretative paradigm in American cultural history, leading many critics and historians to overlook the ambiguity of the term. In particular, I would like to examine the term's relation to contemporaneous debates over intellectual property and the right to privacy.

The close relation between these debates, and the centrality of the term personality to their discussion, is foregrounded in Samuel Warren and Louis Brandeis's highly influential article "The Right to Privacy" in the *Harvard Law Review*. Warren and Brandeis worry that "instantaneous photographs and newspaper enterprise have invaded the sacred precincts of private and domestic life."[27] They lament that "gossip has become a trade." In an uncannily contemporary-sounding panic, they warn that "to satisfy a prurient taste the details of sexual relations are spread broadcast in the columns of the daily papers."[28] In order to protect against this scrutiny, Warren and Brandeis argue for what many legal scholars have agreed was an unprecedented right: "the right to privacy, as part of the more general right to the immunity of the person,—the right to one's own personality."[29] This personality, according to the authors, is both "intangible" and "inviolate."[30]

Their logic turns on the question of whether or not personality can be considered a form of property. At first, they appear to assume that the answer is yes: Those intangible qualities that make up "one's own personality" can be recognized as legal property since the flexibility of common law has gradually expanded the definition of property to include "every form of possession—intangible, as well as tangible."[31] As evidence, they draw an analogy between the "inviolate personality" and intellectual property, affirming "the common law secures to each individual the right of determining, ordinarily, to what extent his thoughts, sentiments, and emotions shall be communicated to others."[32] This common law right has normally been construed as an instance of a right of property in that literary and artistic productions are the product of intellectual labor from which the author has a right to profit.

At this point, however, the authors are forced to concede that "where the value of the production is found not in the right to take profits arising from publication, but in the peace of mind or the relief afforded by the ability to prevent any publication at all, it is difficult to regard the right as one of property."[33] Since it takes no real labor to produce one's "inviolate personality," and it involves no economic loss to have it publicized, it is hard to construe it as a form of property in the Lockean sense. The analogy with copyright breaks down here since personality does not seem to have the same relation as the literary text either to the labor theory of value or the economic system of exchange.

Warren and Brandeis attempt to resolve this difficulty by inverting the relation between copyright and privacy, making the former logically dependent on the latter. First, they confirm that copyright, though a right of property, is independent of an artistic or literary work's actual manifestation in the marketplace and material world. Thus,

> the protection afforded by the common law to the author of any writing is entirely independent of its pecuniary value, its intrinsic merits, or of any intention to publish the same, and, of course, also wholly independent of the material, if any, upon which, or the mode in which, the thought or sentiment was expressed.[34]

Following the established definitions of intellectual property, the authors confirm that ideas are independent of their material expression. By also rendering ideas independent of "pecuniary value," though, they make it difficult to sustain the logic of intangible possession with which they began. If intellectual property is independent of both its material expression *and* its pecuniary value, it is hard to see how it can be construed as property at all. It is at this point that the authors invert the relation between copyright and privacy by claiming that common law understandings of copyright depend on a prior assumption of a right to privacy: "The principle which protects personal writings and all other personal productions, not against theft and physical appropriation, but against publication in any form, is in reality not the principle of private property, but that of an inviolate personality."[35]

Warren and Brandeis's article figures prominently in the conclusion to Mark Rose's important study of the eighteenth-century origins of copyright, in which he alleges that their instinct to establish copyright as a precedent for the right to privacy was sound since "the institution of copyright stands squarely on the boundary between private and public."[36] Yet he neglects to consider why this particular impulse would emerge at this time, or why, a hundred years after what most scholars agree to be the key century in the development of copyright law, Warren and Brandeis felt the need to invert the order of precedent between privacy and property.

In fact, Warren and Brandeis's almost deliberate failure to establish a specific property in which their right to privacy inheres registers a striking transformation in the structure of the U.S. public sphere after the Civil War. With the emergence of new media, an industrial economy, and an urban mass society, public and private realms interpenetrated in new ways. On the one hand, private life increasingly achieved its significance through public exposure in the new metropolitan dailies and mass-market magazines that so distressed Warren and Brandeis; on the other hand, this public exposure was increasingly understood in terms of a mass public engrossed in the private experience of reading and consuming.[37]

Indeed, as the reading public expanded and transformed in the decades following the Civil War, figures in the publishing industry became increasingly concerned about what Henry Dwight Sedgewick designated "The Mob Spirit in Literature." With a nervousness not unrelated to Warren and Brandeis, Sedgewick fears that the audience for literature had become "increasingly vehement in its likes, dislikes, and opinions, forces the book on its neighbors with greater rigor, buys, borrows, gives, and lends more and more with the swift and sure emotions of instinct."[38] Many in the magazine and book industries worried about the effect this mob spirit might have on the reputation of authors, production of literature, and habits of readers in the United States. Established cultural hierarchies seemed to be threatened by the increasing interpenetration of literary and mass cultural fields.

Popular literature had, of course, caused anxiety for the cultural elite over the entire course of the nineteenth century, but the emergence of mass society altered the cultural and institutional coordinates of this concern. For one thing, publishers and editors came to believe that "a large part of our population consists of actual or would-be authors."[39] The national mass public came to consist of potential authors and cultural producers; readers became theoretically interchangeable with the famous authors whose texts they read. Julian Hawthorne decried the fact that

the ease with which [books] are produced in material form, and the cheapness of their price, causes them to be read by everyone, and the familiarity with methods of literary composition thus acquired enables anyone, almost, to write books that publishers will print and the public will read.[40]

How-to and advice columns proliferated for those who wanted to get into print, and editors and publishers trumpeted their openness to and desire for new authors; access to publication and publicity became, at least rhetorically, far more democratic.

As a result of these developments, the very definition of an author underwent a crisis economically illustrated by a brief satiric sketch in the November 1901 issue of the industry journal *Bookman*, titled "An Interview with Nobody." This sketch begins on the same page as a poem titled "A Ballade of Ambition," the envoi of which reads: "Oh, Fame, I ask not gilding bright / Nor brave *éditions de luxe*; / But grant that I may someday write / One of the six Best-selling Books."[41] Thus, the poem emplots a shift from the historically established understanding of literary fame as based in a restricted market of "*éditions de luxe*," to an emergent understanding based in a general market of "Best-selling Books" (*Bookman* instituted the first best-seller list in 1895).[42] By placing the poem directly before the interview, the editors encourage the reader to assume that "An Interview with Nobody" represents someone who has achieved this new form of literary celebrity.

The brief piece promptly confirms this assumption with the claim: "A new star has arisen in the literary firmament in the person of Mr. Zero O. Nobody, whose recent book, *No Matter What* . . . has sold five hundred thousand copies before publication."[43] This opening introduces the two principal tropes of authorial fame: it erases authorial identity, and it inverts the logic of literary value. The article pursues its logic of negating authorial identity throughout, continuing with a standard biographical blurb that "Mr. Nobody was born and erased in Nowhere, New Jersey." Mr. Nobody then boldly asserts that he has "no methods, no style, no knowledge. . . . I depend entirely upon nothing for inspiration, and leave the rest to my publishers."[44] Mr. Nobody's pure, empty generality functions as a revealing caricature of literary celebrity, which clearly is perceived here as having nothing to do with authorial identity or individual talent. Rather, Mr. Nobody is simply a new form of corporate property.

This strategy inverts the calculus whereby the literary value of the text would correspond to the labor and talent of the author. Mr. Nobody concedes that "we sell so many more copies before than after publication," confirming that the value of the book corresponds to the economic investment in its promotion.[45] The article assumes that, traditionally, the value of a text is based on its contents, which can only be judged after the book is read, and which is then critically attributed to the literary labor exerted by the talented author. But in this new corporate calculus, the value of the text is judged purely by the context of its corporate promotion, which precedes actual publication and operates independently of anyone ever actually reading the book. As such, "An Interview with Nobody" economically parodies what happens to authors whose books are marketed like any other brand-name commodity.

In completely erasing the author's identity, "An Interview with Nobody" asserts that neither the biographical specificity nor the literary talent of a writer is a significant factor in corporate marketing strategies. The historical reality was more complicated, however. In the expanding culture industries of the era, real authors responded to the burden of celebrity and the new literary marketplace in which it circulated.

A brief dialogue by Edith Wharton, published in the year 1900 in *Scribner's* and titled simply "Copy," effectively illustrates the cultural anxieties precipitated by the heightened interest in authorial personality during this period.[46] "Copy" was published when Wharton was on the verge of authorial celebrity herself. Her first volume of short stories had just been published, and she was being acknowledged in the literary monthlies as a professional author; she was beginning to see her name in print and to fantasize about the consequences of literary renown. Amy Kaplan briefly mentions "Copy" as an example of how "the figure of the celebrity epitomizes the contradictions that inform the professionalization of authorship."[47] I would like to dwell somewhat more extensively on how this short piece charts out some of the same contradictions that concerned Warren, Brandeis, Sedgewick, and Hawthorne.

"Copy," written in the form of a one-act play, recounts an exchange between a famous female novelist and famous male poet, and it concerns the love letters they wrote to each other during a romance that took place prior to their literary successes. The play begins with a discussion between Mrs. Ambrose Dale, the novelist, and her secretary, Hilda. Wharton's opening description establishes Mrs. Dale's drawing room, "pleasantly dim and flower-scented," as a space of creative privacy enabled by the fruits of publicity: "Books are scattered everywhere—mostly with autograph inscriptions 'From the Author'—and a large portrait of Mrs. Dale, at her desk, with papers strewn about her, takes up one of the wall-panels" (657). Thus, the author sits surrounded by authorial signatures, facing a portrait of herself at work that reinforces the convergence of domestic and professional interior space. Hilda has just brought in the mail:

> Mrs. Dale. Ten more applications for autographs? Isn't it strange that people who'd blush to borrow twenty dollars don't scruple to beg for an autograph?
> Hilda (reproachfully). Oh—
> Mrs. Dale. What's the difference, pray?
> Hilda. Only that *your* last autograph sold for fifty—
> Mrs. Dale (not displeased). Ah? (657)

Mrs. Dale is pleased by the value of her autograph, yet frustrated by the readerly behavior that generates that value in the first place. This authorial ambivalence regarding the commodification of the autograph frames Wharton's exploration of authorial private lives. The author sits surrounded by the autographs of other authors as she is both vexed and pleased by the monetary value of her own. Her secretary, Hilda, monitors and mediates this value: she both handles the distribution of the autographs and keeps track of how much they're worth.

But the subject of this prefatory discussion between author and secretary significantly shifts at this point. When Mrs. Dale tells Hilda that she doesn't need her that evening, the young secretary protests that she'd rather "sit up" since "it's so beautiful to sit here, watching and listening, all alone in the night, and to feel that you're in there (she points to the study-door) *creating*—" (657). This brief exchange expands our view of the apartment's interior. Hilda's private space of "watching and listening" supplements Mrs. Dale's private space of "*creating*." Hilda's importance expands correspondingly: she is both arbitrator of authorial value and readerly witness to the fetishized writerly private life from which best sellers emerge.

But Hilda is not only a reader. Mrs. Dale asks her: "Do you take notes of what you feel, Hilda—here, all alone in the night?" Hilda's response precipitates an awkward moment of almost erotic affection between the two women:

> Hilda (shyly). I have—
> Mrs. Dale (smiling). For the diary?
> Hilda (nods and blushes).
> Mrs. Dale (caressingly) Goose! (657)

This moment of intimacy around the shared experience of private writing is deflected into a discussion of the letters Hilda has brought, almost all

of which concern royalties and publicity. This exchange, in turn, is inter-
rupted by the announcement of Mrs. Dale's visitor, the "great, great
poet" Paul Ventnor. Hilda asks whether she can "stay just a moment" to
"see the meeting between you—the greatest novelist and the greatest poet
of the age." Mrs. Dale grants permission, adding, "You'll make a fortune
out of that diary, Hilda"; to which the secretary responds: "Four publishers have applied to me already" (658). Hilda therefore represents the
democratic audience who increasingly claimed literary celebrity as its
right, both as potential authors and witnesses to the successful author's
private life.

Ventnor arrives as a specter from that private life, or rather, as a reminder of a past when the calculus between privacy and publicity didn't
determine their experiences—a past when, as Mrs. Dale claims, "we were
real people." Seeing her old lover after so many years, Mrs. Dale decides
that "I died years ago. What you see before you is a figment of a reporter's
brain—a monster manufactured out of newspaper paragraphs, with ink
in its veins" (658). Mrs. Dale's rhetorical self-erasure vividly illustrates
the consequences of publicity for the private person who, inevitably, corresponds to the public "monster." As such, even though Ventnor agrees
that both of them have become "public property," their ensuing discussion focuses on private property, on the documentary evidence they pos-
sess of the affair they once had. They discover that they both have kept
the love letters they exchanged. She keeps them locked in a safe; he keeps
them always on his person. If the writers have become public property,
these letters signify a residue of literary private property that both des-
perately keep out of the public eye.

But as they anxiously read over and discuss the letters, they discover,
not surprisingly, that the material in them is the source of much of the literature that made them famous. Mrs. Dale reads her first letter and ex-
claims, "I had a letter of this kind to do the other day, in the novel I'm at
work on now," and she admits that "the best phrase in it . . . is simply
plagiarized, word for word, from this!" (660). Ventnor reads one of his
and declares, "This is the one I made a sonnet out of afterward! By Jove,
I'd forgotten where that idea came from" (661). Both writers find their
fame to be based in a repressed sublimation of love letters into literature.
The private writing is the forgotten source of the published text. Suddenly, the letters take on an entirely different value: "You must see that
these letters of ours can't be left to take their chance like an ordinary correspondence—you said yourself we were public property" (661), Ventnor

blurts out. The two begin to struggle over possession of this valuable property. Each tries to assert their right, not only over the letters they've saved but over those in the other's possession. A veritable crisis of authorial attribution ensues. Ventnor claims that "technically . . . the letter belongs to the writer." But Mrs. Dale retorts, "You couldn't have written them if I hadn't been willing to read them. Surely there's more of myself in them than of you" (662). Once the letters attain literary value, the two writers in essence become each other's public, and they proceed to reenact their anxieties over the agency of the audience in determining that value.

In fact, it becomes clear in the denouement that this is the central anxiety behind the entire dialogue, as both writers admit that without really knowing it until this discussion, they had been saving the letters for their memoirs. These letters, kept so secure over such a long time, represent what the public doesn't know, what the authors have stubbornly kept to themselves. And yet, as the private source of the published literature, their only possible fate seems to be to become public; their current value inheres in their proleptic publication. The writers realize then that there is only one way to keep the letters private: like Lily Bart, they burn them. Apparently, the only way to maintain privacy is to destroy all written traces of it. In the end Ventnor leaves, and Mrs. Dale is left alone, "quietly watching the letters burn" (663).

As Kaplan has discussed at length, the potential revelation of incriminating love letters recurs in both *The Touchstone* and *The House of Mirth*, indicating Wharton's sustained preoccupation with the exchange value that increasingly inhered in the documentary evidence of the private intimacies of public figures.[48] And it is worth further noting that this preoccupation represents a sustained meditation on the relation between copyright and the right to privacy in the wake of the groundbreaking ruling in *Wheaton v. Peters* (1834), which as Meredith McGill has shown, established "a distinction at law between handwriting and print, identifying the former as personal and the latter as public property."[49] "Copy" examines the degree to which writers suffered vocationally specific versions of this distinction. As artists whose personal expression and public self-fashioning is fundamentally mediated by writing, authors obviously had a more complicated relationship to the cultural meanings of handwriting and print. As their work was increasingly expected to be autobiographical, novels were frequently subjected to critical scrutiny for clues to authorial private lives, and letters would increasingly come to signify the written private substrate beneath the public printed texts. Furthermore, through live readings, interviews, and promotional appearances, authors were increasingly expected to offer up their personalities as a promotional component of their work in the literary marketplace. Wharton's condensed dialogue reveals how these claims on authorial privacy problematized the agency behind this personality.

Modernism, Mass Culture, Masculinity

However, "Copy" illustrates why Wharton as well as a host of other authors do not figure centrally in this project. Over the course of "Copy," the private space of writing gets displaced from the solitary author in her room to the romantic love affair between novelist and poet. As such, Wharton anticipates one of the principal mechanisms by which certain modern authors, mostly women, would be excluded from the modernist canon, and consequently, from the mode of literary celebrity that enabled other authors, mostly men, to straddle elite and mainstream audiences. As Nina Miller has recently established in her groundbreaking study, *Making Love Modern*, heterosexual romantic love in the early twentieth century became a crucial arena in which mainly female writers, such as Edna St. Vincent Millay, Genevieve Taggart, and Dorothy Parker, among others, could forge a viable public literary identity. For many of these women, "romantic love was a model of gender relations structurally and historically bound up with artistic sensibility itself."[50] And these women, in particular Millay, enjoyed considerable celebrity in modeling the early-twentieth-century "new woman" along literary lines.

On the other hand, as Miller concedes, "the most visible experience of the situation we are calling modern was one of male crisis, and the most quintessentially modern response was a clearly marked style of masculinity."[51] It would be this "marked style of masculinity" that would decouple the avant-garde literary experimentation of high modernism from the more "feminine" concerns of not only women writers such as Millay but also male writers such as Fitzgerald, whose fame during his lifetime was based much more in his popularization of modern love and the new woman than in literary experimentation. Such writing, revolutionary as it may have been in its treatment of sexuality, tended to be linked by male

writers, academics, and intellectuals to what Frank Lentricchia calls the
"'feminization' of the literary that occurred under the social conditions of
capitalism in the nineteenth century."[52]

Andreas Huyssen has detailed the modernist response to this feminization: male intellectuals concluded that "mass culture is somehow associated with woman while real, authentic culture remains the preroga-
tive of men."[53] Huyssen dialectically links the feminization of mass culture to "the powerful masculinist mystique" among many male
modernists."[54] Huyssen's male modernists are all European, but it is clear
that his argument is, if anything, even more applicable to U.S. modernism, where Emersonian self-reliance and frontier individualism contributed to a modernist image of the hypermasculine male author. Indeed,
Huyssen neglects to consider the degree to which this response to mass
culture also figured as a sort of armor for entering into the mass cultural
public sphere. Starting with London and reaching an apogee with Hemingway, a virile masculinity bordering on caricature became central to the
public image of celebrity authors in modern America. This hypermasculine image of the author emerges simultaneously within and against the
feminized cultural marketplace. On the one hand, the market figures as a
constant psychosexual temptation; on the other, it serves as a devouring
mother/machine. Thus authorial machismo, like genius for Stein, was
both a marketing strategy and a way of configuring resistance to the market.

Huyssen notes the psychoanalytic implications of this relation: the fear
of mass culture becomes a "fear of woman, a fear of nature out of control, a fear of the unconscious, of sexuality, of the loss of identity and stable ego boundaries in the mass."[55] In this study, I will argue that celebrity
itself, in threatening the "stable ego boundaries" of the male author,
figures as a psychosexual trauma in many careers of the modern era, and
that the hypermasculine public posturing of authors such as London,
Hemingway, and Norman Mailer can be understood as a symptomatic response to the feminized, and feminizing, literary marketplace. Psychoanalytic method is useful here, in other words, not so much in revealing the
private traumas of biographical individuals but in unpacking the ways in
which the public personae of celebrity authors are symptomatic of psychosexual anxieties in the culture at large, particularly regarding the status of culture as such.

The celebrity authors under consideration here were all implicated in
this stitching together of masculinity, modernism, and mass culture, and

this is why most of them are men. Indeed, the emergence of this complex triangulation helps indicate the historical parameters of this study. As a wide variety of literary and cultural historians have established, the Progressive Era witnessed the emergence of a masculine reaction to a feminized genteel culture—part of the more general "crisis of masculinity" that emerged in response to the rise of urban industrialism and corporate capitalism.[56] The arenas in which manhood could be forged and affirmed receded from bourgeois life, and an entire series of compensatory spaces emerged in which new, more desperate versions of masculinity could be experienced. Masculine celebrity authorship would become one such space.

Yet as Ann Douglass maintained some time ago, such crises of masculinity were not unique to the turn of the twentieth century.[57] Male authors, as Nathaniel Hawthorne's famous "scribbling women" quote has so often shown, struggled with the feminization of the literary in the antebellum years as well. Indeed, some recent critics have argued that literary celebrity also emerged during this era, with publisher James Fields's management of Hawthorne's career as a signal case. Thus, Michael Newbury contends that in the 1850s, "for the first time, successful authors became public figures in a mass market."[58] Newbury's exemplary illustration is Fields's "Fruit and Flower Festival" at which an audience of three hundred people witnessed a gathering of publishers and authors—an event that though unprecedented, is also quite modest in comparison with later developments. It is worth noting the extent to which Newbury and other critics of this era rely on the term "emergent" in their analysis of the literary marketplace, and Newbury himself concedes that his claims about authorial celebrity have "inevitably been influenced by retrospection."[59] In fact, the public exposure and interrogation of authorial private lives in the antebellum era was nowhere near as extensive and autonomous as it became with the late-nineteenth-century development of the gossip column and human-interest journalism.

The uniformity with which such studies reference the expansion of the mass market as shorthand for their theses indicates the degree to which more nuanced arguments are necessary to account for historical developments in the profession of authorship. As historian Lewis Coser observes, such assertions about the "commercialization of literature" are perennial in publishing, and have occurred from its beginnings as an industry.[60] This is particularly striking since, as Coser elsewhere affirms, publishing was, until quite recently, "largely a cottage industry."[61] Until the post–World War II era of mergers and acquisitions that publishing historian John Tebbel calls the "great change," the publishing world had "functioned as a small community" of predominantly family-owned businesses that was relatively autonomous from the corporate capitalism that surrounded and eventually swallowed it.[62] Clearly, if we rely on the rise of the mass market as an explanatory mechanism for historical claims about or cultural diagnoses of developments in literary history, we risk using a blunt instrument for a complex task.

Nevertheless, the phrase "commercialization of literature" comes directly from Henry Holt's highly influential 1905 review of Walter Hines Page's *A Publisher's Confession*—indeed, it is the term historian Charles Madison uses to designate the period from 1900 to 1945—and it is worth affirming why such a concern would receive a particular urgency at this time, when my own narrative begins.[63] Like critics of the publishing industry both before and after, Holt was concerned with the degree to which books were being marketed like any other commodity, especially in terms of the expanding advertising budgets in the industry. And his argument thumbnails a basic refrain by which publishers attempted to distinguish their industry and its wares from others: "Books are not bricks, and . . . the more they are treated as bricks, the more they tend to become bricks."[64]

Holt places the blame for these developments on the literary agent, who emerged during this era as a middleperson between author and publisher. As Tebbel affirms, the agent was necessary because

> the passage of an international copyright law, the growing importance of first serial rights in magazines and second serial rights in newspapers, the syndication of fiction to newspapers and the dramatization of books—all these were matters too complicated for most authors too handle, years before motion pictures, radio, book clubs, television and mass market paperback rights made it impossible.[65]

In other words, what troubled Holt and others, and what necessitated the emergence of literary agents, was the formation of the corporate culture industry as an economic environment related to, yet distinct from, the genteel culture of publishing. It is this development, I would maintain, that most effectively delineates the historical parameters of my narrative.

One might argue that the appeal of the 1850s for literary historians lies precisely in the absence of this environment. In the antebellum era, book publishing was the only truly national market for the dissemination of culture. After the war, an entire mass culture industry emerged, dwarfing the economic scale and scope of book publishing, despite its considerable expansion during these years. And it would be within and against the emergence of these culture industries that the definition of the "literary" as such would emerge. The key development here would be the "magazine revolution" of the 1890s that according to one influential critic, marks the start of modern mass culture as such.[66] At the turn of the century, magazines shifted from being essentially extensions of the genteel publishing industry to mass-market media funded by the advertising industry. This change was crucial in establishing the split between highbrow and lowbrow culture that would be so essential to the definition and development of literary modernism.

In the Gilded Age and Progressive Era, this definition was arguably somewhat inchoate, and authors such as Mark Twain and London had to struggle to establish "literary" credentials. After World War I, however, we see the emergence of what Tebbel calls "the Golden Age between Two Wars."[67] During this period, key editors and publishers, such as Maxwell Perkins, Bennett Cerf, Horace Liveright, and Alfred Knopf, established the mechanisms whereby modernism could be effectively marketed in the mass cultural public sphere. These men retained their prestige as arbiters of taste while simultaneously immersing themselves in the rough-and-tumble of the mainstream marketplace. They displayed an allegiance and loyalty to modernist authors that helped to nurture as well as sustain their delicate passage between little magazine cachet and mass cultural popularity. As one historian notes, the little magazines during this era served as something of an "advance guard" for the "rear guard" strategies of the commercial publishers, helping to establish the literary reputation of an author that would make him or her worth the investment necessary for mainstream distribution.[68] This reciprocal engagement received crucial mediation from an emerging coterie of influential literary critics, led by the prolific Edmund Wilson and then consolidated around the academic canonization of the new criticism, thereby both establishing literary credentials and promoting the market viability of modernist texts.

In his study of this tight professional relationship between literary critics and modernist authors during this era, Thomas Strychacz remarks that in the twentieth century, "literature and mass culture have come to seem mutually dependent categories: One emerges from and helps determine the shape of the other."[69] The relationship between literature and mass culture, in other words, is one of dialogic interdependence and dialectical engagement, not opposition or mutual exclusion. The foundational work in this regard is Fredric Jameson's "Reification and Utopia in Mass Culture," in which he affirms that modernism and mass culture must be understood as "objectively related and dialectically interdependent phenomena, as twin and inseparable forms of the fission of aesthetic production under capitalism." Jameson offers this approach as an antidote to the traditional evaluative temptations, originated by the modernists themselves, to claim either that "mass culture is popular and thus more authentic than high culture" or that "high culture is autonomous and, therefore, utterly incomparable to a degraded mass culture."[70] Strychacz's adaptation of Jameson's method indicates the crucial importance of literary and cultural institutions in mediating this dialectic between modernism and mass culture. Although neither Jameson nor Strychacz discuss it, literary celebrity was critical to this mediation.

I conclude my study with Mailer in order to illustrate that this dialectic, in the postmodern era, no longer provides the cultural leverage it once had. On the one hand, the ineluctable process of mergers and acquisitions that began in the 1960s has essentially incorporated publishing into the larger structure of the culture industries; it no longer represents a "cottage industry" or "small community" within the larger arena of mass culture. On the other hand, the very category of the "literary" has come under increasing academic scrutiny; it no longer represents a cultural consensus by which to establish "classic" authors and texts. "Literature" itself is, arguably, a residual category.

Furthermore, the dominant masculine pose that enabled authors like Hemingway to straddle elite and popular fields no longer represents a viable literary persona. Kate Millett's attack on Mailer and Henry Miller marks the beginning of a process whereby feminist literary criticism effectively dislodged masculinity from its privileged access to high literary cachet. As historian Michael Kimmel states more generally, in the 1960s and 1970s, U.S. culture witnessed a second "crisis of masculinity" in which "the 'masculine mystique'—that impossible synthesis of sober responsible breadwinner, imperviously stoic master of his fate, and swashbuckling hero—was finally exposed as a fraud."[71] Celebrity authorship was a specific articulation of this mystique that enabled a gendered dialectic between modernism and mass culture; it disappears once that dialectic dissolves with the coordinated emergence of second-wave feminism and literary postmodernism.

Authors Inc. thus argues that celebrity authorship in the United States was a resolutely historical phenomenon that began with the rise of mass culture and the first crisis of masculinity in the late nineteenth century, and ended with the emergence of postmodernity and the second crisis of masculinity in the late twentieth century. Chapter 1, "Modern Consciousness and Public Subjectivity," specifies the emergence of celebrity authorship as a crucial instance of the dialectical engagement between modernism and mass culture. Using the autobiographies and careers of Henry Adams, the aging New England aristocrat who is frequently seen as one of the inaugural figures of American literary modernism, and Edward Bok, the immigrant editor of the *Ladies' Home Journal* from 1889 to 1919, I examine how the modern consciousness of the literary genius emerges in tandem with the public subjectivity of the mass cultural celebrity.

I contrast the literary apprenticeships detailed in *The Education of Henry Adams* (1918) and *The Americanization of Edward Bok* (1921) in order to foreground the dialectical proximity of modernist obscurity and popular celebrity. Both authors recount their careers as the development of a distinctly modern American subject, and both authors use the third person to distance this subject from what they considered to be their private selves. In fact, the autobiographies are striking in their formal similarities. That both books were nonfictional best sellers and won the Pulitzer Prize confirms that the stories they told resonated powerfully with both the modern U.S. audience and the custodians of modern American literary culture. *The Education of Henry Adams*, which almost immediately received literary canonical status and modernist credentials, offers the interior consciousness of the writer as an intellectual insulation from the mass public, whereas *The Americanization of Edward Bok*, which barely entered the horizons of U.S. literary history, offers the exterior subjectivity of the celebrity as a mode of self-fashioning fit for addressing it. I contend that these two autobiographies are only fully intelligible in terms of the dialectical tension between them.

Furthermore, both autobiographies emphasize that transformations in gender roles determined the careers they narrate as well as the form in which those careers are narrated. In the second half of *The Education*, Adams bases his entire theory of the onset of modernity—and his correlative obscurity as an author—in the "liberation" of women into the public spheres of consumption and labor; Bok, of course, was a central figure in this development. Both men, in turn, decided to narrate their texts in the third person—a mode that stresses the masculine pronoun—as a pro-phylactic defense against this feminization of culture. Thus, we see a model of masculine authorship emerging as a method of straddling the divide between modernism and mass culture in the United States. The chapters that follow reveal how American celebrity authors conflate the modern consciousness elaborated by Adams and the public subjectivity innovated by Bok.

Chapter 2, "Trademark Twain," examines the autobiographical reflections of Samuel Clemens in terms of his attempts to retain property in his texts first through registering his pen name as a trademark and later as a corporation. As one of the first U.S. authors to achieve both mass cultural celebrity and canonical literary status, Twain's struggles with fame and his autobiographical responses to it provide a useful template for an exploration of the autobiographical agons of many later modern American authors.

One of the many claims Twain made about his autobiography was that he composed it in order to extend the copyright of his other works after his death, and as critics have noted, the autobiographical reflections themselves reveal his increasing preoccupation with his own death and the posthumous fate of his literary persona. Twain therefore draws a crucial correlation between the formation of an autonomous public image and the death of the biographical private individual. Moreover, he integrates this correlation into the logic of the mass cultural marketplace, whose emerging hegemony both increased the scale and scope of celebrity and threatened authorial agency in the celebrity persona. I argue that Twain's attempts to establish his authorial persona as a legally recognized corporate entity in response to the emergent powers of the culture industries provides a framework for understanding the considerably complex composition, redaction, and publication of his autobiographical works.

London experienced a similar collision between high cultural aspirations and mass cultural conditions. In chapter 3, "Legitimating London," I explore the close relations between the categories of the literary and legitimate in London's career. London's professional attitude toward writing pressured the category of the literary, toward which he had such ambivalent feelings in the first place. As a "brain worker," London viewed his texts as simply lucrative products for the market, but once he became a famous author, he saw how his name alone—aside from the labor he may or may not have exerted—could confer literary value on a book. In

Martin Eden, London introduces the unpleasant possibility that literary value inheres not in the text but in the public perception of the author. And this public perception was as much the product of publisher's promotion and advertising as it was of his own literary efforts.

London's literary legitimacy was also threatened by his legal illegitimacy, which he never publicly revealed during his lifetime. In the second half of this chapter, I detail how Irving Stone, in the biographical novel *Sailor on Horseback* that exposed London's illegitimacy, strove to coordinate legal illegitimacy and literary legitimacy through a model of masculine authorial inheritance. Using never-before-seen correspondence between Stone and London's widow Charmian over the rights to London's archives, I show how Stone tried literally to regain a masculine property and propriety in London's life story—over and against what he saw as the corrupting influence of the women in his life—by attempting to position himself as London's literary heir.

In the 1920s and 1930s, literary modernism began to enter into mainstream culture, and no other figure more effectively managed this migration than Stein. Chapter 4, "Gertude Stein's Money," analyzes Stein's autobiographical meditations on the phenomenal transformation she underwent from unpublished obscurity to mass cultural celebrity after the publication of *The Autobiography of Alice B. Toklas*. I assert that ironically, Stein's work in the 1930s engages the dialectical tensions of celebrity authorship more aggressively and effectively than any other modern U.S. author because her lesbianism—and her age at the time of her fame—enabled her to avoid much of the psychosexual trauma associated with male authorial celebrity. By the time Stein became famous, she had moved beyond her youthful struggles with her father and her brother Leo, the problem of gender and genius, and the challenge of how to represent her relationship with Toklas. Though all of these issues are present in her writings of the 1930s, Stein was able to subordinate their role in her brief identity crisis to the fundamental contradiction between symbolic and economic value at the heart of American authorial celebrity.

Stein's engagements with this contradiction generated a series of meditations on the nature of money whose significance for her work in the 1930s has not been fully appreciated. Stein had been a rentier all her life, living on a fixed income doled out to her by her brother Michael, who was supporting the entire Stein family on money earned from his consolidation of the San Francisco streetcar industry. With the publication of

The Autobiography of Alice B. Toklas, Stein began earning money for the first time, at the age of fifty-nine. Simultaneously, the world was undergoing an economic collapse. Using *Everybody's Autobiography* as my central text, I show how Stein attempted to understand her own transformed economic status in terms of the crisis of the Depression by making money an objective correlative of the writer's mind, thereby calibrating economic to symbolic capital. It is in terms of these efforts that I understand Stein's formulation and deployment of the "continuous present," so key to the critical interpretation and evaluation of her work. I conclude this chapter by arguing that Stein's simultaneous insistence that her genius exists "outside of time" while her writing is fundamentally of her time represents an attempt to accommodate the temporalities of the restricted and general fields of cultural production. If the restricted field mandates that the author be ahead of her time, the general field mandates that she be of her time; Stein wanted to have it both ways. This contradiction in temporality merges with the contradiction in value in Stein's autobiographical style of the 1930s, which works to be both immediate and discontinuous, both popular and obscure. *Everybody's Autobiography*, then, illuminates the contradictions of celebrity authorship with unprecedented clarity, and tries to resolve them with unmatched cleverness.

Chapter 5, "Being Ernest," takes on the career of Hemingway, certainly the most "celebrated" classic American author of the modern era. More than any other U.S. modernist, Hemingway lived the career arc from little magazine cachet to mass cultural celebrity. In the process, his life and "personality" became as important as his work. Using *Death in the Afternoon*, Hemingway's classic study of bullfighting, as my principal text, I analyze his career as a series of hysterical antagonisms, with his audience, his celebrity persona, and the inevitable biographers looming on the horizon of his life.

I read these antagonisms as both socioeconomic and psychosexual; that is, I allege that Hemingway's struggles in the literary marketplace are inextricable from his psychosexual obsessions with women, homosexuality, and death. In a broader sense, then, this chapter explores the possibility that the psychosexual obsessions of the U.S. cultural imaginary are closely stitched into the structural contradictions of the U.S. cultural marketplace, and that this complex imbrication is most evident in the phenomenon of American celebrity culture. It is with Hemingway and his many heirs, in other words, that psychoanalysis becomes a necessary method for fully unpacking the cultural coordinates of celebrity authorship.

Chapter 6, "The Norman Conquest," offers the career of Mailer as the last example of American celebrity authorship; after Mailer, it becomes impossible to occupy this subject position in U.S. public life. Starting with *Advertisements for Myself*, I show how Mailer, explicitly modeling himself on Hemingway, quite self-consciously established a macho persona as a celebrity author. Significantly, Mailer developed this persona in response to his failure as a novelist—his inability to follow up on the success of *The Naked and the Dead*. Mailer was deeply traumatized by the negative reviews of *The Barbary Shore* and *The Deer Park*, and in *Advertisements for Myself*, he introduces an angry and arrogant persona in reaction to this public rejection. The third-person voice Mailer then developed out of this persona in the 1960s was a journalistic one, and his public posturing was specifically designed for the burgeoning mass public of that era. Mailer invented a public subject as both sword and shield, as a way to enter the mass cultural arena without being engulfed by it.

In the second half of this chapter, I describe how this public subject foundered on the emergent controversies over gender and sexuality, to which Mailer attempted to respond in *The Prisoner of Sex* and his biography of Marilyn Monroe. After these fascinating failures to contend with the rise of women's liberation, Mailer abandons his public persona entirely, devoting the rest of his career to a fruitless search for the "great" novel that he clearly will never write.

The failure of Mailer to sustain his celebrity persona into the 1970s reveals that the cultural conditions on which celebrity authorship relied—the dialectical tension between modernist consciousness and public subjectivity delicately bridged by a hypermasculine persona—no longer obtains in the postmodern era. Celebrity obviously persists, and certainly some authors are famous, but the specific articulation of the private authorial genius versus the mass marketplace is no longer possible in a society no longer based on the opposition between art and commerce.

1

Modern Consciousness and Public Subjectivity

In 1919, *The Education of Henry Adams* was posthumously awarded the Pulitzer Prize. Reviewed by T. S. Eliot in *The Athenæum*, selected in the 1930s as one of the *Books That Changed Our Minds* by Malcolm Cowley and Bernard Smith, and heralded in the 1970s as inaugurating "the Emergence of a Modern Consciousness" by John Carlos Rowe, Adams's unusual third-person autobiography has been appreciated ever since its publication as a signal achievement of American literary modernism.[1] Two years later, another third-person autobiography won the Pulitzer Prize, but *The Americanization of Edward Bok* has never achieved the lasting literary canonicity and cultural capital of *The Education*. Both Adams and Bok wrote third-person autobiographies focusing exclusively on their public and professional lives, and both autobiographies won the Pulitzer Prize, yet no literary critic or cultural historian has noted this historical coincidence.[2]

This isn't terribly surprising. Adams—scion of a waning U.S. aristocracy—had spent his privileged literary life in search of an educated U.S. public, while Bok—immigrant editor of the *Ladies' Home Journal* from 1889 to 1919—inaugurated the mass audience against which Adams's modernist *Education* defines itself. As an experiment in modern consciousness, *The Education* located the educated public whose absence it laments; as a formulaic success story, *The Americanization* vanished into the ocean of middlebrow ephemera whose creation it celebrates. The two autobiographies emerged from different social worlds and were addressed to different audiences, and their authors correlatively were subjected to different temporalities of reception. Adams's reputation was established in a specifically American version of the restricted field of cultural production. He initially published *The Education* privately, and circulated it to an exclusive group of friends and colleagues; it achieved both popular recognition and literary canonization after his death. Bok's reputation was established in the general field of cultural production; he achieved great popular recognition during his lifetime, but was essentially forgotten after his death.

For a brief period in the 1920s, however, the two autobiographies appeared side by side in a middlebrow literary marketplace that could accommodate, if not directly acknowledge, their formal similarities. *The Education* was published by Houghton Mifflin, *The Americanization* by Scribner's, both well-respected and well-established publishing houses. Both autobiographies rhetorically addressed themselves to a younger generation of U.S. males, and both were enthusiastically received and reviewed as models of an American education. Since then, they have fallen on opposite sides of the evaluative divide between modernism and mass culture, and the disciplinary organization of cultural knowledge and textual interpretation to which Adams's and Bok's careers contributed has mitigated against any extended comparison of their autobiographies.

The moment would appear to be ripe for such a comparison. Over the last thirty years, the rise of postmodernism has undermined the evaluative distinction between high and low culture, while literary theory and cultural studies have blurred disciplinary boundaries within and beyond the humanities. The historical coincidence of and formal similarities between *The Education* and *The Americanization* can now more easily enter into our field of vision. My reading of these texts exploits this contemporary critical opportunity, which has in recent years revealed how deeply entangled modernism and mass culture have been in the twentieth-century United States. The similarities between *The Education* and *The Americanization* not only reveal the deep dialectical engagement between high and low cultural forms in this country but also the public personality as a specific articulation of this dialectic in the literary marketplace.

In this chapter, then, I will account for how and why two very different literary careers nevertheless seemed to mandate similar formal parameters for their retrospective narration. I will begin with a consideration of the first half of *The Education*, which emplots the literary apprenticeship of its autobiographical subject in the mid–nineteenth century. My objective will be to examine how *The Education* justifies its peculiar form in terms of a protomodernist resistance to the emerging logic of the literary marketplace. Next, I will analyze the first half of *The Americanization*, which emplots the literary apprenticeship of its autobiographical subject in the late nineteenth century. My objective here will be to examine how *The Americanization* justifies its peculiar form in terms of the very market logic that *The Education* resists. Then, I will account for why both Adams and Bok chose to devote the second half of their autobiographies to the relations between gender and modernity—relations that are clearly crucial to both men's personal and professional lives, and that in turn determine the formal peculiarities of their texts. In recounting and analyzing these two literary careers and their retrospective narrations side by side, I will tease out the dialectical relation between them that can account for the simultaneous appearance of *The Education* and *The Americanization* in the post–World War I literary marketplace. I intend to prove that the publication and popularity of these third-person autobiographies illuminates celebrity authorship in the twentieth century as a conflation of modernist genius and mass cultural personality.

Pronouns, Patronyms, Publicity

If, as Philippe Lejeune claims, "the deep subject of autobiography is the proper name," then *The Education* and *The Americanization* advertise their genre almost to the point of parody.[3] In their radically exteriorized third-person narration, these texts perform an almost mantric repetition of the authorial proper name. And yet, to write an autobiography in the third person is also to violate the most basic premise of that genre. As Lejeune also confirms, autobiography in the third person has the peculiar effect that "we read the text from the perspective of the conventions it violates." According to Lejeune, the difficulty of maintaining this relation to the text accounts for why there are "so few modern autobiographies written *entirely* in the third person." He can, in fact, "hardly cite any but the one written by Henry Adams."[4] Nevertheless, within a decade of the publication of *The Education*, Bok, Louis Sullivan, and Stein all wrote third-person autobiographies, clearly qualifying Lejeune's claim. All three of these figures achieved enormous public prominence in cultural fields associated with modernity, and their ambiguous relation to the twentieth-century culture of celebrity in the United States informs their decision to objectify their autobiographical personae.

Self-deprecating as he may have been, Adams was a public figure by his very lineage. Though he cultivated a pose of highly self-conscious obscurity, he knew that the familiarity of his name inevitably interpellated him into the public sphere, expanded and transformed as it may have become over the course of his long life. Adams was legitimately anxious about the legacy of his august patronymic, particularly in relation to the post–Civil War negotiations of U.S. cultural memory in the literary marketplace, and his famous characterization to Henry James of his autobiography as "a shield of protection in the grave" clearly indicates his awareness of public interest in his life.[5] He may not have been as powerful or prominent as his forefathers, but he knew that his name would solicit biographical attention in a literary marketplace obsessed with personalities and life stories.

The Education opens with its subject being "branded" with the name "Henry Brooks Adams" (3), and then explicitly offers the narrative that follows as an attempt to come to terms with the "eighteenth-century inheritance" of Enlightenment republicanism indelibly, if ambiguously, signified by the name "Adams" (7). It is worth briefly dwelling on the complex twentieth-century significance of this deliberately mixed opening metaphor of being branded. Adams begins this paragraph with his famous analogy to the Jew, "born in Jerusalem under the shadow of the Temple and circumcised in the Synagogue by his uncle the high priest," but then he shifts to the metaphor of the racehorse, "handicapped in the races of the coming century" (3). He then blithely dispenses with both of these analogies and, briefly toying with the simple figure of the traveler, "ticketed through life, with the safeguards of the old, established traffic," finally settles on himself as a cardplayer, conceding that "probably no child, born in the year, held better cards than he" (4). Adams's brand name shifts from a bodily mark bestowed by an ancient religious ritual to a card dealt in a modern game, from a metonym written on the body to a metaphor detachable from it. In other words, over the course of a number of restless figurative transformations, the name becomes increasingly attenuated in its link to its bearer, and increasingly susceptible to exchange or loss. And this series of figurative transformations, I hope to argue, mirrors the larger historical transformation of the name in the mass cultural public sphere.

On the other hand, the Adams name—repeated so liberally in the pages of this text—signifies an exclusive social world to which he has privileged access. In fact, all the names associated with the nineteenth-century social and political elite, many of which had acquired a legendary status in Adams's time, appear in these opening chapters, which read like a veritable duty roster of postrevolutionary American politics and high society. The average reader requires a battery of biographical footnotes to orient Adams's individual story in the illustrious procession of U.S. history that the text casually invokes, and certainly part of the text's appeal is as a gossipy memoir of the rich and powerful.

But it is also intended as a trenchant critique of the shared ethos of the class into which Adams was born; an Oedipal animus deeply informs his autobiography as well as his literary career as a whole. T. J. Jackson Lears, in what remains one of the most sensitive psychoanalytic readings of Adams, confirms that "in large measure, *The Education* recounted Adams's efforts to free himself from the authority of his father's liberal, progressive values—whether couched in the eighteenth-century language of the Enlightenment or the nineteenth-century language of positivism."[6] Such a reading has become almost axiomatic in Adams criticism, and Adams's critique of his paternal inheritance remains one of the central interpretative points of entry into this complex autobiography. I would like to use this point of entry to leverage a reading of how *The Education* registers historical transformations in the relationship between authorial subjectivity and the print marketplace. Both as a meditation on and conflicted object within the American literary marketplace, Adams's autobiography tracks the emergence of the modern conditions of celebrity authorship.[7]

In a family that boasted two U.S. presidents, the Adams patronym carried heavy patriarchal burdens, and Adams acknowledges early on that "his father's character was . . . the larger part of his education" (26). Significantly, Adams frames this early sketch of his father as a response to misrepresentations of his family in the popular press: "For a hundred years, every newspaper scribbler had, with more or less obvious excuse, derided or abused the older Adamses for want of judgment. They abused Charles Francis for his judgment" (27). But for the son, the father's "judgment" emerges as an ambiguous trait:

> Charles Francis Adams was singular for mental poise—absence of self-assertion or self-consciousness—the faculty of standing apart without seeming aware that he was alone—a balance of mind and temper that neither challenged nor avoided notice, nor admitted question of superiority or inferiority, of jealousy, of personal motives, from any source, even under great pressure. (27)

Charles Adams shows no evidence of subjective interiority in this description: without "self-assertion or self-consciousness," without "personal motives," he seems to be almost without self or person at all. This peculiar balanced blankness will become the New England type against which the young Henry struggles to individuate himself.

If Charles Adams never deviates from this cool exterior over the course of his son's *Education*, Charles Sumner—a close friend of the family during Henry's boyhood—becomes the substitute whose transformation dramatically reveals the shortcomings of the New England type. In the opening pages, we're told that "Sumner was the boy's ideal of greatness" (31). If Adams is unable to express any real emotion toward or about his father, he readily admits that he "worshipped" Sumner. And if Sumner is something of a father figure in these opening chapters, his schism with the Adams family over Republican policies on slavery and Reconstruction affords Adams the opportunity to critique the sort of authority he once represented. Adams himself became something of a "newspaper scribbler" after the war, and he affirms that Sumner was a "valuable acquaintance for a newspaper-man" (252). Nevertheless, his portrait, if not abusive, is unflattering:

> Sumner's mind had reached the calm of water which receives and reflects images without absorbing them; it contained nothing but itself. The images from without, the objects mechanically perceived by the senses, existed by courtesy until the mental surface was ruffled, but never became part of the thought. Henry Adams roused no emotion; if he had roused a disagreeable one, he would have ceased to exist. The mind would have mechanically rejected, as it had mechanically admitted him. (252)

The "courtesy" of Sumner's mind figures as a perversion or degradation of Charles Adams's "mental poise"; he is a caricature of a caricature. Like Charles Adams, Sumner expresses "no emotion," and the "calm of water" serves as an ironic twist on Charles Adams's "balance of mind." But what in the elder Adams seemed a virtue—if a flawed one—in Sumner has become a "pathological study" (252). The self-discipline that stood as proof of the statesman's "character" in former days has now become a mechanical habit. Sumner's mind has shifted from subject to object, from man to machine. And the more the mind functions like a machine, the more it becomes susceptible to being mechanically reproduced.

In fact, Adams sees his entire family as "modes or replicas of the same type," from which he himself represents "the variation." He deviates from the family type as a consequence of an early bout with scarlet fever. Although "at first, the effect was physical"—he "falls behind his brothers . . . in height"—Adams decides that "his character and processes of mind seemed to share in this fining down process of scale." Adams then affirms that his lifelong

> habit of doubt; of distrusting his own judgment and of totally rejecting the judgment of the world; the tendency to regard every question as open; the hesitation to act except as a choice of evils; the shirking of responsibility; the love of line, form, quality; the horror of ennui (6)

could all be traced to this childhood illness. If the typical Adams judges and evaluates with a mechanical absence of reflection, the young Henry's illness, in generating doubt and hesitation, would seem to figure as consciousness itself. He concludes that "his brothers were the type; he was the variation" (6). Consciousness begins as a peculiar Darwinian epiphenomenon, a freak of family nature.

Interestingly, Adams represents this early illness as a "lesson of taste" since all he remembers of the episode is "his aunt entering the sick room bearing in her hand a saucer with a baked apple" (5). A few paragraphs later, we find a more complicated meditation on "taste" as the young boy chews on "the pages of a spelling book—the taste of A–B, AB, suddenly revived on the boy's tongue sixty years afterward" (8). Adams's illness accrues a figurative relation to writing and print through a literalization of the "lesson of taste." This rare convergence of authorial and narrative subject on "the boy's tongue" confirms the dense significance of this memory as an intimation of Adams's literary career. The spelling book, as a text in which one copies by hand from printed letters, specifically registers the anxieties Adams will have about being simply a copy of the family type.

In fact, Adams formulates his variation from type in terms of writing and his choice of a literary career. This career began, inevitably for an Adams, at Harvard College, which he condemns for creating men very much like his father: Harvard graduates "were objectiveness itself; their attitude was a law of nature; their judgment beyond appeal, not an act either of intellect or emotion or of will, but a sort of gravitation" (56). Like

Charles Adams, Harvard grads lack any evidence of subjective interiority. Their judgment is mechanical; they haven't contracted the illness of doubt.

It is in his accounts of Harvard that Adams explicitly couches his criticism of the New England type in metaphors of print technology. He thus claims that Harvard

> graduates could commonly be recognized by the stamp, but such a type of character rarely lent itself to autobiography. In effect, the school created a type but not a will. Four years of Harvard College, if successful, resulted in an autobiographical blank, a mind on which only a watermark had been stamped. (55)

Here, Adams associates the quasi-scientific concept of the type with the technology of print. His metaphoric use of the terms "stamp" and "watermark" indicates the mechanical reproduction of "type." Although he concedes that "the College Catalogue for the years 1854 to 1861 shows a list of names rather distinguished in their time"—names that he of course proceeds to enumerate—he nevertheless represents the college as a publishing factory for the mass production of blank type. And the sameness of this type precludes autobiographical writing. Adams's figuratively reduced references to print foreground the densely important etymology of this sole reference to writing. While "stamp," "type," "blank," and "watermark" all metaphorically indicate relations of monotonous reproducibility, the term "autobiographical" stands out for its cluster of semantic references to self, life, and writing—arenas of variability and unpredictability that seem to be excluded by the technology of print reproduction.[8]

As it emplots the development of an ostensibly failed literary vocation, *The Education* generates considerable tension between the private *process* of writing and its published (printed) products. Adams both generates and negotiates this tension through self-consciously dwelling on the problem of literary form. Reflecting on his undergraduate work for the college's magazine, Adams self-deprecatingly appraises that "at best it showed only a feeling for form; an instinct of exclusion" (66). Later on, commenting on his early published correspondence from Europe, he elaborates: "The habit of expression leads to the search for something to express. Something remains as a residuum of the commonplace itself, if one strikes out every commonplace in the expression" (89). If print is a matter of reproduction, writing is a process of "exclusion." Literary form, which Adams repeatedly identified as the key challenge of *The Education*, emerges in the ambiguous space between the private process and public reproduction. Form appears as the "residuum" that survives the instinctive habit of striking out—a residuum that becomes the final printed product, a residuum that, ideally, links writer to reader in the public sphere.

On the other hand, Adams himself felt literally residual for much of his career. Exclusion was both a literary technique and concrete political experience. As a private secretary to his father, who was in the vexed position of being ambassador to England for the Union during the Civil War, most of Adams's writing took the form of mindless and anonymous copying. Although he was at the center of some of the most complicated and crucial diplomatic negotiations, he had no real agency except to reproduce and record: "The private secretary copied the notes into his private books, and that was all the share he had in the matter, except to talk in private" (172). This iteration of the term "private" complicates the meanings of "exclusion" in Adams's developing sense of literary vocation. If literary form developed out of an "instinct of exclusion," that instinct itself would appear to be partly inculcated through the concrete experience of being excluded from the exercise of public authority while simultaneously being interpellated into it as a consequence of his name. This ambiguous convergence of public interpellation and exclusion centrally informs Adams's entire career, and in fact came to determine the meaning of his name for modernism and modernity.

When Adams returned from Europe, he found that only one option was available to "the educated poor who could not be artists and would not be tutors": he moved to Washington, D.C., and began a career as an investigative journalist, hoping to use his pen as a tool for political reform. At this point, the literary concerns of *The Education* shift from the boundary dividing writing from print to the new stratifications of the print marketplace that characterized the postwar journalistic world. Although he mostly published in elite journals such as the *North American Review*, Adams was confident that his opinions expanded beyond the periodical's tiny circulation. As he says in *The Education*,

> the *North American Review* stood at the head of U.S. literary periodicals; it was a source of suggestions to cheaper workers; it reached far into societies that never knew its existence; it was an organ worth

playing on; and, in the fancy of Henry Adams, it led, in some indistinct
future, to playing on a New York daily newspaper. (234)

Adams re-creates a youthful optimism that the growing mass public exists in concentric contiguity to his high-reputation yet low-circulation literary endeavors. He hoped that the literary quality and moral clarity of
his work would give it the centrifugal force to expand out from the "five
hundred" to the "five hundred thousand" (259).

Adams envisioned this expansion happening through plagiarism and
piracy. Looking back on why he published "The New York Gold Conspiracy" in the *Edinburgh Review*, Adams wistfully recaptures the optimism of his brief journalistic apprenticeship:

> Any expression about America in an English review attracted ten times
> the attention in America that the same article would attract in the *North
> American*. Habitually the American dailies reprinted such articles in full.
> Adams wanted to escape the terrors of copyright; his highest ambition
> was to be pirated and advertised free of charge, since, in any case, his
> pay was nothing. Under the excitement of the chase, he was becoming a
> pirate himself, and liked it. (283)

In the absence of an international copyright or any organized system of
syndication, material printed in prestigious British journals could be
taken "free of charge" by New York dailies, which Adams assumes to be
eager for such a scoop. Piracy would bridge the gap between the elite and
the mass public, comfortably sheltering the principles of truth from both
the profit motives of print capitalism and corrupted interests of political
patronage.

But Adams's actual experience of this centrifugal transmigration from
elite to popular venues didn't work out quite the way he wished. In 1870,
he caused something of a stir with the publication of his article on "The
Session" in the *Review*. In a letter to Charles Milnes Gaskell, he boasts
that

> for once I have smashed things generally and really exercised a distinct
> influence on public opinion by acting on the limited number of culti-
> vated minds. As evidence of this in a small way, I enclose to you a long
> slip from a Massachusetts newspaper, probably the most widely circu-
> lated of all these Massachusetts papers, in which I am treated in a way

that will, I think, delight you. Of course it is all nonsense. I am neither a journalist nor one of the three best dancers in Washington. . . .

This leader was condensed into a single paragraph of half a dozen lines by a western paper, and copied among the items of the column "personal" all over the country. From this it came back to New York. Hitherto my skill as a dancer was kept a mere artistic touch to heighten the effect of my "brilliant" essay. Now however the paragraph is compressed into two lines "H.B.A. is the author of article &c &c &c. He is one of the three best dancers in W." The next step will be to drop the literary half, and preserve the last line.[9]

The shift from the *North American Review* article to the New York daily column supplements literary recognition as an "author" with social recognition as a "dancer," and presents the possibility of the latter completely occluding the former. Adams literally witnesses himself precariously straddling the divide between being an elite subject of political discourse and a popular object of personal gossip. Adams was a prominent DC socialite, but he wouldn't have considered this a fact of public significance. In the new postbellum literary marketplace, however, with burgeoning personal columns filled with society gossip, the passage from private writing to public circulation effected its own volatile patterns of exclusion and reproduction: Adams's exhilarated ambivalence is clear.

In fact, this would be the last article he would publish as a freelance journalist. As he affirms in *The Education*, "The fateful year 1870 was . . . at hand, which was to mark the close of a literary epoch, when quarterlies gave way to monthlies; letter press to illustration; volumes to pages" (259). As it became increasingly apparent that the literary marketplace that came into being during the Gilded Age had little place for him, Adams married and retreated to Harvard as a professor of medieval history. *The Education* breaks off at this point to begin again twenty years later, after the suicide of his wife and the publication of his monumental nine-volume *History of the United States under the Administrations of Jefferson and Madison*.

(Re)Collecting the Past

It just so happens that 1870 is also the year with which *The Americanization of Edward Bok* begins, when the six-year-old Dutch boy arrives with his family in the United States, inaugurating an immigrant success story that would replace the Republican statesman as a staple of American social mythology. And by the year 1891, when *The Education* picks up again, Bok had just been installed as editor of the *Ladies' Home Journal*. I would like to insert Bok's literary apprenticeship somewhat gratuitously into this twenty-year gap in *The Education*. Bok's career encapsulates the epochal shift in the literary marketplace that Adams associates with his own obscurity, and also inaugurates the transformations in gender roles so central to the second half of *The Education*. I can only hope that Adams would appreciate the ironic appropriateness of such a move.

Bok arrives in the United States as Edward William Bok, but he quickly clarifies that "the American public was, in later years, to omit for him the 'William.'"[10] If U.S. history branded Adams with his name, the U.S. public gave Bok his by taking part of it away. And *The Americanization* proceeds to dwell almost obsessively on the circulation of the proper name in the new mass cultural public sphere. Here is Bok's account of the start of his career in journalism:

> One evening Edward went to a party of young people, and his latent journalistic sense whispered to him that his young hostess might like to see her social affair in print. He went home, wrote up the party, being careful to include the name of every boy and girl present, and next morning took the account to the city editor of the *Brooklyn Eagle*, with the sage observation that every name mentioned in that paragraph represented a buyer of the paper, who would like to see his or her name in print. (12)

From a young age, Bok is sensitive to the thrill associated with publicity, so economically encapsulated in the experience of seeing one's "name in print." This thrill neatly translates, according to Bok's "sage observation," into the desire to consume, as "every name mentioned in that paragraph represented a buyer of the paper." The partygoers, in essence, consume themselves.

This excitement of seeing one's name in print derives from a prior understanding of what it means socially to be the subject of publicity in the age of the gossip column: to appear in print is to join the ranks of those already appearing there. Bok's sage observation is thus based on his appreciation of the emergent social value of celebrity. Like *The Education*, *The Americanization* has its gossipy side, and the opening chapters are peppered with famous names that represent educational influences on its autobiographical subject as a young man. But unlike Adams, Bok was not born into these ranks; he worked his way in through his youthful hobby of collecting autographs, which he pursued with astonishing aggressiveness. *The Americanization* reports on and reproduces in great detail the autographs—of ex-presidents, literary figures, and noteworthy Americans—that Bok collected when he was a young man. This hobby not only earned him his first public notoriety but it also ended up supplying him with considerably helpful business and political connections later in his career. Bok was not dealt his hand; he won it in the card game.

This particular game—collecting American authorial autographs—became a popular fad over the course of the nineteenth century. Starting with the generation of Henry Wadsworth Longfellow and James Russell Lowell, both of whom were regularly solicited with requests for autographs, U.S. authors had to contend with readers who fetishized their pens. Autographs provided a way of achieving an intimacy with authors that seemed unavailable in the public sphere of print. Hence, Richard Henry Stoddard opens his discussion of his autograph collection with the claim that "there is a personal nearness, a human interest in manuscript which is denied to print, and the hands with which we touch it seem to press the hands of its writers."[11] At one point, Bok considered publishing a description of his collection, and Oliver Wendell Holmes offered to write an introduction, which Bok cites in *The Americanization*. According to Holmes,

> An autograph of a distinguished personage means more to an imaginative person than a prosaic looker-on dreams of. Along these lines ran the consciousness and the guiding will of Napoleon, or Washington, or Milton or Goethe. His breath warmed the sheet of paper which you have before you. The microscope will show you the trail of flattened particles left by the tesselated epidermis of his hand as it swept along the manuscript. Nay, if we had but the right developing fluid to flow over it, the surface of the sheet would offer you his photograph as the light pictured it at the instant of writing.[12]

The autograph thus functions metonymically as a material conduit linking the productive inspiration of the "distinguished personage" to the receptive dedication of the "imaginative person." Holmes cleverly confirms this metonymic logic through attributing to writing the indexical qualities of a photograph. The authorial signature in this economy straddles the divide between precapitalist and capitalist modes of fetishism as designated by Michael Taussig:

> The fetishism that is found in the economics of precapitalist societies arises from the sense of organic unity between persons and their products, and this stands in stark contrast to the fetishism of commodities in capitalist societies, which results from the split between persons and the things that they produce and exchange.[13]

On the one hand, the value of the authorial autograph clearly inheres in an "organic unity" between writer and manuscript based on a metonymic chain physically linking the author to the page; on the other hand, the value of the autograph depends on "the split between persons and the things that they produce and exchange" once it enters into a capitalist market economy. The collectability of autographs encouraged a sense that authorial identities could literally be bought and sold, but this sense was based on an auratic conviction of a palpable linkage between the signature and signatory. Autograph collecting, in other words, exploits what Derrida identifies as the paradox of the signature, its simultaneous singularity and iterability. The authenticity of the signature, the fact that it marks the "having-been-present" of the signer, undergirds its value as a fetish. Yet the iterability of the signature, the fact that it must have "a repeatable, iterable, imitable form," allows these written fetishes to circulate as mass-produced commodities in the print marketplace. Derrida, significantly, makes no reference to authorial celebrity or the literary marketplace, even though both have fundamentally contributed to the reception of his text.[14]

Indeed, the nature and importance of the autograph has varied relative to the socioeconomic organization of the literary marketplace. As Tamara Plakins Thornton affirms in her fascinating cultural history, *Handwriting in America*, the rise of an urban industrialized society in the United States after the Civil War generated a shift in the cultural meaning of the written signature.[15] If autograph collecting began as a practice that confirmed the unique character of celebrated figures, it gradually developed into an activity that in essence rendered celebrity generic. As handwriting came to be seen as an idiosyncratic expression of anybody's individual personality, everybody's signatures became unique and interesting. Articles on autographs began to discuss both celebrities and the average person. As signatures lost their auratic resistance to commodification, they came to represent the peculiar fungibility of celebrity itself in a democratic age.

Bok never got around to publishing his collection, but in a sense *The Americanization* is his collection in narrative form. He reproduces many of his autographs in all their apparent authenticity in *The Americanization*, and goes to considerable trouble to narrate their acquisition and its consequences. In essence, then, Bok builds his own subjectivity out of the metonymic traces of these other, more illustrious authors.

After having achieved some notoriety as "the well-known Brooklyn autograph collector" (20), Bok decides to take a trip to New England to collect the autographs of famous U.S. literary and political figures, many of whom appear in the opening pages of *The Education*. The ensuing episodes narrate Bok's appropriation of an entire literary and cultural heritage through a gradual recontextualization of the signatory act. First he goes to Holmes himself, who gladly writes out a four-line poem with his signature on the flyleaf of one of his books. Next Bok goes to Longfellow, but this time he dictates his favorite poem—"so familiar to every schoolboy" (42)—to the poet as he writes and signs it. Afterward, Bok visits Adams's second cousin and Harvard classmate, Phillips Brooks, who instead of copying an original work, writes Bok a thank-you note for an article recounting an earlier visit. Slowly but surely, Bok's own writing recontextualizes the signatures of these New England sages; the cultural capital of their names becomes an investment in his own.

The most remarkable illustration of Bok's tactics would have to be his encounter with Ralph Waldo Emerson, aptly titled "Emerson's Mental Mist." Bok claims that "the philosophy of the Concord sage made a peculiarly strong appeal to the young mind," but by this time Emerson is old and senile, hardly capable of engaging this "young mind" at all (34). The results, both poignant and telling, are worth reciting in full:

> "Mr. Emerson, will you be so good as to write your name in this book for me?" and he brought out an album he had in his pocket.
> "Name?" he asked vaguely.
> "Yes, please," said the boy, "your name: Ralph Waldo Emerson."
> But the sound of the name brought no response from the eyes.
> "Please write out the name you want," he said finally, "and I will copy it for you if I can."

> It was hard for the boy to believe his own senses. But picking up the pen he wrote: "Ralph Waldo Emerson, Concord; November 22, 1881."
> (57–58)

After one failed attempt, Emerson achieves a moment of lucidity and is able to copy his own signature from Bok's "original." Both the failed and successful attempt are duplicated in *The Americanization*. Increasingly, it is Bok himself who dictates the form and context of the signatures, until Emerson is actually copying his own signature from Bok's version of it. Bok both rehearses and extends this appropriation though duplicating these signatures in his published autobiography. *The Americanization* brings Derridean iterability to its furthest extreme, mass-producing signatures like little written commodity fetishes lodged in its printed narrative stream. Conveniently, for my purposes, Bok's last visit is to Henry Adams's father, where he acquires "autograph letters" of John and John Quincy Adams.

In fact, it is not only the signatures that Bok collects and appropriates; he always tried to make sure that he acquired "actual letters which would tell him something useful" (18–19). And it is the so-called personality of each author, as expressed in these letters, that really interests Bok, as he later admits:

> Edward Bok was always interested in the manner in which personality was expressed in letters. For this reason he adopted, as a boy, the method of collecting not mere autographs, but letters characteristic of their writers which should give interesting insight into the most famous men and women of the day. He secured what were really personality letters. (204)

Bok then reproduces a series of these "personality letters"—from such figures as Twain, Henry Ward Beecher, William Dean Howells, and Rudyard Kipling—and this time, significantly, he renders them in print instead of facsimiles of the original handwriting. By this point in the narrative, Bok has been installed as editor of the *Ladies' Home Journal*, where he would perfect his methods of mediating the passage from private writing to publication. The recontextualization is complete, then, when the signature essentially sublimates into print to become a marketable personality. And Bok's reproduction of these letters in his autobiography makes these personalities part of his own.

Bok's contact with celebrities had more tangible effects. In 1887, he took advantage of his friendship with Beecher to start a weekly syndicate of "comment on current events" (80) by the enormously popular Brooklyn preacher. The success of this enterprise led Bok to organize his own syndicate and start his own column of "literary chat," titled "Bok's Literary Leaves" (108). Bok's connections, many of them established through assiduous autograph collecting, were paying off, and he was becoming well known in the newspaper and publishing industry.

Yet Bok's eagerness to circulate his name in the literary marketplace led to serious reservations about the relationship between authorship and audience in a market culture. In an 1895 article titled "The Modern Literary King," Bok laments the closing of an era when "the 'needs' of the publisher, the 'requirements' of the public, were far from the mind of the writer when he wrote."[16] Adopting a somewhat different attitude toward the professionalization of publishing from that expressed twenty-five years later in *The Americanization*, Bok claims that "the successful authors of the day are under the thraldom of the modern literary king,—the almighty dollar" (335). Under these conditions, the author "is driven by a force he neither understands nor stops to analyze"; he is "simply 'under contract': his time, his brain, his mind is mortgaged" (335). And the responsibility for this mental mortgaging lies with none other than "the agency known as the 'newspaper syndicate' [which] has done much to infuse this commercial aspect into our literary affairs." According to Bok, "the newspaper syndicate is the sewer of the author" (340).

Clearly knowing whereof he speaks (he started "Bok's Literary Leaves" in 1886), Bok continues, "The syndicate is in business for money: for literature it cares very little. It is the author's name it is after, pure and simple" (341). Uncannily referencing his own early hobby, Bok affirms that "we have all of us by far too present the feeling that a certain effect can be had by the juggling of a great name, despite the material behind it" (342). Bok's high moral tone in this essay is belied by his own admitted role in the commodification of literary endeavor—both at the time of the essay's publication and in his later career—and his decision to distance his private from his editorial self becomes more intelligible in the context of his ambivalence about this role.

For the commodification of literature not only degrades content, it also vitiates authorial agency. Bok asserts that "the result is that most of our authors are nothing more or less than a species of literary telegraph-operators who transmit to their public a certain number of words in a given time at so much a word" (337). Once again, Bok knows whereof he speaks: his apprenticeship in publishing was in the capacity of a stenographer, passively taking the dictation of another's words (not entirely unlike Adams's apprenticeship to his father). Bok worked as a stenographer during the period he was marketing the Bok syndicate, first at Henry Holt and then at Scribner's, where as he observes in *The Americanization*, "he was given as close an insight as was possible for a young man into the inner workings of one of the largest publishing houses in the United States" (110). This "insight" into the "inner workings" nevertheless involves a sacrifice of agency analogous to being "literary telegraph-operators," and Bok is happy to eventually find himself "directing a stenographer instead of being a stenographer himself" (112).

Thus, by the time Bok took the helm at the *Ladies' Home Journal*, against the advice of all his friends and colleagues, he was already conflicted about his role in the literary marketplace. He had exploited the current interest in "names," and had to a degree become one himself, and yet he was anxious about the effects this fascination had on the relationship between authorship and audience. Bok's characterization of the emergence of his editorial persona is deeply contradictory:

> The method of editorial expression in the magazines of 1889 was distinctly vague and prohibitively impersonal. The public knew the name of scarcely a single editor of a magazine: there was no personality that stood out in the mind: the accepted editorial expression was the indefinite "we"; no one ventured to use the first person singular and talk intimately to the reader. Edward Bok's biographical reading had taught him that the American public loved a personality. . . . He felt the time had come . . . for the editor of some magazine to project his personality through the printed page and to convince the public that he was not an oracle removed from the people, but a real human being who could talk and not merely write on paper. (163)

The almost glaring contradiction here between the intimacy that Bok endorses and impersonality through which he projects his endorsement is telling. On the one hand, he wants a "real human being" who will "use the first person singular and talk intimately to the reader." On the other hand, the marked iteration of the third-person pronoun in reference to this intimate personality belies the apparent sincerity of Bok's claims. The sincere and intimate "personality" that Bok projects "through the printed page" is rendered artificial and impersonal by the form through which he chooses to project it. The public subject of Edward Bok emerges out of this contradiction in the performative practice of personality.

This contradiction in turn anchors the formal peculiarities of Bok's autobiography. Bok alleges in the preface and then stresses throughout the text that the editor of the *Ladies' Home Journal* was a separate, public personality who dominated his life for a time:

> This method came to me very naturally, in dealing with the Edward Bok, editor and publicist, whom I have tried to describe in this book, because, in many respects, he has had and has been a personality apart from my private self. . . . His tastes, his outlook, his manner of looking at things were totally at variance with my own. In fact, my chief difficulty during Edward Bok's directorship of *The Ladies' Home Journal* was to abstain from breaking through the editor and revealing my real self. (vii–viii)

Bok concludes: "I learned to subordinate myself and let him have full reign" (vii). "Myself"—Bok's private subjectivity—is subordinated to "him"—Bok's public personality—by a mediating "I," which in Bok's schizophrenic self-fashioning, plays the role of the editor in his autobiographical narrative. This schizophrenic power struggle is explicitly textual or, I would even say, editorial insofar as it is played out in the realm not only of print discourse but, more significantly, in terms of Bok's development of an editorial policy and agenda appropriate to a family magazine. Bok's desire to keep his public personality "apart" from his private life, to "subordinate" the private self to the public in his book and life, recapitulates in the printed narration of his professional life the editorial role that defined that life.[17] In *The Americanization*, Bok describes the editor's role as consisting of monitoring and managing the entry of private issues into the public forum of the magazine; his autobiography reveals how this can become a model for the self.

Third-Person Masculine

Just one year before Bok left Scribner's to take the helm at the *Ladies' Home Journal*, Henry Adams was negotiating with his boss, Charles Scribner, over the publication of the *History of the United States*. Adams had similar concerns about literary profit motives:

As I am not a publisher but an author, and the most unpractical kind of an author, a historian, this business view is mere imagination. In truth the historian gives his work to the public and publisher; he means to give it; and he wishes to give it. History has always been, for this reason, the most aristocratic of all literary pursuits, because it obliges the historian to be rich as well as educated. I should be very sorry to think that you could give me eight thousand a year for my investment, because I should feel sure that whenever such a rate of profit could be realised on history, history would soon become as popular a pursuit as magazine-writing, and the luxury of its social distinction would vanish.

I propose to give the work outright to the public and the publisher, but I have some objection to admitting the publishers' share in producing it to be greater than my own. This may be a fad, but I have seen the author squeezed between the public and the publisher until he has become absolutely wanting in self-respect, and I hold to preserving the dignity of my profession.[18]

Adams endorses a "gift" economy as autonomous from—if not subversive of—the profit economy undergirding even the more prestigious publishing houses. Such an endorsement anticipates the call Marcel Mauss would make in the conclusion to his influential study *The Gift* for a return to "habits of aristocratic extravagance."[19] For both Adams and Mauss, aristocratic benevolence provides a necessary check on the utilitarian ruthlessness of the capitalist economy. Correlatively, as Adams is quick to note, such benevolence helps sustain the "social distinction" on which it is based.

This figure of the "aristocratic" historian both perpetuates and eulogizes the Adams family's vexed relationship to republicanism and the American Enlightenment. The family name that once denoted revolutionary principles now confers class privilege. Adams can trade on the latter to reinforce his authority to judge the former. Both the aristocratic and Enlightenment extensions of Adams's name, however, support his resistance to seeing his text as a property from which he can personally profit. If the aristocrat looks down on the literary marketplace with class disdain, the Republican man of letters opposes private property in texts as contrary to the Enlightenment diffusion of knowledge. The text as gift to the public accommodates these attitudes to each other. This economy of the gift bears some similarity to the "theft" economy that Adams had proposed for his political journalism insofar as both offer alternatives to the corporate organization of the publishing industry and print marketplace; both propose that profits not accrue to the author, and both were ways for Adams to formulate his work as public property. Both, in other words, would appear to be ways of reconstructing a public sphere in the absence of the socioeconomic conditions that sustained it in the era of republicanism.

However, if piracy was a way of maximizing the circulation of the text at the expense of the author, the gift ended up being a way of maximizing the prestige of the author at the expense of the circulation of the text. If the piracy of anonymous texts was a way of subtracting the author from the calculus of the print marketplace, the gift was, conversely, a way of making sure that the author wasn't "squeezed between the public and the publisher." And certainly, the word on which the difference turns is the authorial name—in this case that august patronymic that for Adams was so complexly suspended between familial specificity and U.S. typicality. As authorial subject, Adams needed to preserve the "social distinction" and "dignity" of his name, but the history that his name unavoidably referenced as an object of study caused such differences to dissipate into the "democratic ocean" of the United States.[20] The solution to this problem was *The Education of Henry Adams*, in which Adams is both the dignified authorial subject and generic object of historical narrative.

It would be in the second half of *The Education* that Adams would explicitly fashion himself as a modernist author in response to transformations in gender relations that had much to do with the rise of figures like Bok and magazines like the *Ladies' Home Journal*. Adams's complex musings on gender exhibit the tendency Andreas Huyssen has identified in this period among male authors to view mass culture and mass society generally as feminine.[21] Commenting on the women of his own class, Adams claims that

> one had but to pass a week in Florida, or on any of a hundred ocean steamers, or walk through the Place Vendome, or join a party of Cook's tourists to Jerusalem, to see that the woman had been set free; but these swarms were ephemeral like clouds of butterflies in season, blown away and lost, while the reproductive sources lay hidden. (444–45)

Here, Adams figures the freedom of leisure-class U.S. women in terms of geographic mobility. They participate—along with Adams, who spent most of his widower years abroad—in the late-nineteenth-century rise of global tourism that was a harbinger of America's twentieth-century economic and cultural expansionism.

But in a telling simile, Adams discounts the historical significance of these "clouds of butterflies," implying that the deeper questions concern the more sedentary caterpillars, the working-class women who metaphorically represent the "reproductive sources" in the above passage on the social elite:

> In every city, town, and farmhouse, were myriads of new types—or type-writers—telephone and telegraph-girls, shop-clerks, factory-hands, running into millions on millions, and, as classes, unknown to themselves as to historians. (445)

Although the reference to "factory-hands" sustains a sense of the production ethos of the nineteenth-century United States, the addition of "telephone and telegraph-girls" and "shop-clerks" indexes the rise of a communications- and consumption-based economy. The seemingly incidental, yet crucial substitution of the hyphenated "type-writers" for "types" replaces the synecdoche of type—individual for community, part for whole—with the metonymy of the type-writer—tool for worker—and shifts the literal reference from nationality to occupation. These occupations—whose appended referents ("girl," "clerk," "hand") recursively humanize the possible meanings of "writer" in "type-writer"—further index a shift from productive source to communicative media. These jobs involve the mediation of goods and information; they are, in a sense, contemporary versions of the "private secretary." This somewhat indirect correlation with Adams's own career is reinforced by his final claim above, which juxtaposes these women's apparent lack of self-consciousness with the ignorance of "historians," presumably like himself.

A correlative shift from production to mediation is evident in Adams's meditations on the problem of self-consciousness.[22] Avowing that "no one could follow the action of a vivid dream, and still need to be told that the actors evoked by his mind were not himself," Adams continues with a passage that is critical to understanding the structure and significance of his text:

> The new psychology went further, and seemed convinced that it had actually split personality not only into dualism, but also into complex

groups, like telephonic centers and systems, that might be isolated and called up at will, and whose physical action might be occult in the sense of strangeness to any known form of force. (433)

Referencing an intellectual debt to the work of William James, Adams dispenses with the more coherent models of subjectivity that grounded his prior writing. Certainly this decentered dispersion bears little similarity to the rational subject of the public sphere or volitionless type produced by a machine culture. Rather, as a "complex group" of "telephonic centers and systems," personality bears a resemblance (if not a relationship) to the "telephone and telegraph-girls" who so vitally mediate and enable the new culture of communications.

Thus, N. Katherine Hayles's assertion that the third-person form of *The Education* "constitutes as a possibility the belief that some authorial self lingers beyond the reach of textuality, autonomous, self-determined in a way that a character obviously is not," should be read in gendered terms.[23] The need to posit an autonomous consciousness outside the text emerges from the text's structural resemblance to a feminized culture in which autonomous agency is vitiated.

Bok arrived at similar conclusions. First of all, the magazine editor is by his very nature something of a medium as opposed to a source of literary production; for Bok, however, this subversion of agency was compounded by the fact that he was a man editing a women's magazine. In his early editorials, Bok felt the need to justify this incongruity, and his language is revealing. Claiming that he benefits from his mostly female editorial staff, he remarks, "*They* know, even if *I* do not, and their counsels are my laws. So, like the phonograph, I am only the mouthpiece of hearts and minds of your own sex behind me."[24] The similarity to his earlier characterization of modern authors as "literary telegraph-operators"—or Adams's representation of consciousness as "telephonic centers"—is striking, strongly implying that an additional reason for his decision to objectify his editorial self is that he felt he had subordinated—even prostituted—his voice to the needs and desires of his female readership. Thus, the prophylactic objectification of the autobiography—which shields the private author from the public editor—mirrors the actual objectification as the "mouthpiece" of U.S. women.

This is more than simply a textual strategy of self-fashioning. Subordination to the public was part of the actual editorial and commercial structure of the magazine. Bok based both his editorial personality and decision-making process on correspondence from his readers; in a sense, he constructed his entire readership as a massive focus group. In other words, Bok bothered to get to know Adams's millions of new women. His early editorials exhibit his tactics in action. One of his first editorial decisions was to offer prizes for answers to these questions: "What did you like best in the last issue, and why? What least, and why? What would you like to see?"[25] Soon after, Bok used the editorial page to describe the relationship he wanted with his readership:

> We believe in a close friendly relation between an editor and his readers. Too often the editor of a magazine stands aloof from his subscribers and no communication is offered between them. With us, it will be different. If at any time there is something which you think might interest me to know for the good of the *JOURNAL*, write and tell me of it.[26]

Bok realized that the active participation of his readers was key to the magazine's popularity. As he maintains in *The Americanization*, he strove "to accustom his readers to writing to his editors upon all conceivable problems" (174). He insisted that his editors respond to all correspondence, regardless of whether or not it was printed in the magazine; on certain occasions, he even sent people out to assist readers personally. Therefore, he contends that

> it was the comprehensive personal service, built up back of the magazine from the start, that gave the periodical so firm and unique a hold on its clientele. It was not the printed word that was its chief power. . . . Thousands of women had been directly helped by the magazine; it had not remained an inanimate printed thing, but had become a vital need in the personal lives of its readers. (179)

What gives life to this "inanimate printed thing" is an enormous network of handwritten things—letters running back and forth between the editorial staff and readership—that both invest the printed word with personality and mobilize the participatory agency of the readership.

This epistolary substrate not only problematizes Bok's agency as an editor—through obligating him at least partially to base his decisions on reader correspondence—but it also works to mask the corporate and commercial origins and objectives of the magazine. Richard Ohmann, speaking of early magazine advertising, claims that "markets were an impersonal medium of human relationship. Manufacturers had to overcome buyers' uneasiness at dealing with complete strangers."[27] Bok's editorial strategies are analogous in their purposes. Bok strove to personalize the magazine, to render it "animate" and "vital." He did this not solely through adopting an "intimate" first-person voice—significantly different from the impersonal, third-person narration of his autobiography—but by rendering this voice as the mouthpiece of its readers through encouraging their active correspondence. As a medium, Bok's personality distills itself into the magazine, which in turn comes alive as an intimate correspondent, adviser, and counselor to its readership.

Furthermore, Bok was acutely aware of the association of the *Journal* with vapid middlebrow culture, and this conflicted with the literary self-image he had established at Holt and Scribner's. Thus, he has a genuinely schizophrenic relation to the enormous success of his editorial policies:

> The editorial Edward Bok enjoyed this hugely; the real Edward Bok did not. The one was bottled up inside the other. It was a case of absolute self-effacement. The man behind the editor knew that if he followed his own personal tastes and expressed them in his magazine, a limited audience would be his instead of the enormous clientele that he was now reaching. (377)

The "editorial Edward Bok" appeals commercially to an "enormous clientele"; the "real Edward Bok" wants only a "limited audience." The narrative voice of *The Americanization* registers a textual schizophrenia that in his second autobiography, *Twice Thirty* (1925), Bok describes as an actual split personality. In a chapter recounting the end of his editorial tenure—titled "Twice-Born at Twice Thirty"—Bok portrays the struggle between his "selves" as "a mental battle which I distinctly remember as peculiarly exhausting, and resulted in a nervous breakdown."[28]

It is worthwhile rehearsing once again the nominal and pronominal shenanigans necessary to represent this "mental battle." In this far-more-rambling and episodic autobiography—published five years after the more successful *Americanization*—Bok briefly narrates "a period extending some six months when my own personality was undoubtedly dominant in the conduct of *The Ladies' Home Journal*" (374). He tries to give the magazine a "highbrow atmosphere" by publishing articles by famous authors (Kipling, Lyman Abbott, and Jane Addams, among others) on "the best and most trenchant questions of the day"; unfortunately, "the people revolted" (375). Bok remains vague as to the specific nature of the articles or responses, but eventually things return to normal:

> It was not long, however, before I felt that unconsciously my real self had lost my grip on the editorial helm, Edward Bok had risen to the surface and I was submerged. The contents went back to its former standard, the circulation leaped forward, and the subscription and advertising departments were happy once more! Edward Bok was in the saddle. But during the time I did function I felt no interference from the editorial personality; I was in full sway. Nor was I conscious of the time or the fact when I lost control and was submerged. But for a brief period I had my innings, and did an incredible amount of damage to the circulation. (375)

The editorial self is a creature linked to "subscription," "advertising," and "circulation," institutional entities that seem literally to take possession of Bok's body and name. Consequently, the textual construction of an artificial self refers to and reenacts a psychological story of possession by a public self—one that is generated autonomously as a proper name in the print marketplace.

If Bok chose to write his autobiography in the third person because of his enormous audience, Adams seems to have made his choice partly for the opposite reason. In a now-famous letter to his old friend Charles Milnes Gaskell justifying his decision to privately publish *The Education*, Adams claims:

> As my experience leads me to think that no one any longer cares or even knows what is said or printed, and that one's audience in history and literature has shrunk to a mere band of survivors, not exceeding a thousand people in the entire world, I am in hopes a kind of literary art may survive, the freer and happier for the sense of privacy and *abandon*.[29]

Adams anticipates the little magazine mentality—the resolute opposition to the middlebrow cultural marketplace—that would enable and sustain the rise of literary modernism. *The Education* was required reading for the generation of writers who published in these magazines, and it has since been canonized by U.S. academics as an inaugural expression of the modern alienated consciousness.

In the very year of the above letter's composition, though, one of the "young men, in universities or elsewhere" (*xxx*) to whom the preface to *The Education* is addressed got his hands on a copy of it and immediately realized that this public prefatorial rhetoric was more accurate than the private epistolary rhetoric of the author. Ferris Greenslet, assistant editor of the *Atlantic Monthly* and literary adviser to Houghton Mifflin's book division, spent the next decade trying to persuade Adams—now a cranky octogenarian—to publish *The Education*. Greenslet, a young easterner with a PhD from Columbia and an illustrious future in U.S. publishing, was a perfect accommodation of the conflict between Adams's elite and populist forms of audience address. As Greenslet himself reports in his own autobiography, *Under the Bridge*, his pursuit of *The Education* was his "most exciting professional experience."[30] Over the course of an extensive rhetorical courtship, he gradually wore Adams down to permitting posthumous publication—a compromise that seems particularly appropriate to *The Education*'s rhetorical reliance on absences. Posthumous publication would ensure that the gap between private subject and public persona remained permanently unbridgeable.

Such a decision also takes Adams's economy of the gift to its furthest degree, assuring that on the one hand, he will never personally profit from the book's entry into the marketplace, while on the other, his public will owe him a literary and cultural debt that in a sense can never be repaid. Adams told Greenslet that the book would lose money, but in a final and appropriate irony, *The Education* won the Pulitzer Prize in 1919 and became the leading nonfictional best seller of that year. Once his private self had passed away, the U.S. public would breathe new life into the autobiographical "manikin" of Adams's posthumous preface.

Both *The Education of Henry Adams* and *The Americanization of Edward Bok* can be seen as attempts at formulating and enacting a subject as well as a mode of intersubjectivity fit for cultural authority in a modern mass-mediated world. Both texts envision this subject as an effect of the tension between private writing and public circulation—an effect whose trace is iteratively marked through the repetition of the proper name. Both texts locate this subject at the anxious intersection between gender identity and commercial culture—an intersection that is iteratively marked through the repetition of the masculine pronoun. And both texts confirm the reputation of their authors as representative men in the modern world.

Nevertheless, they came to represent considerably different segments of the U.S. middle class, and their divergent reception over time mirrors the mode and manner through which they both solicit readerly attention and envision representative authority. *The Education* centripetally recedes into a space of writerly privacy and literary form, while *The Americanization* centrifugally expands into a horizon of print publicity and literary formulas. As such, *The Education* persists in the canon of American literary classics—in fact, Modern Library recently deemed it number one on its list of the one hundred most important nonfictional books of the twentieth century—even as *The Americanization* vanished into the archives of the American success story. Adams thus inaugurates the modern consciousness that would provide an intellectual insulation from the mass audience, while Bok inaugurates the public subjectivity that enabled that very audience to come into being.

2

Trademark Twain

As the cases of Adams and Bok indicate, the rise of consumer capitalism in the United States coincided with a notable increase in the publication of autobiographies by writers and journalists. According to Louis Kaplan's *Bibliography of American Autobiographies*, only twenty-six autobiographies were published by authors, journalists, or novelists between 1800 and 1880. In the forty years between 1880 and 1920, however, thirty-four authors, sixty-one journalists, and eighteen novelists each published at least one autobiography. Many published two or more.[1] Thus, in half the time, well over three times as many autobiographies of U.S. writers were published. Twain, Louisa May Alcott, London, James, William Dean Howells, and countless others less prominent felt the need to account for their careers through autobiographical reflection. It became almost imperative in these years for authors to write some sort of memoir. Furthermore, novels themselves, from *Little Women* to *Martin Eden*, became more conventionally autobiographical in both form and content, and critics and reviewers increasingly looked for biographical sources and parallels in novels published by well-known authors. Imaginative writing increasingly became understood as expressing the marketable personality of the writer, and modern authorial autobiography emerged as a generic recognition of this interpretative paradigm.

No American writer more completely and enthusiastically embodied this overlap between the cultural performance of authorial personality and the generic reliance on authorial autobiography than the man known as Mark Twain. More than any other author of the nineteenth century, Twain's life story was inextricably entangled with his writing, and this informing autobiographical impulse has in turn dictated the popular and critical reception of his texts to this day. This critical credo was established by Twain's friend, Howells, in 1882, when in an essay for the *Century Magazine* that Twain's official biographer Albert Bigelow Paine called "a kind of manifesto," Howells affirmed that "in one form or another, Mr. Samuel L. Clemens has told the story of his life in his books."[2] Three decades later, Stuart Sherman, in a review of Paine's three-volume biography, confirmed that "Twain had been writing autobiography in one form or another for fifty years."[3] Twain's most well-known post–World War II biographer, Justin Kaplan, concedes that Twain himself was "always his own biographer" and that "the central drama of his mature literary life was his discovery of a usable past."[4] More recently, Richard Lowry has maintained that Twain "never repudiated . . . the authorial autobiography that shaped his early work."[5] From his first explosion onto the national scene in 1869 with the publication of his hugely popular travel narrative, *The Innocents Abroad*, up through the theoretically sophisticated criticism of the present day, Twain's literary output has been understood as fundamentally autobiographical.

And yet, ironically, his actual autobiography was never completed, never fully published, and has received little critical appreciation in comparison to his more well-known work. Paine's two-volume version, published in 1924, was not a critical or popular success, and Paine felt compelled to concede that the text "was not really autobiography at all."[6] Paine's successor as Twain's literary editor, Bernard DeVoto, in his introduction to *Mark Twain in Eruption*—a selection of dictations excluded from Paine's edition of the autobiography—agreed that although Twain is one "of the most autobiographical of writers, he is least autobiographical when he tries to be."[7] Since DeVoto, the editorial approach to the autobiographical dictations has split between those who endorse some version of fidelity to Twain's intentions and those who believe that their own editorial intentions should intervene. Hence, Charles Neider, for his version of *The Autobiography of Mark Twain*, decided to completely reorganize the autobiographical material into a chronology that he felt was "the order functional to it, inherent in it, the order which is in harmony with its subject"—a claim that met with almost universal critical skepticism.[8] Nevertheless, Michael Kiskis's more recent claim that his republication of the excerpts that originally appeared in the *North American Review* can be treated "as the text of Clemens's life story" seems equally dubious.[9] Each of Twain's editors has felt the need to apologize for his edition, to clarify its problematic relation to Twain's intentions and the genre in which Twain himself placed it, and as Robert Atwan notes, to criticize the version(s) that preceded it.[10]

One other element that all of the editions—as well as any other critical work that uses previously unpublished materials—have in common is the copyright of the Mark Twain Company to which Twain assigned all of his literary property. Originally formed in 1908, the Mark Twain Company became the Mark Twain Foundation on the death of Clara Clemens Samassoud in 1962, under the trusteeship of the Manufacturers Hanover Trust, and pledged to enable "mankind to appreciate and enjoy the works of Mark Twain."[11] In other words, Twain's posthumous existence is now overseen by one of New York's largest investment banks.

Twain was always anxious about the legal disposition of his intellectual property, and this chapter argues that his autobiographical project was conceived as and developed quite literally into this incorporation of authorship. First, I show how Twain based the formal innovations of his autobiography in the ostensibly democratic foundations of authorship, and specifically autobiography, in the United States. But these formal innovations, though based on a democratic philosophy of authorship, did not meet with a democratic readership; the unusual form actually impeded the book's success in the literary marketplace. In order to account for this apparent contradiction, I examine Twain's peculiar location, late in life, between a restricted field of cultural production that mandates a posthumous reputation and a general field of cultural production that mandates contemporaneous mass cultural celebrity. Part protomodernist genius, part populist icon, Twain's syncretic public image illuminates the autobiography's reception problems, as well as Twain's intention to publish it posthumously. Finally, I contend that Twain's decision to bequeath the voluminous autobiographical dictations to his editors reveals how celebrity makes authorship a corporate affair. I thus conclude by discussing Twain's attempts to trademark his pen name as signaling a new model of U.S. authorship—one that legitimates literary property less as a mark of intellectual labor than as an index of cultural recognition. In this way, Twain could envision authorial autobiography in a democracy as a corporate project that would persist long after his physical death.

The Republic of Letters

If on the one hand, authors in the late nineteenth century were increasingly expected to account for themselves autobiographically, the rise of autobiography in the United States, on the other hand, challenged conventional notions of who, in the end, could claim to be an author in the first place. In a society increasingly integrating the discourses and practices of universal literacy and democratic citizenship, autobiography came to be understood as the generic expression of literary democracy. In a 1909 editorial column for *Harper's*, Howells, affirming that "we would not restrict autobiography to any age or sex, creed, class, or color," declared the genre to be the "most democratic province of the republic of letters."[12] According to Howells, the writer of autobiography need not meet any of "the ordinary specifications for authorship." Howells then makes a peculiar plea for an autobiography that he believes would validate these democratic claims. He would

> like to have some entirely unknown person come out with his autobiography and try if it will not eclipse the fiction of the newest novelist whose work we sometimes see commended by its advertiser because it is new. For once we should like to have such an autobiographer wreak himself upon the very truth, and we should not join any detective force in compelling him to put off his mask, if he chose to remain anonymous.[13]

In hoping that an anonymous autobiography can outflank the publicity apparatus that the advertiser exploits to promote the "newest novelist," Howells contrasts his "democratic province" with the emerging corporate order that increasingly influences the logic of the literary marketplace. And yet, he also implicitly connects them insofar as both the democratic and corporate logic rely on the basic assumption that anyone can be an author. His call for an autobiography of an unknown person dialectically links the literary ideal of a "republic of letters" to the literary culture of celebrity in the United States that emerged in the late nineteenth century.

Howells omnivorously dwells on a wide variety of autobiographies, but he makes a point of emphasizing that "the most popular autobiography of our time, outcirculating and outselling any fiction, was the story of a soldier," Ulysses S. Grant.[14] *The Personal Memoirs of Ulysses S. Grant* was one of the most popular autobiographies published in the nineteenth century, at least partly because Twain convinced Grant to publish it on a subscription basis with his newly formed publishing house, Charles L. Webster and Company. In fact, Grant's memoirs were the most successful venture of Twain's ill-fated foray into publishing. And at least according to Twain's first biographer, Paine, it was his negotiations with Grant that prompted Twain to begin dictations for his own autobiography.

For both Twain and Howells, the success of Grant's memoirs was proof that one need not be a professional author to write great literature. In a public dispute with stockbroker and literary critic Edmund Clarence Stedman over the existence of "literary genius," Howells claimed that Grant's autobiography, "written as simply and straightforwardly as his battles were fought, couched in the most unpretentious phrase, with never a touch of grandiosity or attitudinizing, familiar, homely, even common in style, is a great piece of literature."[15] In an equally public dispute with Matthew Arnold over "General Grant's Grammar," Twain agreed that "General Grant's book is a great and, in its peculiar department, a unique and unapproachable literary masterpiece," a verdict later confirmed by U.S. literary figures from James to Stein.[16] *The Personal Memoirs of Ulysses S. Grant* became something of a flash point for proving that "great literature" need not be written by great writers, and for further affirming autobiography as the genre in which this proof is illustrated.

Moreover, the astonishing success of Grant's memoirs confirmed for Twain the wisdom of the subscription method of publishing that had established his own fame—a publishing method that explicitly bypassed the literary centers of Boston and New York, and focused instead on the U.S. heartland. As his own critics and biographers have repeatedly observed, Twain's unprecedented success in the subscription market established him as the "people's author," and gradually transformed American understandings of the literary marketplace. The subscription audience, in effect, came to represent the literary masses.[17] Twain himself repeatedly asserted that he wrote for "the masses"; however, commenting to Andrew Lang on the negative reviews he had been receiving in England for his *Connecticut Yankee in King Arthur's Court*, he complained that this "audience is dumb; it has no voice in print" (*MT*, 2:895).

If it was an audience without public voice, though, it was not without private income, and in an interesting exchange with Robert Louis Stevenson, recounted in his autobiography, Twain reflects on the economic and cultural clout of these anonymous literary masses. Stevenson asks Twain if he can "name the American author whose fame and acceptance stretch widest and furthest in the States." When Twain modestly refuses to answer, Stevenson mentions an unknown author named "Davis," whose compilations of speeches, poetry, and the like need "to have freight trains to carry them, not baskets." According to Stevenson,

> Nobody has heard of Davis; you may ask all round and you will see. You never see his name mentioned in print, not even in advertisements; these things are of no use to Davis. . . . You never see one of Davis's books floating on top of the United States, but put on your diving armor and get yourself lowered away down and down and down till you strike the dense region of eternal drudgery and starvation wages—there you will find them by the million. The man that gets that market, his fortune is made, his bread and butter are safe, for those people will never go back on him. (*MTA*, 2:249)

Stevenson and Twain coin a new term for Davis's literary reputation: "submerged renown" (*MTA*, 2:249). In this depth metaphor, the literary marketplace acquires a heavy ballast of readers in the rapidly expanding and increasingly literate working classes, but the names and needs of this audience, and the authors who address them, never rise to the surface of the public sphere.

Twain's own celebrity, derived from a subscription audience suspended somewhere between the genteel surface and proletarian depths, implicitly emerges as a passage between them. Unlike Davis, Twain's name is frequently mentioned in print; yet like Davis, his principal audience has no public voice. Twain's enthusiastic endorsement of Grant's literary credentials, as well as his lifelong promotion of himself as the people's author, represent an attempt not only to give voice to this unknown audience but to elevate its cultural currency in the public sphere as a ballast for his own popularity.[18]

However, Twain's own rambling, shapeless autobiographical reflections could not have been more different in form from Grant's rigidly linear narrative, nor did they ever achieve a comparable popularity. *The Personal Memoirs of Ulysses S. Grant* methodically and emotionlessly recount the military campaigns and political developments that led to Grant's enormous public prominence, and this prominence in turn made it one of the great publishing successes of the nineteenth century. Twain's wandering reflections, in contrast, follow no apparent temporal order, and the U.S. public was generally disappointed with the version Paine published in 1924. Thus, Grant focused on the objective unfolding of events in a manner that appealed to the American audience's almost insatiable desire for fact-based historical narrative, while Twain concentrated on his own subjective ordering of memory in a manner that violated the audience's expectations of the genre as well as its expectations of him.

Nevertheless, Twain conceived of his formal innovations in democratic terms. He intended his autobiography to "become a model for all future autobiographies when it is published," because it

> deals merely in the common experiences which go to make up the life of the average human being, and the narrative must interest the average human being because these episodes are of a sort which he is familiar with in his own life and in which he sees his own life reflected and set down in print. The usual, conventional autobiographer seems to particularly hunt out those occasions in his career when he came into contact with celebrated persons, whereas his contacts with the uncelebrated were just as interesting to him and would be to his reader, and were vastly more numerous than his collisions with the famous. (*MTA*, 2:245)

Twain's argument links his defiance of autobiographical conventions with his emphasis on "the life of the average human being." Unlike Grant's memoirs, his autobiography must be *formally* exceptional in order to be *culturally* representative. In 1904, Twain decided on and described these formal innovations:

> Finally . . . I hit upon the right way to do an Autobiography: Start it at no particular time of your life; talk only about the thing which interests you for the moment; drop it the moment its interest threatens to pale, and turn your talk upon the new and more interesting thing that has intruded itself into your mind meantime. Also, make the narrative a combined Diary *and* Autobiography. In this way you have the vivid thing of the present to make a contrast with memories of like things in the past, and these contrasts have a charm which is all their own. (*MTA*, 1:193)

Instead of being ordered chronologically, the dictations would follow the order of his own spontaneous train of thought, constantly bringing the present into associative contact with the past. For him, the text followed "the law of *narrative*, which *has no law*" (*MTA*, 1:237).

Twain's critics have generally tended to legitimate this form in high modernist terms. Jay Martin offers it as proof that "Twain was the first writer able to reflect the structure of the modern mind, his own, in literature"; Robert Atwan remarks that "Twain's preoccupation with mental processes and his deliberate rejection of conventional narrative sequence make his book not so much a failed autobiographical effort but an important precursor of modern self-consciousness"; and Henry Nash Smith contends that Twain's autobiography should be "considered a flawed but magnificent anticipation of Proust."[19]

But the memories that Twain strives to recollect are resolutely more broad based than Proust's. Twain wanted to recall and record not only his own memories but those of his audience, an audience that seemed to encompass the entire world. In fact, his agenda was at least partly to trouble the difference. Thus, in the opening pages of the second volume of Paine's edition of the *Autobiography*, Twain comments on the many individuals who claim to have known him personally in the past:

> If a person thinks that he has known me at some time or other, all I require of him is that he shall consider it a distinction to have known me; and then, as a rule, I am perfectly willing to remember all about it and add some things that he has forgotten. (*MTA*, 2:4–5)

For Twain, one of the protocols of democratic fame is to participate politely in the imagined intimacies it generates, to assist his fans in spinning stories about a shared past that never happened. His elderly solicitude for the fantasies of his audience bleeds over into the structure and intent behind the autobiography itself, which is casually to recount his "contacts with the uncelebrated" (*MTA*, 2:245).

These contacts are not restricted to personal encounters; Twain is equally concerned to incorporate epistolary correspondents. He alleges that "for thirty years, I have received an average of a dozen letters a year from strangers who remember me, or whose fathers remember me as boy and young man" (*MTA*, 2:173), further confirming how celebrity engenders imagined memories. More significantly, letters to someone as well known as Twain need not be addressed with any precision; he claims to have received one from Europe addressed simply to "Mark Twain, Somewhere" (*MTA*, 1:241). According to Paine, Twain also received letters addressed to "Mark Twain, United States," "The World," and "Anywhere"; that these letters were successfully delivered underscores, for

Paine, "the farthest horizon of fame" (*MT*, 2:566). On this far horizon, the resolute specificity of the name Mark Twain bleeds into the abstract generality of "Somewhere" and "Anywhere." His "surface" notoriety diffuses out into the anonymous depths of his audience.

And yet, the autobiography's failure in the literary marketplace would seem to belie the democratic philosophy that informs its composition. Twain may have hit on a democratic method of producing an autobiography—he bragged that "no talent is required to make a Combined Diary and Autobiography interesting" (*MTA*, 2:193)—but it was not destined to be democratically received. Twain had violated his mass audience's expectations by producing a modernist text. It is not clear, however, that Twain intended the autobiography to be a popular text, or that in the end, popularity would be the only index of the project's success. In fact, Twain knew that the autobiography could never really be published as a single, authoritative text. Rather, he conceived of its publication as a fragmentary and gradual affair that would be supplemental to, as opposed to independent of, the popularity of his more well-known texts. In order to unpack Twain's complex and often contradictory intentions regarding the publication, as opposed to the composition, of his autobiography, it is necessary to examine his ongoing efforts to accommodate mass cultural and modernist understandings of the U.S. literary marketplace.

BeTwain Two Deaths

In September 1893, Twain published a short story in *Cosmopolitan* titled "Is He Living or Is He Dead?" The story recounts a discussion between Twain and a man he calls "Smith" at the Hotel des Anglais on the French Riviera.[20] The two notice another man who Twain identifies as Theophile Magnan, "an old, retired and very rich silk manufacturer from Lyons. . . . I guess he is alone in the world, for he always looks sad and dreamy, and doesn't talk with anybody" (109). Smith proceeds to narrate Magnan's story, a story that usefully illuminates the peculiar cultural conditions out of which Twain's autobiographical project would emerge.

Smith—whose real name is never given—claims that he and Magnan were starving artists in their youths, when they came up with a clever plan to artificially inflate the value of their paintings. The friends are confident that their works are of "such great and high merit, that, if an illustrious name were attached to them they would sell at splendid prices." All they need to do, Smith reasons, is "*attach* an illustrious name to them!" (112). Smith bases his plan on a widely shared assumption about the value of art:

> The merit of many a great artist has never been acknowledged until after he was starved and dead. This has happened so often that I make bold to found a law upon it. This law: that the merit of *every* great unknown and neglected artist must and will be recognized and his pictures climb to high prices after his death. My project is this: we must cast lots—one of us must die. (113)

Smith's friends are initially astonished and chagrined at this apparently macabre plan, but he assures them that "the man doesn't really die; he changes his name and vanishes" (113). Smith bases his ruse on one of the fundamental tenets of Bourdieu's restricted field of cultural production: that "asceticism in this world is the precondition for salvation in the next," or in other words, that the true reputation of an artist, and the value of his or her work, is only established after death.[21]

The rest of Smith's plan is firmly situated in the general field of cultural production, though, as he lays out a program for mass-producing the artist's work prior to his death:

> During the next three months the one who is to die shall paint with all his might, enlarge his stock all he can—not pictures, *no!* skeleton sketches, studies, parts of studies, fragments of studies, a dozen dabs of the brush on each—meaningless, of course, but *his*, with his cipher on them; turn out fifty a day, each to contain some peculiarity or manner-ism easily detectable as his. (113)

Smith's plan, in essence, surreptitiously inserts a U.S. logic of mass production into a European (more specifically French) logic of artistic production through exploiting one crucial element they share: the value of the name. The "cipher"—in art, the signature on the artwork; in business, the brand name on the product—ensures value and authenticity in both fields. And almost astonishingly, the only thing necessary to leap from one field to another is to change names. Smith's plan is a success; he and his "dead" friend become rich for life. "Is He Living or Is He Dead?" economically illustrates what Bourdieu calls "the miracle of the signature or personal trademark . . . [as] a *valid imposture*," a designation that in many ways sums up Twain's entire career.[22]

This brief story exhibits a revealing structural apposition to Twain's discovery of his own famous "cipher," at least according to the versions recounted in Paine's biography and DeVoto's *Mark Twain in Eruption*. According to Paine, when the young journalist Sam Clemens first began writing anonymously for a public, he

> was not altogether satisfied. His letters, copied and quoted all along the Coast, were unsigned. They were easily identified with one another, but not with a personality. He realized that to build a reputation it was necessary to fasten it to an individuality, a name. (*MT*, 2:221)

Significantly, Clemens chooses the pen name of a dead man, Isaiah Sellers, who "would never need it again." Paine celebrates the appropriateness of this choice:

> The name of Mark Twain is as infinite, as fundamental as that of John Smith, without the latter's distribution of strength. If all the prestige in the name of John Smith were combined in a single individual, its dynamic energy might give it the carrying power of Mark Twain. (*MT*, 2:222)

The notoriety of the name therefore accrues from a concentration of the average, and the simple addition of this name augments the value of the work, which "was neither better nor worse than before, but it had suddenly acquired identification and special interest" (*MT*, 2:222).[23]

This now almost mythical tale of origins resonates quite remarkably with the cultural logic of "Is He Living or Is He Dead?" and clarifies Twain's own complex identification with both the teller and subject of the tale. On the one hand, by giving his companion the quintessentially American name of Smith and endowing him with the characteristically Yankee qualities of entrepreneurial inventiveness, Twain establishes an identification between himself and the narrator. On the other hand, by giving the subject of the tale a name with the same initials (reversed) as his pen name and representing him as an artist who fakes his death in order to elevate the value of his work, he implies a parallel critique of his own literary reputation.

In the years after he wrote this tale, Twain realized that his work had acquired a value that according to a high cultural logic of taste, should only be achieved after the author's death, and he inserted this contradiction quite self-consciously into his autobiographical project. Furthermore, by the time he began his autobiographical dictations, Twain knew that his public image would persist far after his death. The dictations themselves, consequently, are not only marked by a preoccupation with death but also were mobilized by Twain's desire to extend his own agency in his posthumous public image. As Alan Gribben puts it, Twain "virtually *willed* the creation of his posthumous legend."[24] This preoccupation is, of course, not uncommon for literary autobiographers; in fact, it could be said to characterize authorial autobiography. But Twain's particular interpretation of his autobiographical mandate reveals how acutely contemporary mass cultural celebrity inflects the more high cultural obsession with posthumous reputation.

Twain addressed an audience that was intimately familiar with the tragedies of his domestic life, and a considerable portion of his autobiographical dictations were prompted by the brief biography of him written by his daughter Susy when she was thirteen. Twain's preoccupation with his deceased daughter's biography, and his insertion of excerpts from it throughout this portion of his dictations, foregrounds the contrast between the domestic harmony of his years in Hartford, Connecticut, and the painful loneliness of the conditions under which the autobiography was conceived. But his discussion of the biography also reveals the degree to which he perceived of his public persona as both penetrating into and emerging from the private space of his household. He notes that he has "had no compliment, no praise, no tribute from any source, that was so precious to me as this one was and still is" (*MTA*, 2:65), aligning his daughter's text with the overwhelming accolades he had received over the course of his public career. Furthermore, he admits that once he discovered her project, he began "posing for the biography," much as he was doing for Paine at the very time he dictated these lines (*MTA*, 2:65). And this interpenetration of private life and public persona increasingly turns on death, as Twain figuratively resurrects Susy in order to forge his own posthumous image.

It would be these sections, prompted by Susy's biography and tenderly dwelling on Twain's Hartford family life, that Colonel George Harvey would choose to publish in the *North American Review* in 1906–7, the money from which Twain would use to build his last home, Stormfield, which he called "Autobiography House." Harvey's choice confirms the degree to which the private life—now only an elegiac memory—was gradually being absorbed into the public persona. Hamlin Hill, whose meticulous study *Mark Twain: God's Fool*, is the best account of Twain's final years, claims that these dictations represent his attempt "to speak as Samuel Clemens rather than as Mark Twain," but I would say that it's more accurate to understand the autobiographical project as a gradual conflation of the two into a composite posthumous image that was already in the process of formation.[25] Certainly, the *North American Review* articles confirmed that the private tragedies of Clemens had become part of the public image of Twain.

These articles violated Twain's original intentions not to publish any portion of his autobiography until after his death, and his intentions in this regard would form both the handwritten frontispiece and printed preface to Paine's edition of the *Autobiography*, which wasn't published until 1924. The frontispiece, a facsimile of Twain's handwriting, simply states, "I am writing from the grave." The much-quoted preface reads: "In this Autobiography I shall keep in mind the fact that I am speaking from the grave. I am literally speaking from the grave, because I shall be dead when the book issues from the press" (*MTA*, 1:xv). Both claims strive to link the posthumous text to the absent physical body of the author—the preface through emphasizing the text as a transcript of his spoken words, and the frontispiece through stressing the material trace of his own hand.

In fact, the degree to which Twain's written signature continues to be fetishized as a mark of his authorial intention is remarkable. Facsimiles of Twain's signature and/or handwriting appear on the flyleaf not only of Paine's version of the autobiography but also his biography, and are embossed on the cover of his edition of the notebooks; a facsimile of Twain's handwritten statement "this is the authorized Uniform Edition of all my books" appears with his signature on the flyleaf of every volume of Harper's Uniform Edition and his signature is embossed on the cover of every volume of the Stormfield Edition; the flyleaf of DeVoto's *Mark Twain in Eruption* has a facsimile of Twain's handwriting on a card he sent to the Young People's Society of Brooklyn; the flyleaf of Kaplan's *Mr. Clemens and Mark Twain* has facsimiles of both signatures; and Twain's signature is embossed on the cover and reproduced on the flyleaf of every volume of University of California Press's ongoing publication of the Mark Twain Papers. Thus, we continue to authenticate the value of Twain's work through the fetish of his signature as a lingering mark of his authorial presence and intention.

The autobiography further links the function of the signature to the function of the voice. Twain himself felt dictation to be the perfect method for autobiography, gushing to Howells, "What a dewy & breezy & woodsy freshness it has, & what a darling & worshipful absence of the signs of starch, & flatiron, & labor & fuss & the other artificialities."[26] Henry Nash Smith and William Gibson, commenting on this oft-quoted letter, view it as

> yet another expression of Mark Twain's delight in a prose style having the ease and apparent spontaneity of the spoken language. All his best work—including many passages of the Autobiographical Dictation—is written in such a vernacular mode.[27]

As a writer who got his start on the lecture circuit and whose specific method of literary realism relied heavily on the accurate transcription of spoken vernacular, Twain himself established the critical habit of authenticating his works through their imagined proximity to his own spoken voice.[28]

Twain reveals the link between this impulse to authenticate and the related impulse to be authentic when in the rest of his preface, he compares his autobiography to a love letter. According to Twain, "The frankest and freest and privatest product of the human mind and heart is a love letter; the writer gets his limitless freedom of statement and expression from his sense that no stranger is going to see what he is writing" (*MTA*, 1:xv). He concludes that "it has seemed to me that I could be as frank and free and unembarrassed as a love letter if I knew that what I was writing would be exposed to no eye until I was dead, and unaware, and indifferent" (*MTA*, 1:xvi). By withholding publication until after his death, Twain hopes to forge a generic syncretism between the most private and public of literary genres: the love letter between two private individuals and the autobiography of a famous figure addressed to a limitless public.

Most critics of the autobiography have, to varying degrees, interpreted it as a failure relative to these revelatory intentions, and certainly Twain exposes little of what we might consider to be his private life. I think that the significance of his stated intentions shifts, however, if we interpret the entire project in terms of Jacques Lacan's distinction between biological and symbolic death. Slavoj Zizek explicates Lacan's distinction "between the two deaths as the difference between real (biological) death and its symbolization." According to Zizek, "This gap can be filled in various ways; it can contain either sublime beauty or fearsome monsters."[29] Twain, I would like to argue, filled it with his autobiography.

First of all, that Twain was explicitly aware of this distinction for his public reputation in old age is clear from his astonishing plan to advertise antemortem obituaries for himself in *Harper's Weekly* in 1902. In terms of his literary reputation, Twain knew that he was, in a sense, already dead, and was therefore enjoying the somewhat paradoxical experience of witnessing his own posthumous existence. Twain's autobiographical voice emerges from this experience, this peculiar suspension between his literal death, which he knows is fast approaching, and his symbolic death, which given his enormous worldwide fame, he knows will take much longer to occur. This location is strangely devoid of the very intentionality that frames it:

> It is understandable that when I speak from the grave it is not a spirit that is speaking; it is a nothing; it is an emptiness; it is a vacancy; it is a something that has neither feeling nor consciousness. It does not know what it is saying. It is not aware that it is saying anything at all, therefore it can speak frankly and freely, since it cannot know that it is inflicting pain, discomfort, or offense of any kind. (*AMT*, 272)

Without the biological being in which his consciousness is housed, Twain's words become constitutively unmoored from their source. Pronominally, he shifts from "I" to "it"; phenomenologically, he becomes "nothing," an "emptiness," a "vacancy." Zizek elsewhere portrays the space between two deaths as "a demand that is not caught up in the dialectic of desire," and I think we can understand Twain's posthumous autobiographical persona in these terms, as an impossible drive for a form of authentic expression uncomplicated by the exigencies of subjectivity.[30] Twain wanted to create, in essence, a subject without subjectivity, for which duplicity would be impossible.

In this sense, the structural incompleteness and exhausting length of the autobiography is more important than any specific content it might reveal, as Twain was mostly concerned to expand the temporal gap between two deaths in which this subject "lives." For this, Twain needed some cooperation. He therefore continues the passage above, in which he is defending certain vengeful comments he made about his old business partner, Charles Webster:

> I am talking freely about Webster because I am expecting my future editors to have judgment enough and charity enough to suppress all such chapters in the early editions of this book, and keep them suppressed, edition after edition, until all whom they could pain shall be at rest in their graves. But after that, let them be published. (*AMT*, 272)

What Twain has said specifically about Webster seems less significant here than his confident expectation that his "future editors" will issue "edition after edition" of his autobiography to correspond with the deaths of those maligned in its pages. He knows his editors will keep his drive alive after his body dies, continually expanding the gap between his biological and symbolic deaths. The autobiography, in other words, was never intended to be a single, marketable text. Rather, it was conceived of as a corporate affair continuously ballasting the ephemerality of mass cultural celebrity with the posthumous persistence of high cultural fame.

Incorporating the Author

Twain was not the only person to exploit the freedom of speaking of himself from the gap between two deaths. In 1909, the year before his actual death—when he was still dictating the rambling autobiography that he would never finish—an article was published in the *North American Review* titled "Is Mark Twain Dead?" Eugene Angert, whose comparative obscurity significantly contrasts with Twain's public ubiquity at the time, opens his clever satire with the claim, "Mark Twain is dead. Not dead in any literary sense, but literally dead."[31] Angert alleges that Twain couldn't possibly have written the book most recently attributed to him, *Is Shakespeare Dead?* He therefore decides that Twain "died in the year 1906," the very year in which Twain started dictating the bulk of his autobiography and publishing portions of it in the *North American Review*. Angert argues that Twain's publishers have replaced him with "an impostor" in order to continue to reap the profits accruing to any text associated with his famous name: "If his death, when it occurred, could be kept secret, books written by the publishers' hacks might be given to the gullible public year after year as the latest offerings of Mark Twain."[32] Angert's article indicates the degree to which, in the words of one Twain scholar, "Twain's era had a consciously vivid picture of him apart from and, in some minds, above the caliber of his writings."[33] In his final years, everyone knew who he was, but few bothered to read his "latest offerings," and those who did were frequently disappointed. Furthermore, impersonating Twain had, by this time, become a profession in and of itself.[34] It would thus seem easy enough to fool the public into accepting an "impersonator for Mark Twain himself."[35] The most significant evidence that Angert offers for his tongue-in-cheek conspiracy theory is that "Mark Twain's latest works have been copyrighted in the name of the Mark Twain Company." Declares Angert, "The creation of this corporation is a convincing proof that Mark Twain is no longer alive" since there is "no reason for incorporating a live Mark Twain; but there [is] the strongest motive for incorporating the dead Mark Twain."[36] And Angert's nail in the coffin, so to speak, is the fact that "*Mark Twain was not one of the organizers of the Mark Twain Company. His signature does not appear to the agreement which constituted him as a corporation.*"[37] By dislodging the name from the signature, Angert breaks the metonymic chain that would link Mark Twain to the Mark Twain Company. According to Angert's clever conceit, the "Mark Twain" who emerges between two deaths—between 1906 when he began publishing excerpts of his autobiography and 1910 when he really died—is a corporate Mark Twain, a trademark name that ensures property in and elevates the value of books written by anonymous hacks.

Is Shakespeare Dead? which Twain originally intended to be part of his autobiography, relies on a similar signature logic. Twain opens with the statement that "scattered here and there through the stacks of unpublished manuscript which constitute this formidable Autobiography and Diary of mine, certain chapters will in some distant future be found which deal with 'Claimants.'"[38] Twain offers a variety of arguments for his assertion that Shakespeare is such a claimant, most of which were derived from two recent books, *The Shakespeare Problem Restated* by George Greenwood and *Some Characteristic Signatures of Francis Bacon* by William Stone Booth. And one of his most important pieces of evidence is that besides five stray signatures attributed to Shakespeare, "there are *no other specimens of his penmanship in existence*" (315). Twain further bases his contention on a comparison between the apparent silence of Stratford's residents on the occasion of Shakespeare's death and what he knows will be a considerably different response to his own death on the part of Hannibal's residents: "If Shakespeare had really been celebrated, like me, Stratford could have told things about him; and if my experience goes for anything, they'd have done it" (332). Significantly, Twain compares himself to Shakespeare not in literary terms but in terms of popularity. The authenticity of Shakespeare's signature is dubious because it is not ratified by contemporaneous public acclaim.

Is Shakespeare Dead? was the first book to be copyrighted by the Mark Twain Company, which was incorporated in 1908, with Clemens, his secretary Isabel Lyon, his business manager Ralph Ashcroft, and his two daughters Clara and Jean as the original officers. There are two main reasons offered for why Twain took this unprecedented legal step. According to Paine, Clemens "incorporated his pen name, Mark Twain, in order that the protection of his copyrights and the conduct of his literary business should not require his personal attention" (*MT*, 3:1485). By this time, Twain was getting old, and his business dealings were complicated and time-consuming; the company allowed him to delegate many of the tasks involved in managing and maintaining his property. Yet according to the *New York Times* article reporting on the formation of the company, Twain incorporated his name "in order to keep the earnings of [his] books continually in the family, even after the copyright on the books expires."[39] Twain was increasingly preoccupied with the financial fate of his daughters after his death, and he hoped that the company might provide them with legal leverage to extend his copyrights in the future. The formation of the Mark Twain Company, then, signified a legal consolidation of his literary property at the same time that in anticipation of his death, it vitiated his agency in determining the disposition of that property.

In fact, the story of the Mark Twain Company quite melodramatically documents the transformations in the relationship between literary property and authorial agency precipitated by the rise of corporate capitalism in the United States—transformations that are, in turn, crucial to understanding the complex agenda behind the autobiographical project. The company is only one element in this melodrama, the major characters of which are its original officers. Its formation briefly united these players, already entangled in a web of complex economic and domestic relations, into a single agency, an agency whose unity inhered in the problematic property known as Mark Twain.

The exigencies of the melodrama can be effectively traced through a trail of signatures—both absent and present—left on a series of key legal forms during these years. On May 7, 1907, Clemens apparently signed a form granting full power of attorney over all of his affairs to Isabel Lyon. On November 14, 1908—one month before the formation of the Mark Twain Company—this form was amended to include Ralph Ashcroft. Clemens later vigorously denied signing either of these forms, and his signature does not appear on the copies that are housed with the Mark Twain Papers. Nor does his signature appear on the extant copy of the Certificate of Incorporation of the Mark Twain Company, dated December 22, 1908. The legal status of Clemens's literary property during these years is thus constitutively ambiguous.

On March 18, 1909, Ashcroft married Lyon, and at the prompting of his daughter Clara, Clemens became violently suspicious of their intentions. After a series of confrontations and threats, Clemens revoked the power of attorney on June 1, 1909, broke off relations with the Ashcrofts, and the Mark Twain Company board was rearranged without them as officers. The *New York Times* published a brief article recounting the resolution of these affairs, and the details of this article so enraged Clemens that he began a letter to its publisher, Adolph Ochs, to clarify matters. The result is an unpublished document that has as much of a right as any to be considered Clemens's "real" autobiography: a four-hundred-plus-page rant that is known to Twain scholars as the "Ashcroft-Lyon Manuscript."

The manuscript, marked "private" in Clemens's own hand, is addressed three times and signed twice. The first address is to Ochs, above a letter refuting a number of details in the *Times* article; this letter is signed "S. L. Clemens."[40] Immediately after this letter, however, is an address "To the Unborn Reader," followed by a series of prefatorial remarks inviting the future reader to witness "an intimate inside view of our domestic life of today." The value of ensuing narrative, according to Twain, inheres in its "authenticity," in the fact that its characters "are not inventions . . . [but] are flesh and blood realities." And obviously echoing the preface to his autobiographical dictations, Twain claims that he has decided to write this history in "the form of a letter to an old and sympathetic friend" in order to have "limitless freedom, liberty to talk right out of my heart, without reserve." This letter, which Clemens surely knew would be read by future scholars of his autobiography, is signed "Mark Twain."[41]

The voluminous document that follows is addressed to Howells, and amid the paranoid petty ravings at slights real and imagined emerges a fascinating story of a private individual losing control over his public persona. Once again, the linchpin of the drama is the authorial signature. As for the power of attorney, Clemens insists that "if my signature to it is genuine, it was procured by fraud."[42] Furthermore, he contends that the Mark Twain Company was "organized at a meeting which was never held, a meeting whose minutes are a fraud."[43] These two frauds are in fact closely related, as Clemens suspects that Ashcroft had abused his status as secretary and treasurer of the company to fraudulently obtain his signature on the power of attorney. As such, he claims that "I had signed a document which transferred my copyrights, real estate, and everything else, to Ashcroft, disguised as the Mark Twain Company."[44]

The result, according to Clemens's paranoid logic, is a complete inversion of agency, as his new relation to Ashcroft and Lyon is "that of master to slave, I being the slave."[45] Correlatively, he shifts from proprietor to property: "I had been their property, their chattel."[46] The formation of the Mark Twain Company did consolidate his property, but at the sacrifice of his control over and possession of it. Once his signature becomes dislodged from his agency, he ends up on the other side of the equation it legally signifies.

Clemens gradually realizes that the very power of his signature to signify possession has shifted. The last document in the manuscript is a letter dictated to Paine from Bermuda, dated March 2, 1910, little over a month before Clemens's death, in which he warns his official biographer that after he dies, it will "rain swindles and forgeries from the Ashcroft camp" since "Ashcroft has a supply of genuine signatures of mine in his possession on blank sheets of paper." The letter concludes with the question: "How much money has the Mark Twain Co. in [sic] bank?" It is initialed "SLC per HAS" since Clemens had dictated the letter to Helen Allen.[47] Thus, Clemens's signature doesn't appear on the letter conceding that his "genuine" signature can be as easily mass-produced as his books. By the end of his life, Clemens had almost entirely lost confidence in and control over the conventional function of his signature as a mark of both possession and personality—the peculiar combination of which form what we call intellectual property.

Twain had, of course, a lifelong fascination with the cultural and economic exigencies of intellectual property law. He invested in numerous patents—the Paige typesetting machine is only the most well known of many—and had been active in and frustrated with copyright reform over the entire course of his career. Twain never respected the constitutional mandate granting the government the right to set time limits on patents and copyrights, and all of his published arguments endorse perpetual copyright. Late in his life, though, Twain's anxieties about copyright took on a particular urgency as he was greatly concerned about the livelihood of his daughters after his death, the congressional Committee on Patents was meeting to consider extending the copyright limit, and he was negotiating for the publication of an official version of his works.

It was certainly an appropriate time to issue such a collection, but a good portion of his books were still the property of the American Publishing Company, the original subscription publisher that had issued many of his most popular works. As with so many of his former business associates, Twain had completely lost faith in the management of the firm that had essentially made his career, and he was attempting to shift the rights to all his works to Harper and Brothers, the company that did, in the end, become the official posthumous publisher of Mark Twain for the duration of his copyrights. The shift to what Twain, in an unpublished dictation, called "the great corporation of Harper and Brothers" indicates a broader transformation in literary distinction.[48] In fact, in many ways it signifies Twain's elevation to the status of the literary as such insofar as the subscription books were frequently perceived more as the works of a frontier humorist than an accomplished novelist. With the consolidation of all his works in Harper's hands, Twain's contradictory location on the cusp between the restricted and general fields of cultural production was assured. After his death, the Harper ads for the national edition lauded him as, on the one hand, "the greatest prose writer we had," a homegrown "genius." On the other hand, the books were bound in "a beautiful dark-red vellum book cloth, with blue title labels stamped in gold," and loudly offered at half the former price; Harper's bragged that "never before has a copyrighted library of a standard author's works been issued at such a low figure."[49]

Nevertheless, Twain did not feel that this canonized status was adequately recognized by the current laws of intellectual property, and the logic of his copyright arguments quite strikingly anticipates the type of property he himself would become for Harper's after his death. Prior to the extension of the copyright limit shortly before Twain's death, the limit was forty-two years, and as Twain pointed out in his speech before the congressional Committee on Patents, only "one author per year produces a book which can outlive the forty-two-year limit."[50] What Twain quite astutely recognized is that only authors who achieve classic status, whose literary reputations consolidate after their deaths, are affected by the copyright limits. Furthermore, Twain alleges that the apparent intention to bequeath these classics to the public is only a ruse under the conditions of the literary marketplace: "The Government does not give the book to the *public*, it gives it to the *publishers*."[51] And as he remarked in his speech, "They live forever, publishers do."[52] Since authors generally don't live forever, it seemed necessary to Twain to provide some protection for their literary property after their death.

Twain conceived of his autobiography as precisely such a protection. For one thing, he intended "to distribute it through my existing books and give each of them a new copyright life of twenty-eight years."[53] In 1904, he wrote Howells that the autobiography would "not be published independently, but only as *notes* (copyrightable) to my existing books. Their purpose is, to add 28 years to the life of the existing books."[54] At best, this must have seemed like a stopgap measure, and Twain in his later years explored other regions of intellectual property law for ways of establishing perpetual copyright through his autobiographical project. For one thing, he was intrigued by the practical limits of the government's seventeen-year limit on patents:

> The Government *can't* seize the really great and immensely valuable ones—like the telegraph, the telephone, the air-brake, the Pullman car, and some others, the Shakespeares of the inventor-tribe, so to speak— for the prodigious capital required to carry them on is their protection from competition.[55]

Generally speaking, the maintenance of literary property requires no such capital. During these same years, however, he began to conceive of his autobiography as precisely such a project: a form of literary invention as groundbreaking and capital intensive as the great technological inventions of the industrial era. Thus, as he wrote to his friend and financial adviser Henry Huttleston Rogers,

> I would like the literary world to see . . . that the *form* of this book is one of the most memorable literary inventions of the ages. And so it is. It ranks with the steam engine, the printing press, and the electric telegraph. I'm the only person who has ever found out the right way to build an autobiography.[56]

Not only does Twain conflate inventors and authors, patents and copyrights, but he compares his autobiography to those very inventions whose capital-intensive nature enables their owners to subvert the intellectual property laws. The autobiography, then, is a literary invention designed to subvert the time limit on copyright through requiring the continuous labor and investment of the officers of the Mark Twain Company (and now, the editors of the Mark Twain Project).

Twain had earlier considered another closely related and equally novel avenue to establishing perpetual property in literary works—one that clarifies the significant ambiguity around the term "Shakespeare" in his comments above. Is the name an object of or appositive to the "inventor-tribe"? In other words, does it refer to an invention or inventor? In the legal logic that undergirds patent and copyright law, a name like Shakespeare would indicate the owner of the intellectual property in question. Yet a new region of federal legislation emerged in the late nineteenth century around a third category of intellectual property, one never mentioned in the Constitution: the trademark. The idea of the authorial name as a trademark proposes a new relationship between author and text—one appropriate to the emergent corporate order in the United States. If copyright recognizes property in the text based on the author's labor in creating it, trademark registration recognizes property in the text as a commodity produced in the author's name. As legal scholar Bruce Bugbee maintains, trademarks have generally been considered different in kind from copyrights and patents since little or no creative inspiration or effort is assumed to have gone into their design.[57] Moreover, trademarks, unlike copyrights or patents, are granted in perpetuity and never expire.

Critics have long recognized the appropriateness of understanding the name "Mark Twain" as a trademark, but few have bothered to analyze fully the fundamental transformation this implies in our basic notion of literary property.[58] According to Louis Budd, Clemens considered registering the name Mark Twain as a trademark as early as 1873.[59] His first effort to legally establish his pen name as a trademark, however, was made in an 1883 lawsuit against Belford Clark and Company, which had published a collection of his writings that were not protected by copyright. But Twain's claim to trademark status did not fare well in the courts. In *Clemens v. Belford Clark and Co.* (1883) U.S. Circuit Court Judge D. J. Blodgett determined that the invention of a *nom de plume* gives the writer no increase of right over another who uses his own name. Trademarks are the means by which the manufacturers of vendible merchandise designate or state to the public the quality of such goods, and the fact that they are manufacturers of them; and one person may have several trademarks, designating different kinds of goods or different qualities of the same kind; but an author cannot, by the adoption of a *nom de plume*, be allowed to defeat the well-settled rules of the common law in this country, that the "publication of a literary work without copyright is a dedication to the public after which anyone may republish it."[60]

The judge affirms that "vendible merchandise" and "literary work" are distinct forms of property, and their distinctness justifies the separation between trademark registration, which is perpetual, and copyright registration, which is limited. Thus, in 1907, when Ashcroft resuscitated the idea of a Mark Twain trademark, his plan was to use it for such "vendible merchandise" as "tobacco, whiskey, shirt, corset, hair restorer, etc., etc."[61] In the end, Ashcroft only registered the trademark for whiskey and tobacco; the approach failed as a legal protection of Twain's literary property.[62]

The idea of the authorial name as a trademark did gain *cultural* currency at this time, however, and Twain conceived of and executed his autobiographical project in terms of these experiments in extending and consolidating his intellectual property beyond his death. His autobiographical dictations were an effort to pursue perpetual copyright according to a different legal reasoning than that which continued to undergird literary property theory. The autobiography, then, can at least partly be considered an attempt to pursue the logic of the trademark by different means.

In fact, it is interesting to note that legal scholars frequently explicate the legal logic of the trademark by way of analogy with the authorial signature. According to Rosemary Coombe, the trademark "operates as a signature of authenticity that the good that bears it is true to its origins— that the good is a true or accurate copy." Furthermore, "it registers a real contact, a making, a moment of imprinting by one for whom it acts as a kind of fingerprint: branding."[63] The trademark therefore relies on an indexical and metonymic logic not unlike that of the signature, and this "signature of authenticity" registering a point of "real contact" is necessary in the emergent "national market in which the distances between points of mass production and points of consumption might be vast."[64] Unlike copyright or patent law, trademark legislation was an emergent legal discourse recognizing the new conditions of a national mass market in which commercial transactions between strangers were becoming the norm.

Twain's inspiration that his name could be considered a trademark or brand name reveals his acute understanding of how this emergent legal discourse corresponded to changes in the cultural meanings of authorship. Unlike copyright, the authorial name or signature as a metaphoric form of trademark explicitly acknowledges a cultural relation of recognition between the public and text, as opposed to a legal relation of property between the author and text. The public need not be familiar with the author's name for copyright purposes, but for that name—or any other chosen pseudonym—to function as a trademark, it is necessary that the audience recognize and invest in it as the mark of a distinct textual product. This mutual recognition between author and public would have seemed much more adequate to Twain's relation with his audience than conventional copyright and its assumptions of authorial originality.

Indeed, Twain was never completely comfortable with the concept of originality as the basis for property in ideas. As Susan Gillman notes, he was obsessed with plagiarism and "rejected the possibility of originality in art."[65] Twain frequently recounted his consternation at discovering that he had "unconsciously plagiarized" the dedication to *Roughing It* from Oliver Wendell Holmes, and his consequent relief at Holmes's reassurance that everyone commits plagiarism, that "all our phrasings are spiritualized shadows cast multitudinously from our readings" (*MTA*, 1:241). On the other hand, Twain knew that such theories of creativity troubled the basic informing assumptions of literary property. In a brilliant essay discussing Twain's attacks on Christian Science and its founder, Mary Baker Eddy, Cynthia Schrager has shown how plagiarism for Twain "threatened the ethos of autonomous individualism central to his notion of authorship and the integrity of intellectual property."[66] Yet Schrager neglects to consider Twain's clever response to this threat. The authorial name as a trademark relieves the burden of originality on which this notion of authorship is based, enabling Twain to maintain his intellectual property without necessarily basing it on an autonomous individualism.

Furthermore, unlike with copyrights and patents, property in the trademark does not require any labor on the part of the proprietor. It is significant, in this regard, that Twain always emphasized that he was a lazy man, who did not consider writing as a form of labor. As he confirms in an unpublished dictation: "My life for the past thirty-five years and more has really been nothing more nor less than one long holiday, with three months' scribbling in each year which other people dignified with the great name of 'work,' but which to me was not work at all, but only play, delicious play."[67]

And he quite specifically conceived of his autobiographical dictations in these terms. When, some two hundred pages into Paine's edition, Twain hits "upon the right way to do an Autobiography," he declares that his dictations make "my labor amusement—mere amusement, play, pastime, and wholly effortless." And he observes that "no talent is required" to dictate an autobiography in this manner (*MTA*, 2:235). Rather, the writing simply bears the (trade)mark of his signature literary personality.

Twain's signature may not be a legally registered trademark, but the trademark, as a signifier of corporate ownership, is the best description of its significance for U.S. public culture. The facsimile of his signature has become the imprimatur of projects undertaken in the name of the Mark Twain Company, now the Mark Twain Foundation, and continues to mark the residue of his agency in publications selected, edited, and revised by others. Moreover, seeing the authorial signature and name as a trademark provides a conceptual register for understanding the cultural meanings of celebrity authorship more generally in the United States. As Coombe elsewhere asserts, "The names and likenesses of the famous are constitutive of our cultural heritage and resonate with meanings that exceed the intentions or the interests of those they identify or resemble."[68] Unlike copyright, the name and signature of the celebrity author as a trademark acknowledges and appropriates these other meanings by incorporating them into its nature as intellectual property.

More broadly, the shift from copyright to trademark can be seen as analogous to the shift from the restricted field to the general field of cultural production. In the restricted field of high cultural production—a field in which Twain's status was frequently tenuous—the cultural value of the text is seen to inhere in the intellectual labor and genius of the author. If copyright registers the legal recognition of this literary labor, trademark becomes the recognition of literary mass production, where cultural value depends as much on audience desire and demand as it does on authorial genius. The author as celebrity emerges in the ongoing tension between these two conflicting fields of production and evaluation in the U.S. literary marketplace. And no author negotiated this tension more effectively than Twain.

3

Legitimating London

When Jack London claimed, in an early letter to his friend Cloudesly Johns, that "to satisfy my various sides I should be possessed of at least a dozen astral selves," he couldn't have anticipated the peculiar manner in which his fame would ambiguously effect such a possession.[1] Almost as soon as London became well known, people started to impersonate him, and he entertained a persistent fascination with his doubles. Unlike with Twain, these impersonations tended not to be for entertainment purposes. In fact, London's first epistolary reference to another "Jack London" comes in the form of a criminal impostor using his name to cash checks at the Yellowstone National Bank in Billings, Montana, after convincing the local paper that London was actually in town. In his letter to the bank president, however, London claimed that he had long been plagued by doubles:

This double of mine is always getting me into trouble. Last year, while I was in Cuba, he was in Washington, entering into an engagement to deliver a lecture at the Congressional Library. Of course, he jumped the lecture, and I got the blame for being an "erratic genius," from the newspapers.

When I was East in January this year, he was making love to a married woman with two children in Sacramento, in my own State. And now I have his love-troubles on my shoulders, too.

When I was in Boston last year, he was in San Francisco, my native city, entering into engagements with school-teachers to gather data for a volume on Education that he was writing.

When I was in California, he was lugging away armfuls of books from the Astor Library in New York, on the strength of his being I.

When I was in California, in 1900, he was in Alaska, and when I was in China, in 1904, I was meeting the people who had met him in Alaska in 1900.

These are only a few of the instances of this miserable double of mine. I don't know what to do with him.[2]

London acknowledges not only that his authorial personality—his "erratic genius"—is at least partly a by-product of fame but that this famous personality also transcends the temporal and geographic limitations that normally determine the boundaries of the self. As an erratic genius, London can appear in two (or more) places at once. In fact, in this letter he chooses instances that almost symmetrically straddle the frontiers of the United States—California, Alaska, Boston, New York, Cuba—as if unwittingly recognizing how such impersonation affirms his national notoriety.

London henceforth made it something of a pet project to pursue his doubles. It took him four years from the date of the above letter to get an address. He promptly wrote to his double, assuring him that "we've a lot of experiences to swap," and emphasizing that he "is dreadfully anxious to have you tell me the ins and outs of the game you have been playing."[3] London assumes his invitation will be accepted since anyone impersonating him must have "read my stuff. I know it. I know you know it like a book; therefore, I am confident that you will know that this is a straight deal I am giving you."[4] London's invitation wasn't accepted, but the terms of the offer are revealing. His desire to "swap" experiences only partly masks a literary profit motive. Indeed, four years later London wrote to Edgar Sisson, editor of *Colliers*, claiming that "I have been pestered by 'doubles' from the beginning of my career. How would 50,000 words on the subject strike *Collier's*? I assure you that it will be very human, intensely interesting, and most sensational."[5] Unfortunately, London never wrote what would surely have been a fascinating narrative.

Nevertheless, London's desire to publish an account of his doubles is understandable since he knows that such impostures only become possible through the familiarity bred by publication. Thus he can write, "You know who I am, and you know who wrote the stuff that has appeared above my name," only because that name, which appears both above and below the letter in which this sentence appears, has become so public.[6] Having never met his double, London can still maintain that they have a prior bond through his published work, which he somewhat tautologically assumes his addressee knows "like a book." The entire relationship is based on the public circulation of texts associated with the universal familiarity of London's name. In this way, Jack London can "know," even if he never met, "Jack London."[7]

This desire to know and, in essence, be "Jack London," both for London himself and his various impostors, emerges from the same fascination with authorial names and personalities that both enabled and troubled Twain's career. Still, while Twain's fame remained rooted in genteel nineteenth-century literary institutions, with London we see emerging a more properly modern response to literary celebrity: the cult of the virile author in combat with a feminizing culture industry.

In this chapter, I will analyze this emergence in terms of London's struggles with legitimacy, both literary and biological. On the one hand, London had trouble establishing the legitimacy of his work as literature; he was himself seen as something of an impostor, and much of his work was accused of being plagiarized. For London, these attacks on this authorial legitimacy were intimately entangled with his anxieties over his legal illegitimacy, which he deliberately hid from public knowledge. As such, London's attempts to base the legitimacy of his authorship on a labor theory of literary value were closely related to his sense of himself as a legitimate son and father. In *Martin Eden*, London tried to resolve these anxieties through an allegory offering a feminized middle class as the source of the fictitious value of celebrity and a masculine working class as the source of the labor value of literature. But London was left with a contradiction: his recognition as an autonomous male author depended on his appeal to a feminizing mass audience. Indeed, when he died his reputation, at least in the United States, was uncertain. I conclude this chapter by showing how Irving Stone's controversial biography, *Sailor on Horseback*, resuscitated London's legend through exposing his illegitimate birth. Stone attempted to attribute London's talent to his inheritance from his "real" father, correlatively relating his decline later in his career to the women in his life. With London, then, we begin to see how the celebrity author in the United States is only intelligible as a conflation of literary and psychosexual anxieties. The celebrity image of the male author as an ersatz working-class hero—inaugurated by London, and then elaborated by Hemingway and Mailer—is constitutively overdetermined because the threat in both private and public spheres is the same: a loss of authorial agency.

Plagiarism, Primitivism, Publicity

Plagiarism accusations plagued London from the very beginning of his career, when he became well known as the "Kipling of the Klondike." One early reviewer contended that every publisher is trying

> to discover or create or boom into existence another Kipling. This is
> why the name Kipling creeps into the ads and why every new book,
> from a collection of love sonnets to a series of animal tales, is sure to be
> compared sooner or later with the author.[8]

Of London he asserts, "In this particular case there has been an evident attempt on the part of the author to duplicate Kipling's success, whose style he has studied so conscientiously that his own has become a mere echo." The reviewer supports his allegation with a series of parallel paragraphs from Kipling and London—a technique that would be used by all of London's accusers.[9]

One of the more sensational and symptomatic accusations involved London's short story "Love of Life." On March 25, 1906, Joseph Pulitzer's *New York World* published an article titled "Singular Similarity of a Story Written by Jack London and One Printed Four Years before a New Literary Puzzle." The article noted a "similarity in thought and phraseology" between "Love of Life" and Augustus Bridle and J. K. McDonald's "Lost in the Land of the Midnight Sun."[10] Since both narratives had been published in *McClure's Magazine*, Samuel McClure himself wrote to London requesting clarification. London's response provides a significant counterpoint to his attitude toward his doubles. If he resented the new mass public for circulating fantastic impostors of him, his defense of his methods of gathering material for his fictions turned the table on this process, allowing him to plagiarize from that very public for the material that they would consume.

His explanation begins with an indictment of the newspaper industry:

> Life is so short and people so silly, that from the very beginning of
> my career, when I first began to get newspaper notoriety because of
> my youthful socialism, I made it a point to deny nothing charged
> against me in the newspapers. On the other hand, I have made it a
> courtesy to deny such things when requested to do so by my
> friends.[11]

London implies that the journalistic quest for notoriety and sensation compromises the accuracy and reliability of the newspapers in which so many stories about him had appeared. But his ensuing explanation of the similarity between his "Love of Life" and Bridle and McDonald's "Lost in the Land of the Midnight Sun" seems to contradict this claim: "It is a common practice of authors to draw material for their stories from the newspapers. Here are the facts of life reported in a journalistic style, waiting to be made into literature."[12] London bases his defense on the apparent reliability and veracity of the very industry that circulates fictions about him. When papers use his life as a source for material, it is a question of "newspaper notoriety"; when he in turn uses them as a source for material, it is a question of "the facts of life."

Plagiarism—or at least the implication of it—would appear to result from the inevitable confusions between these two. In other words, if London uses material that has already been altered or falsified in some way by someone else, then literary "use" of journalistic raw material becomes literary "theft" of another's fictions. Later in the letter, London acknowledges that the difficulty in ascertaining and maintaining such distinctions makes for good copy:

> It might be well to explain how that half-page of deadly parallel was published in the *World*. In the first place, SENSATION. Sensation is the goods demanded by a newspaper of its space-writers. The suggestion of plagiarism is always sensational. When a half-page of deadly parallel is run in a newspaper, plagiarism is certainly suggested. The loose meaning of words in the average mind would make ninety percent of readers of such a parallel infer that plagiarism had been charged.[13]

Apparently the "deadly parallel" (the *World* had published passages from "Lost in the Land of the Midnight Sun" alongside passages from "Love of Life") between the facts of life and fictions of London results in "SENSATION." It is almost as if their proximity on the page provokes a palpable response in the "average mind," which can only negotiate the "loose meaning of words." If London can perceive the difference between public fact and proprietary fiction, he feels obligated to acknowledge that "ninety percent of readers" cannot, and that their inability can easily be exploited to sell newspapers.

For it is the value—both economic and cultural—of published words that is at stake here. And for London, this problem of value has less to do with profits than with paychecks. Here is the last paragraph of his letter to McClure:

> In conclusion, I, in the course of making my living by turning journalism into literature, used material from various sources which had been collected and narrated by men who made their living by turning the facts of life into journalism. Along comes the space-writer on the *World* who makes his living turning the doings of other men into sensation. Well, all three of us made our living; and who's got any kick coming?[14]

Here are three writers who "make their living" by "turning" certain raw material into published text; the important thing to keep clear—according to London—is the proprietary relation each writer maintains to the material once he has "turned" it. Otherwise he can't get paid. The problem is that one man's publication is another man's raw material, such that it becomes difficult to ascertain what belongs to who once it all circulates in the newspapers and magazines of the day. A reporter takes the "facts of life" and turns them into "journalism"; then London takes this journalism and turns it into "literature"; finally, along comes a space-writer and turns the confusion between these two into "sensation."

Conceding that this disorienting circulation of similar texts might make it difficult for "ninety percent of readers" to distinguish one man's raw material from another man's fiction, London added a postscript permitting McClure to publish his explanation: "You are at liberty to use the whole foregoing letter any way you see fit. I should like to see it published in the *World*, incidentally. But I should not like to see it 'revised.'"[15] This crucial codicil highlights London's anxieties about the unreliable trajectory from authorial intention to mass cultural publication. And the entire episode illustrates the degree to which both accusations of and defenses against plagiarism were functions of the intense publicity surrounding London's career—a career that required ongoing public negotiations of the relation between his textual productions and famous name.[16]

Indeed, the *New York World* article, which covers the entire editorial page for Sunday, March 25, 1906, questions London's claim to his name. In a subsection titled "What Manner of Man Jack London Is," the article alleges, "His family name is London, and he was christened Jack. At least, that is the record so far as anyone has been able to discover it. Able critics went so far as to call him John London, and reproach him with the taunt of Barnumizing."[17] This opening gambit throws doubt on the entire minibiography that follows—a biography that replicates all the standard clichés that were appearing on book jackets and promotional pieces across the nation. The article thereby links the publicity apparatus around London's biography to the sensational implication of plagiarism, illustrating how London's tenuous claim to his textual productions is associated with his claim to his name.

In fact, as the article notes, the name "Jack London" was suspected as a pseudonym from the very beginning. One early reviewer asserted that

> the announcement by Messrs. Houghton, Mifflin, and Co., that one of their spring books, bearing the title "The Son of the Wolf," may seem to bring forward a new *nom de plume*. As a matter of fact, Mr. London is a very real person, not yet twenty-five years old.[18]

This accusation was repeated so often that the Houghton Mifflin bulletin of 1900 reports that "Mr. Jack London (who claims this is not a pseudonym though it looks wonderfully like one) is a young man with a remarkably varied group of experiences."[19] London himself wrote a letter to the *Post-Express* of Rochester, New York, on March 8, 1900, stating that his name is not a pseudonym: "This is certainly away off from the truth. Jack London is my real name."[20]

Significantly, one of the principal differences between "Love of Life" and "Lost in the Land of the Midnight Sun" involves the proper name. Both narratives recount the experiences of a man lost in the arctic who is brought to the extremity of human endurance before he is discovered. Bridle and McDonald's version is based on the actual experience of Charles Dunn, who "had arctic geological records of the Canadian government to bring out to civilization."[21] Dunn gets lost during this geologic expedition, and nobly drags a bag of rock specimens and scientific records through the arctic wastes until, at the brink of death, he finds an Indian camp and is saved by four Indian boys.

London's story is similar in structure, and it is not surprising that it raised some eyebrows, but London made crucial changes in content that illuminate his assertions to McClure. First of all, the major character has no name. In fact, the story gradually and completely strips him of nominal specificity, wrenching him out of any category to which one might affix a name. He starts out as "a strong man in distress."[22] Then, as his search for food repeatedly fails, he finds himself "crunching and munching, like some bovine creature" (18), until toward the end, "he as a man, no longer strove. It was the life in him, unwilling to die, that drove him on" (28). He is finally discovered by a scientific expedition, who see "simply a strange object" that they are "unable to classify" (38). London inverts the content of the narrative, having his nameless protagonist actually discovered by a scientific expedition like that to which Dunn belonged.

Furthermore, unlike Dunn, London's hero is a gold prospector. His sack of minerals is a private possession, not a public property, and his journey has been one of private gain, not professional obligation. And he, again unlike Dunn, eventually leaves his rocks behind in order to reduce his burden. Even as Dunn hangs onto his specimens and records, thereby stubbornly remaining a professional scientist throughout the narrative, London's hero divests himself of all material traces of humanity, and is gradually reduced to being an object that defies the classificatory powers of the scientific expedition that discovers him.

We now begin to see how London can affix his name to other people's material. He does it by first *unfixing* the name that would give the material any identifiable specificity, any orientation in the social world. In recounting the reduction of a man to raw material—in the end, "his knees had become raw meat like his feet" (35)—London's story seems also to be narrating its own defense against accusations of plagiarism. "Love of Life" reduces the narrative of "Lost in the Land of the Midnight Sun" to pure raw material, after which London can stamp it with his own signature style. Indeed, the reduction of specific people to brute matter *is* London's signature style.[23]

Literary Value and Class Consciousness

The reverse process—sublimating brute matter into "pure" proper name—would appear to indicate the correlative phenomena of authorial celebrity. *Martin Eden*, the autobiographical novel that London wrote after he had become immensely famous, stages an interesting inversion of the narrative of "Love of Life": here, the famous author is gradually reduced to being nothing but a name:

> He drove along the path of relentless logic to the conclusion that he was nobody, nothing. Mart Eden the hoodlum, and Mart Eden the sailor, had been real, had been he; but Martin Eden, the famous writer, did not

exist. Martin Eden, the famous writer, was a vapor that had arisen in the mob-mind, and by the mob-mind had been thrust into the corporeal being of Mart Eden the hoodlum and sailor. But it couldn't fool him. He was not the sun-myth that that mob was worshipping and sacrificing dinners to. He knew better.[24]

London figures literary fame as a literal possession of the writer's "corporeal being" by a "vapor that had arisen in the mob-mind" of his bourgeois readership. This vaporous being effectively muscles out his former selves such that if he refuses to acknowledge the legitimacy of his fame, he becomes "nobody, nothing." According to this "relentless logic," there is only one admittedly drastic solution: kill the body into which has been thrust the "vapor" of "Martin Eden, the famous writer." In essence, the suicide that concludes the novel turns the famous writer back into "the hoodlum," the raw material with which the novel began.

But there is a narrative problem built into this relentless logic. According to the lines quoted above, an innocent, young, working-class stiff named Mart Eden who had previously existed has now been replaced by the fantasy of a famous writer. Yet who wrote the material that made him famous in the first place? The answer to this question is Martin Eden's real dilemma since the material that makes him famous was written by the hoodlum and sailor. Continuously and obsessively over the concluding pages of the book, he reminds himself that "the work was already done—all done" (445). Like London himself, Martin has been publishing previously rejected work to satisfy the public desire generated by his fame. The irrationality of the fact that work performed by Mart Eden could be worthless and work performed by Martin Eden could make him rich starts to drive him mad: "His thoughts went ever around and around a circle. The center of that circle was 'work performed'; it ate at his brain like a deathless maggot" (453).

It is this chronological inconsistency that leads him to believe that his work can't have any real value at all, and that his famous self can at best be a vapor in the mob mind:

He had not changed. He was the same Martin Eden. What made the difference? The fact that the stuff he had written had appeared inside the covers of books? But it was work performed. It was not something he had done since. . . . Therefore, it was not for any real value, but for a purely fictitious value, that Judge Blount invited him to dinner. (437)

The problem of Martin's fame is one of value, more specifically the "purely fictitious value" of literary work. This value is a problem, it is fictitious, because it apparently has nothing to do with its authorial source, but everything to do with its public circulation. This circulation—through a sort of fantastic retroactivity—then creates an authorial source—the famous writer—who occupies the helpless body of the original author. Apparently, the only "real value" inhered in the raw material of the original Mart Eden, hoodlum and sailor.[25]

Unsurprisingly, it's not so simple, since the "original" Mart Eden (London must have purposefully given him a name that reads as an abbreviation for the market) seems himself to be a product of the bourgeois imagination insofar as he comes into being through the experience of contact with the middle class. The narrative of *Martin Eden* is structured such that the protagonist only attains self-consciousness through the process of cross-class contact and conflict. In this text, the self is a product of movement and struggle between classes. This is clear from the beginning, when Martin's awkward introduction to the bourgeois household is figured in terms of a heightened awareness of his body:

> He did not know what to do with those arms and hands, and when, to his excited vision, one arm seemed liable to brush against the books on the table, he lurched away like a frightened horse, barely missing the piano-stool. He watched the easy walk of the other in front of him, and for the first time realized that his walk was different from that of other men. (31–32)

As Martin enters this alien bourgeois interior, he becomes acutely aware of his gendered body, particularly of his appendages. His "arms and hands," metonyms for his male laborer's body, become cumbersome and difficult to negotiate. He also becomes sensitive to his legs, and the awkwardness of his walk anticipates the painfully literal recalibration of the physical self to different gestures and environments that constitutes class mobility in this text. In oblique opposition to the narrative of "Love of Life," Martin Eden's body moves from being brute matter (he is significantly compared to a "frightened horse"), beneath social or literary notice, to becoming a social individual and, eventually, a literary author. The corporeal exigency of this cross-class interloping then generates self-awareness:

All his life, up to then, he had been unaware of being either graceful or awkward. Such thoughts of self had never entered his mind. He sat down gingerly on the edge of the chair, greatly worried by his hands. They were in the way wherever he put them. (37)

Only by placing his body in a different class milieu does Martin become aware of its palpable public presence as something that might appear "graceful or awkward" to others. The psychic result is that "thoughts of self . . . entered his mind" as if from somewhere outside him. From the outset, then, Martin Eden's self-consciousness is thrust into his body by contact with the bourgeoisie.[26]

But the agency behind this whole process remains ambiguous since Martin *wants* to enter this class, and his desire to court favor with the bourgeoisie rapidly becomes figured in terms of his love for Ruth Morse, whose house he is entering in these opening pages. If this process of cross-class desire makes Martin intensely aware of his own body, it correlatively creates problems for his understanding of hers:

He did not think of her flesh as flesh, which was new to him, for of the women he had known that was the only way he thought. Her flesh was somehow different. He did not conceive of her body as a body, subject to the ills and frailties of bodies. Her body was more than the garb of her spirit. It was an emanation of her spirit, a pure and gracious crystallization of her divine essence. (58)

Martin's new awareness of his own embodiment corresponds to this inability to embody Ruth. If Martin feels himself awkwardly overembodied, Ruth is correspondingly underembodied; her flesh seems constantly in danger of vaporizing into an "emanation" or hardening into a "crystallization." Significantly, neither of their bodies really fits comfortably in the world. In fact, it would seem to be this very lack of fit that allows Martin to become conscious of embodiment in the first place—hers or his.

This libidinally invested and corporeally figured consciousness of class difference generates the repeated mirror scenes that punctuate the narrative:

He got up abruptly and tried to see himself in the dirty looking-glass over the washstand. . . . It was the first time he had ever really seen himself. His eyes were made for seeing, but up to that moment they had been filled with the ever-changing panorama of the world, at which he had been too busy gazing ever to gaze at himself. He saw the head and face of a young fellow of twenty, but, being unused to such appraisement, he did not know how to value it. Above the square-domed forehead he saw a mop of brown hair, nut brown, with a wave in it and hints of curls that were a delight to any woman, making hands tingle to stroke it, and fingers tingle to pass caresses through it. But he passed it by as without merit in Her eyes, and dwelt long and thoughtfully on the high, square forehead, striving to penetrate it, and learn the quality of its content. (67–68)

In this densely overdetermined passage, London figures Martin's self-consciousness in terms of his attempts to mimic Ruth's consciousness of him. His consciousness of himself comes from his efforts to imagine what it would be like for a middle-class woman to be attracted to him; it develops out of his partially failed attempts to inhabit *her* consciousness of him. Thus we see Martin, in psychoanalytic terms, struggling to adapt his ideal ego to his ego ideal, struggling to identify with a positive image of himself *from the position of* another who is, in terms of both gender and class, the Other.[27]

Martin's desire for the bourgeoisie is never purely libidinal though; it is also literary. The two tend to correspond to each other as correlative ways of either entering or being possessed by the middle class. As a result, the romance that ensues between Martin and Ruth is punctuated by scenes of reading in which cross-class contact is figured through and as literary pedagogy:

When she returned with the grammar, she drew a chair near his . . . and sat down beside him. She turned the pages of the grammar, and their heads were inclined towards each other. He could hardly follow her outlining of the work he must do, so amazed was he by her delightful propinquity. But when she began to lay down the importance of conjugation, he forgot all about her. He had never heard of conjugation, and was fascinated by the glimpse he was catching into the tie-ribs of language. He leaned closer to the page, and her hair touched his cheek. He had fainted but once in his life, and he thought he was going to faint then. He could scarcely breathe, and his heart was pounding the blood up into his throat and suffocating him. Never had she seemed so accessi-

ble as now. For the moment the great gulf between them was bridged.
(101–2)

The "great gulf between" the working-class hoodlum and middle-class
debutante is "bridged" by the "tie-ribs of language" in a brilliant ex-
ploitation of the various embedded meanings of "conjugation." London
partially displaces the problematic sexual union between the two onto a
scene of grammatical coupling, thereby figuring language almost literally
as consisting in libidinal investment. But the displacement is only partial,
as the bodies and book all clustering in "delightful propinquity" cause
Martin to teeter between being oblivious to and acutely aware of Ruth's
closeness to him. It is as if the attempt to sublimate desire into language
results in an almost vertiginous oscillation between them.

This oscillation intensifies as the reading material progresses from
grammar to classic literature to Martin's own efforts at writing. Ruth is
shocked and dismayed by Martin's early literary endeavors, and London
figures this shock in terms of her unwillingness to acknowledge the real
nature of her desire for him. Once again, the literary and libidinal are
hopelessly entangled:

> The paradox of it was that it was the story itself that was freighted with
> his power; that was the channel, for the time being, through which his
> strength poured out to her. She was aware only of the strength, and not
> of the medium, and when she seemed most carried away by what he had
> written, in reality she had been carried away by something quite foreign
> to it—by a thought, terrible and perilous, that had formed itself unsum-
> moned in her brain. She had caught herself wondering what marriage
> was like. (170)

This passage again figures linguistic and libidinal conjugation in terms of
each other, as Martin's attractive "strength" appears to Ruth through the
"channel" of his story. The couple needs this channel to enable their own
budding conjugal relations, but Ruth is crucially unaware of the maieutic
function of the "medium." The story seduces Ruth into acknowledging
to herself her desire for Martin, but the seduction depends on her being
"carried away by something quite foreign" to the story itself.

For if literature in *Martin Eden* provides a means for cross-class contact, it does this through a certain pattern of misrepresentation and mis-
interpretation that is key to the narrative's denouement. If Martin learns

of the middle class through books, and Ruth discovers her attraction for Martin through his stories, and the two of them plight their troth through scenes of reading, literature itself nevertheless sustains an ambiguous relation to the cross-class romance it enables. If Ruth must forget the medium for the man, Martin too eventually discovers that the version of the middle class that he has received in the genteel literature they read together critically misrepresents the carnal realities of bourgeois courtship:

> And all the while there was running through his head Kipling's line, "And the Colonel's lady and Judy O'Grady are sisters under their skins." It was true, he decided, though the novels he had read had led him to believe otherwise. His idea, for which the novels were responsible, had been that only formal proposals obtained in the upper classes. (229)

If genteel fiction had led him to Ruth, and his vulgar attempts at writing had cemented her attraction to him, this literary enabling of their union must be disavowed for them to admit the resolutely carnal nature of the attraction, which the literature in the first place had inevitably misrepresented. Repeating to himself Kipling's adage—as a harbinger of the type of "realistic" fiction he will write—Martin decides, "Her dear flesh was as anybody's flesh—as his flesh. There was no bar to their marriage. Class difference was the only difference, and class was extrinsic. It could be shaken off" (230).

And yet, the literary misrepresentations that facilitated this revelation are not so easily "shaken off." London concludes the scene of the couple's declaration of love:

> The cloud masses on the western horizon received the descending sun, and the circle of the sky turned to rose, while the zenith glowed with the same warm color. The rosy light was all about them, flooding them, as she sang, "Good-bye, Sweet Day." She sang softly, leaning in the cradle of his arm, her hands in his, their hearts in each other's hands. (230–31)

London's dilemma—that will presently become Martin's—is that he must rely on the sentimental literary conventions he despises to represent the cross-class romance that was originally enabled by such mawkish literary language in the first place. The above lines, in their cliché sentimentality, belie Martin's comfortable certainty that class is "extrinsic." After all, the

"Colonel's lady and Judy O'Grady" are not sisters under their *clothes* but under their *skins*, which is not so easily shaken off. Likewise, literature is still necessary as, crucially, a way of changing skins.[28]

For if Martin's crude realism allows Ruth to acknowledge a carnal desire that she had previously disavowed, it is Martin's reading of high literature that quite literally allows him to embody a bourgeois self that moves comfortably in her world. In another mirror scene later in the book, Martin contemplates his former hoodlum self and wonders if he really has changed:

> As if in reply, the vision underwent a swift metamorphosis. The stiff-rim and the square-cut vanished, being replaced by milder garments; the toughness went out of the face, the hardness out of the eyes; and the face, chastened and refined, was irradiated from an inner life of communion with beauty and knowledge. The apparition was very like his present self, and, as he regarded it, he noted the student-lamp by which it was illuminated and the book over which it pored. He glanced at the title and read, "The Science of Aesthetics." Next, he glanced into the apparition, trimmed the student-lamp, and himself went on reading "The Science of Aesthetics." (319–20)

"The Science of Aesthetics" literally transforms Martin's physiognomy from within, making his body, like Ruth's in the beginning of the novel, more like an irradiation of his spirit. And yet this physiognomic transformation remains an "apparition," whose simultaneous likeness to and difference from his "present self" is foregrounded during a break in the act of reading. Like Jack London, Martin Eden is slowly becoming a double of himself.

As a private apparition, this bourgeois double can still function as an imaginary ideal ego, a model of what Martin wants to be, but as a public spectacle, it vertiginously descends into the symbolic realm of mass cultural celebrity in which he becomes what everyone else wants. Suddenly, everyone desires this phantasm of himself for which he feels compelled to disavow responsibility. Martin describes the new situation to Ruth in the following terms:

> I am personally of the same value that I was when nobody wanted me. And what is puzzling me is why they want me now. Surely they don't want me for myself, for myself is the same old self they did not want.

Then they must want me for something else, for something that is outside of me, for something that is not. Shall I tell you what that something is? It is for the recognition that I have received. That recognition is not I. It resides in the minds of others. Then, again, for the money I have earned and am earning. But that money is not I. It resides in banks and in the pockets of Tom, Dick, and Harry. And it is for that, for the recognition and the money, that you now want me. (460)

Again, what maddens Martin (and London) is the sheer circularity of the public's desire, the essential bootstraps structure of his popularity. The paradox of this structure is wrapped up in the word "recognition," which implies seeing something or someone *familiar*—that is, seeing someone again who you already know. But this famous author is a new person, a fantasy that presumably should be familiar to no one. And yet, in a key revelation, Martin acknowledges that it is not even the famous author that the public wants, but rather the recognition itself, which they displace and confer onto him, as a kind of placeholder for their own desire for recognition. In other words, the public wants recognition, and is using his name as a marker of it. Or more accurately, the public simply *is* this desire for recognition, in which everybody participates through wanting people like Martin Eden.

This public desire seems to leave the "original" Mart Eden entirely out of its economic and social calculus. Hence, in becoming famous, Martin Eden loses his sense of property both in his textual products and authorial identity. But London, by having his literary double commit suicide rather than submit to this paradoxical fate, can both confirm his own proprietary claim over his public image *and* disavow the identity between this public image and his private self. By figuratively killing his double, London can confirm that he literally owns him. *Martin Eden* thereby allows London to have his famous cake and eat it too; responding to those who would equate him with Eden, London declares: "Martin Eden killed himself; I am still alive."[29]

The problems that generated *Martin Eden*, however, would not die, and London later returned to the genre of fictional autobiography with *John Barleycorn* (1913), which dwells on the homosocial world of London's earlier youth, the period that in *Martin Eden* figures as the "edenic" prehistory of the class interloper.[30] *John Barleycorn* begins with a trope of psychic possession that will be repeated throughout: "My brain was illuminated by the clear, white light of alcohol. John Barleycorn was on a truth-telling rampage, giving away the choicest secrets on himself. And I was his spokesman."[31] As the mind of alcohol that speaks through London, Barleycorn is not only an impersonation of the masculine public sphere that will be narrated in the book but also a figuration of the narrative *process* itself:

> There moved the multitudes of memories of my past life, all orderly arranged like soldiers in some vast review. It was mine to pick and choose. I was a lord of thought, the master of my vocabulary and of the totality of my experience, unerringly capable of selecting my data and building my exposition. For so John Barleycorn tricks and lures, setting the maggots of intelligence gnawing, whispering his fatal intuitions of truth, flinging purple passages into the monotony of one's days. (2)

To have Barleycorn on the brain is to have one's memories ready for narrative, to see the "monotony of one's days" punctuated by "purple passages." Suddenly, the hodgepodge of memories becomes "all orderly," and the criteria of selection for the purposes of narration becomes clear. Barleycorn, here, figures for authorial propriety and control: over personal "experience," over the "vocabulary" in and through which to represent that experience, and over the process of selection critical to autobiographical "exposition."

The resulting exposition outlines a semi-utopian, yet at the same time crucially pathological homoerotic world that is passing away. It is the world of the saloon, where every man and boy is welcome:

> A newsboy on the streets, a sailor, a miner, a wanderer in far lands, always where men came together to exchange ideas, to laugh and boast and dare, to relax, to forget the dull toil of tiresome nights and days, always they came together over alcohol. The saloon was the place of congregation. Men gathered to it as primitive men gathered about the fire of the squatting-place or the fire at the mouth of the cave. (2)

The saloon is a homosocial world of "exchange" and "congregation," a place autonomous from the "toil" of labor as well as the "dull" nights at home. For London, it was the beginning of the adventures that would form the bulk of material for his later fiction:

> As a youth, by way of the saloon I had escaped from the narrowness of
> women's influence into the wide free world of men. All ways led to the
> saloon. The thousand roads of romance and adventure drew together in
> the saloon, and thence led out and on over the world. (3)

In the homosocial world of the saloon, storytelling and adventure draw
"together," the truths of experience are reconstructed as narratives, and
these narratives expand out into further "romance and adventure." A
"wide free world of men," it figures as the deceptively "innocent"
utopian homoerotic fantasy that Leslie Fiedler claims is the identifying
characteristic of classic American fiction.[32] In the opening pages of his autobiographical fiction, London extols the pleasures of this world. In the
saloon, "men talked with great voices, laughed great laughs, and there
was an atmosphere of greatness. Here was something more than common
every-day where nothing happened" (24).

And yet, *John Barleycorn* is also a temperance tract; London ostensibly wrote it as a condemnation, not an endorsement, of the saloon and all
it represented. This is at least partly because alcohol, like fame, indicates
the apparently arbitrary, potentially shameful, and crucially disorienting
social construction of the self. London's accounts of his early exposure to
alcohol are telling in this regard. At the age of seven, he is forced to drink
at an Italian picnic:

> I was frozen, I was paralyzed, with fear. The only movement I made was
> to convey that never-ending procession of glasses to my lips. I was a
> poised and motionless receptacle for all that quantity of wine. It lay inert
> in my fear-inert stomach. I was too frightened, even, for my stomach to
> turn. So all that Italian crew looked on and marveled at the infant phe-
> nomena that downed wine with the *sangfroid* of an automaton. (16–17)

Alcohol comes to London from a foreign culture, an "Italian crew" who
are "mysterious" and "unknown" (15). His ambiguous representation of
his own agency in this passage foregrounds this distance between the
drinker and drink. Paralyzed by fear, the young boy becomes "a poised
and motionless receptacle," oddly alienated from the one "movement" of
conveying the glasses to his lips. This movement itself is so mechanical as
to make him seem like "an automaton" to his Italian audience. The scene
becomes an eerie spectacle: London drinks not because he wants to but
because he feels obliged to *perform* for a foreign audience. Not only is

drinking a social practice, then, it is also a performative obligation, a price the young boy must apparently pay to enter into the (homo)social world.

In the rest of the narrative, the Italian crew is replaced by the men of the saloon, but the structure of obligatory performance remains:

> They were men. They proved it by the way they drank. Drink was the badge of manhood. So I drank with them, drink by drink, raw and straight, though the damned stuff couldn't compare with a stick of chewing taffy or a delectable "cannonball". I shuddered and swallowed my gorge with every drink, though I manfully hid all such symptoms. (28–29)

Drink is "the badge of manhood," or really, more accurately, manhood is performed ("proved") through drinking in front of other men and "manfully" hiding the fact that you can't stand the stuff. Manhood is less something you are or have than something you do in front of other men. As he later admits, "My manhood, according to their queer [!] notions, must compel me to appear to like this wine" (38).[33]

But what London really likes and wants is "chewing taffy," and this "secret and shameful" desire for candy constantly threatens to expose his manhood as simply a performance (58). Not surprisingly, candy is associated with private pleasures, one of which is reading:

> I would go up to the Free Library, exchange my books, buy a quarter's worth of all sorts of candy that chewed and lasted, sneak aboard the *Razzle Dazzle*, lock myself in the cabin, go to bed, and lie there long hours of bliss, reading and chewing candy. (59)

Although London maintains, "I would have died before I'd let anybody guess it" (58), he constantly treasures these private, almost onanistic retreats, which couple the gustatory delight of "chewing candy" with the intellectual joys of "all the great world beyond the skyline" that he discovers through reading (23).

Thus, both reading and drinking gain one access to "the great world" of adventure and romance. The difference, however, is the *cost*, and as in *Martin Eden*, it is on the question of value that the whole problem turns: "And those were the only times I felt that I got my real money's worth. Dollars and dollars, across the bar, couldn't buy the satisfaction that twenty-five cents did in a candy store" (59). And yet, if candy was cheap and reading was essentially free, drinking was important for another activity: writing. For it was on the drunks that the material for stories occurred: "As my drinking grew heavier, I began to note more and more that it was in the drinking that the purple passages occurred. Drunks were always memorable. At such times things happened" (59). London has a problem, and it is, significantly, one that he locates in the physiological economies of his body: "Intenseness and duration are as ancient enemies as fire and water. They are mutually destructive. They cannot co-exist" (31). By assuming that each individual has been allotted a set amount of life energy, London can claim that intense moments of experience literally drain time off a person's life expectancy. The intensity of the "purple passages" during which memorable events occur uses up energy necessary for the duration of life, and one "pays according to an iron schedule" (31).

But at the same time, it is these purple passages that are marketable as stories. "Duration" itself is essentially boring. As in *Martin Eden*, the contradictions of the authorial economy are palpably manifest in the body of the author. The author pays for the experience he narrates with his very life, losing quantities of duration for each quantity of "intenseness." For each royalty London has apparently sacrificed increments of life expectancy.

London's own life and death both reflect and complicate this logic. On the one hand, it is arguable that London died at forty because he refused to abandon his appetite for adventure, or to change his diet regimen of hard alcohol and semicooked meat. When he died—officially of uremia—he had only recently failed in an attempt to sail around the world, during which his health was devastated by tropical disease. He continued, to the end, to insist on living the adventures represented in his writing. On the other hand, his egomaniacal faith in his ability to continue to live such a life can be seen as based on his own confusion of himself with his public image that, after all, is unkillable. One could argue that Jack London the private individual died because he thought he could be "Jack London" the public figure.

Literature and Legitimacy

Both *Martin Eden* and *John Barleycorn* try to split the author into an authentic original who precedes public acclaim and a fake copy who follows it. They fail in this attempt because, as Jonathan Auerbach remarks, "for London the writer's 'self' does not so much serve as the basis for literary success and reputation as it is the consequence of the very quest for public approval."[34] Nevertheless, Auerbach still traces this "consequence" to a relatively unproblematic authorial agent, affirming that "Jack London wrote to become 'Jack London.'"[35] However, both the narrative emplotment of *Martin Eden* and *John Barleycorn* and the historical career of their author indicate a more complex agency. Given the elaborate publicity machinery that enabled London's emergence, it would be more accurate to spread the responsibility around a bit.

The *Jack London Journal* recently acknowledged this distributed agency when it published a collection of "Jack London Promotional Booklets"; editor James Williams estimates "the amount of material actually written by London to be about 40 percent."[36] The object of this estimate is a booklet titled "Jack London: A Sketch of His Life and Work," issued by Macmillan in 1905, and widely distributed by both author and publisher. Commenting on the booklet's style, Williams asserts that "the voice of the narrator is familiar, easy going, the voice of an early twentieth-century advertising man."[37]

In fact, the source of over 50 percent of this promotional booklet was Ninetta Eames's biographical article for the *Overland Monthly* in May 1900, arguably the first nationally distributed version of London's life story. Eames—at the time married to the editor of the *Overland Monthly*, which published London's first widely recognized Klondike story, "The Man on Trail"—was also Charmian Kittredge's aunt, and therefore responsible for introducing London to his second wife. Eames would become London's business manager during the peak years of his fame, at which time she had power of attorney to sign his name. After his death, she would claim to have received instructions from London's spirit to publish his love letters to Charmian. The line that Williams cites as characteristic of an "advertising man"—"The backing of sturdy ancestral stock enabled young Jack early to prove his mastery over the environment"—is only slightly revised from Eames's earlier article.[38]

This line also reveals how crucial the myth of paternal inheritance was to London's public identity. Although London discovered that he was illegitimate before he became well known, he nevertheless provided Houghton Mifflin with false biographical information for their promotion of *The Son of the Wolf*:

My father was Pennsylvania-born, a soldier, scout, backwoodsman, trapper, and wanderer. My mother was born in Ohio. Both came west independently, meeting and marrying in San Francisco, where I was born January 12, 1876.[39]

Eames clearly had access to this letter when she wrote her biographical article, but she played fairly fast and loose with its contents. Her version reads:

"Jack London" proves to be no adroitly chosen pseudonym, but the name a fortuitous fate bestowed upon the subject of this sketch at his birth. His father, John London, a nomadic trapper, scout, and frontiersman, in 1873 came to San Francisco, where Jack, the youngest of ten half brothers and sisters, was born January 12, 1876. "Once I essayed a climb among the branches of the family tree," he writes in answer to a query from an Eastern publisher, "and traced both parental lines back to American residence prior to the Revolution." . . . With this backing of sturdy ancestral stock, it is no marvel that young Jack proved his mastery over environment. He seems, indeed, to be endowed with the executive and resistant force that enables a man not only to withstand untoward circumstances, but to shape them ultimately to his own ends.[40]

Eames's "family tree" quotation does not appear in London's letter to Houghton Mifflin, or in any other extant letter from this period. Not surprisingly, then, the Macmillan booklet, issued five years later, no longer attributes these lines to him:

His father, John London, a nomadic trapper, scout and frontiersman, came in 1873 to San Francisco, where Jack, the youngest of ten half-brothers and sisters, was born three years later. He once essayed a climb among the branches of the family tree, and traced both parental lines back to an American residence prior to the Revolution. . . . The backing of this sturdy ancestral stock enabled young Jack early to prove his mastery over environment, very much as Buck does in *The Call of the Wild*. He seems endowed with the force that enables a man not only to prevent being pushed out of his true self by untoward circumstances, but even to shape them to his own ends.[41]

Hence, this affirmation of London's masculine agency and ancestry emerges from a process of revision and invention that undermines both. His "sturdy ancestral stock" and "true self" were creatures of a publicity process over which, in the end, he had at best partial control.

London's illegitimacy remained an underground rumor until the publication of Stone's "biographical novel" *Sailor on Horseback*. The negotiations between Stone and Charmian London over this early biography, the considerable controversy that followed its publication, and the force with which it eclipsed recognition of London's daughter Joan's own biography, reveal how masculinity grew to legitimate the literary status of a celebrity author's career between the wars.

In the foreword to Doubleday's reissued version of *Irving Stone's Jack London*, Stone explains, "I had always loved Jack London. I grew up in San Francisco, where I read *Martin Eden* as a young boy, and from it gained the concept that I too could become a writer. . . . I knew that one day I would write Jack London's story."[42] Charmian, who controlled the rights to the materials Stone would need to compose such a story, learned of Stone's childhood dream after the enormous success of *Lust for Life*, his biography of Vincent van Gogh. In fact, in their early correspondence, Charmian addresses Stone as "Vincent," very much with the implication that he may, in the future, become "Jack":

> With the greatest difficulty I think or write your name IRVING, as YOUR name. Perhaps it is a shying away from the familiar name of Irving Shepard. Anyway, I have a funny feeling that I'll never get away from calling you Vincent in my mind. Didn't I try that out on you involuntarily in the flesh up here?[43]

Stone enthusiastically encouraged this confusion in a complex rhetorical seduction of Charmian, clearly with the objective of getting unrestricted access to London's papers. Thus he answers the above letter:

> It is difficult for me to say now just how much of that book is mine—I want to talk to you about this at length—and how much is Vincent's, because, during the period of two years that I was thinking about and writing the book, Vincent and I became one and the same person. Don't you agree that I had to identify myself with him utterly in order to understand him?[44]

He signs the letter, "With love, Irving (Vincent)." Stone's implication is obvious: if he can become Vincent van Gogh, he can become Jack London. And in their initial contact and correspondence, Charmian was convinced. One month later, she gave Stone access to all of London's papers:

> I am writing this letter granting you permission to go ahead with a biography of Jack London. My intention is to cooperate with you in every possible way, rendering to you my valuable memories and giving you access to papers, letters, files and unpublished matter. It is my earnest desire that you make a complete and honest book of Jack London's life and work. To that end I offer you permission to use and publish about myself, in relation to Jack London, anything which in your judgment seems necessary and suitable.[45]

Charmian had originally drafted the last phrase as "in our combined judgment," but at Stone's insistence that "in the judgment of the critics, the public and of God I must stand responsible for every line in this book," she would grant him complete control of her portrayal in the biography.[46] It was a decision she would come to regret.

As Stone researched the biography, he insinuated himself into the London family's private life, simultaneously uncovering material that deeply troubled that private life. Principal among that material was the revelation of London's illegitimacy. Sensing the family's uneasiness, Stone wrote a remarkable letter to London's stepsister Eliza Shepard, whose own son was named Irving. The letter is addressed to "Dear Mama":

> Please put this note under your pillow and read it every night before you go to sleep:
>
> Every truth I fail to uncover renders me incompetent to that very extent.
>
> Every truth I fail to trace renders me dishonest to that extent.
>
> Truth alone must be the judge of my material, not its pleasantness or unpleasantness, its agreeableness or disagreeableness. I am not uncovering gold nuggets every time I find something complimentary about Jack, and digging up filth every time I find something

uncomplimentary, or something which on the surface does not look complimentary.

I have been absolutely honest with you. I have told you no lies and practiced no deceits. From the very start I have believed you when you said that there is nothing in Jack's life which you would want to have concealed.

You must be on your guard when people attack me who have something to gain from that attack, such as Joan, or who have something to fear from my work, such as Doctor P—, and who would consequently like to destroy that work.

Please do not become violently angry at me when I discover things that you thought were buried forever. Please do not stop loving me because I insist upon finding the whole truth, not merely part of it. For only from that whole, that complete truth, can we create a book that will live, and that will do Jack justice.

I love Jack London. I love you. That love will permeate the entire book.

Astonishingly, he signs his letter, "Really, your son, Irving."[47] In this way, Stone's exposure of London's illegitimacy parallels his own rhetorical insinuation into the dead author's family, literally substituting himself for the author's nephew.

During the same year that Stone was perpetrating this peculiar substitution, Henry Maule of Doubleday and Doran was negotiating with London's real daughter Joan regarding a biography of her father that she had been working on for many years. Maule was understandably distressed when he received the following letter from Charmian:

It has been called to my attention that one of your editors, Mr. Burton Rascoe, has made the statement that your company has contracted with Joan London for a biography about her father, Jack London. I wish to bring a few facts to your attention so that all future trouble may be avoided. All of Mr. London's private papers, notes, correspondence, files, and documents are here on my ranch at Glen Ellen. Joan London has never had access to any of these papers. All copyrights to Mr. London's work are held by me. Joan London has never been granted the right to use any of the material copyrighted by her father. Bessie London, as guardian of Jack London's children, Joan and Bess London, assigned all rights they may have had in their father's literary estate to me at the time his estate was settled and distributed by the court. Irving Stone, author of *Lust for Life*, has been given authority by me to write a biography of my husband, Jack London. I have given him free access to all of Mr. London's papers.[48]

Charmian reminds Maule that her legal relationship to Jack London trumps Joan's blood descent. Consequently, Stone's "free access" to her estate would seem to give him an "authority" over London's life that his real descendant lacks.

In fact, Joan London's real estrangement from her famous father provides a revealing parallel to Stone's imagined intimacy. In an unpublished autobiographical sketch, she poignantly recounts growing up in the shadow of her prominent father, who after marrying Charmian when Joan was just a girl, rarely saw his daughters. As a result, she grew up with "two conceptions of Jack London":

There was a man whose only name, at first, had been Daddy, and there was a man named Jack London who wrote books. Just when I learned about Jack London, I do not know, but, by the time I was seven, the two conceptions of father and author were distinct. That "Daddy" and "Jack London" were two names for one person, I knew, but so greatly did the connotations of each name differ that I did not try to put them together. "Daddy" belonged to me and to my sister, Bess. "Jack London" belonged, apparently, to everyone who read his books. I considered each separately; when I thought or spoke of one, the existence of the other was ignored.[49]

After her father died when she was still a teenager, the fission turns to fusion, as her father's public fame impinges on her personal life. Thus she discovers that

the name promptly secured excellent theater tickets, opened charge accounts with miraculous ease, and performed innumerable wonders that any amount of cash in hand would have failed to do. To my young mind, it seemed invested with the magic I found in fairy tales, like "abra-cadabra" and "open sesame."[50]

As she grew to adulthood, however, she found that the magic of the name was as much a curse as a blessing: "Anyone bearing the name comes in for his, and especially *her* share of publicity if they marry or divorce or do anything that hundreds of others do scarcely observed."[51] Joan London's two divorces were highly publicized. One scrapbook headline reads: "Jack London's Daughter Too Much like Her Father: The Same Qualities and Habits of Life Which Made the Novelist a Success Worked out Disastrously in Daughter Joan's Matrimonial Ventures."[52] Joan's personal life unfolded in the public shadow of her father's fame. She would, in turn, make a career for herself as a lecturer and writer analyzing that popularity.

Ironically, then, Joan, as London's real daughter, would strive to understand the historical and cultural significance of her father's fame, while Stone, London's symbolic son, would strive to represent his private personality. Maule had a sinking feeling about which would sell better. He therefore writes to Joan,

> Will there be room in the book market for a second biography of Jack London coming six months or a year after the Stone one? There is no use kidding ourselves. Irving Stone is a fine writer and has a very fine standing in the trade. His book will sell even though it may not as a biography have the material in it which you, as another biographer of Jack London, think it should have. As we know, the public is more interested in a good story than it is in completeness.

He concludes, "I cannot help but wonder whether the social history aspect will be interesting enough to sell it after so good a book as Stone's will be, has fairly completely covered the market."[53] As Maule had anticipated, *Jack London and His Times: An Unconventional Biography*, a remarkable interweaving of biography and social history, was completely overshadowed by *Sailor on Horseback*.

Significantly, *Sailor on Horseback*, which had little "social history aspect," was deeply informed by Stone's discovery of London's illegitimacy. Stone assumed that London's real father was "Professor" William Chaney, an itinerant astrologer with whom London's mother lived for a brief period in San Francisco. With access to the letters

Chaney wrote in response to queries from London, Stone avers in *Irving Stone's Jack London,*

> His writing of the name Jack London on the envelopes of the letters he sent Jack cannot be distinguished from Jack's own signature. Jack inherited from his father his strong, handsome Irish face, his light hair, high forehead, deep-set mystical eyes, sensuous mouth, powerful chin, and short, husky torso. (18)

In the biography that follows, this presumed inheritance explains Jack's character and literary talent. As Stone claims, "It was here too the boy discovered the authentic passion of his life, which was in truth passed down to him by Professor Chaney, the one talisman that never failed him, that brought him meaning and direction: the love of books" (26). Later, he notes that, "the thousands of astrological divinities Professor Chaney had written were short stories, pure creations of fiction. Jack came legitimately by his passion to spin yarns for a living" (69). Even London's socialism is inherited: "Professor Chaney was inherently a socialist before Jack was born. . . . Professor Chaney had all these attributes; they made him a socialist; similar traits made his son a socialist" (74). Thus does legal illegitimacy bestow literary legitimacy.

Astonishingly, Stone bases this entire presumption on a series of letters in which Chaney vehemently denies paternity. In 1897, London wrote to Chaney, asking him to clear up the issue of his parentage. Chaney responded:

> I was never married to Flora Wellman, of Springfield, Ohio, but she lived with me from June 11th 1874 till June 3rd 1875. I was impotent at that time, the result of hardship, privation and too much brain-work. Therefore I cannot be your father, nor am I sure who your father is.[54]

Chaney then mentions a number of possible candidates, affirming that "a very loose condition of society was fashionable at San Francisco at the time and it was not thought disgraceful to live together without marriage. I mean the Spiritualists and those who claimed to be reformers."[55] Nowhere does Chaney even imply the possibility that he is London's father. The main thing, in fact, that Chaney shared with London is unwanted publicity. Hence, the *San Francisco Chronicle* carried the screaming headlines in June 1875, "A Discarded Wife. Why Mrs. Chaney Twice

Attempted Suicide. Driven from Home for Refusing to Destroy Her Unborn Infant—A Chapter of Heartlessness and Domestic Misery."[56] The following article reads, in part, "Husband and wife have been known for a year past as the center of a little band of extreme Spiritualists, most of whom professed, if they did not practice, the offensive free-love doctrines of the licentious Woodhull." In his letter to London, Chaney complains that this article was "copied and sent broadcast over the country," disgracing him and ruining his career.[57] Clearly, Stone based his assumption that Chaney was London's father on the flimsiest of evidence.

Indeed, Stone's assumption has more to do with his own identification with London, as both a writer and man—an identification that would come at Charmian's expense. Stone's tenuous attempt to establish London's paternity parallels his more vicious and misogynistic effort to distance London's talent and success from the key women in his life. Flora London, Ninetta Eames, and Charmian Kittredge are all represented as shrewd, cunning women whose desire to benefit from London's fame simultaneously cripples his talent. The story begins with London's meeting with Ninetta over her biographical article for the *Overland Monthly*. Stone describes Ninetta as "a clinging vine with flexed fingers of steel beneath her softness and sentimentality" (127). Declaring that Charmian, who also met London at this time, was "a fairly good replica of her aunt," Stone contends that "it is not impossible that Mrs. Eames hoped that Jack and her niece might become interested in each other" (128). Eames's article, whose text Stone neglects to analyze, becomes simply part of a feminine subterfuge to capitalize on London's talent and allure.

Charmian is held directly responsible for the melodramatic excesses of London's later work. Stone claims that Charmian's love letters to London "are artful and coquettish, fluttery and flowery, but beneath the façade of verbiage can be detected the hand of a shrewd and clever woman" (172). These letters, according to Stone, excite a peculiar contagious imitation in London's own writing:

Under the spell of Miss Kittredge's thousands of words beating daily against his eyes, he begins to sound like a fifth-rate Marie Corelli. Mesmerized by her literary style, he replies in her own florid-purple nineteenth-century effusion, a manner against which he had asserted his revolt since the days of his earliest writing; a style of effervescing about love from which he was never to recover, and which was to mar so many of his books. (172)

Stone maligns the role in London's life of the very woman to whom he owes his access to that life.

Charmian was, unsurprisingly, outraged by Stone's portrayal of her in *Sailor on Horseback*, and the Stone materials held at the Huntington Library include a draft of a letter, dated August 2, 1938, angrily attempting to rescind the permission she had given him:

> Some time ago I granted to you, without profit or the desire or expectation of profit to me, the privilege of examining all my precious Jack London documents and of preparing a Life of Jack London with the use of such documents and of writing a free and untrammeled judgment of him and of myself in relation to him. This privilege was extended to you— freely and without hope of personal advantage—in the faith that you would use that privilege fairly, cleanly and with the sensitive understanding of an intelligent and cultured man. You have abused that privilege; and you have converted what you assured me would be a distinguished appreciation of Jack London and his place in Life into a scandal-mongering serial, aimed to secure sensationalism without justice. I now withdraw and cancel that privilege and any privilege or right I have hereto extended to you. If you published another word defamatory of me or tending to hold me up to scorn or ridicule or contempt, you do so at your own peril. There is protection in the laws of the United States and Canada against malicious and unprivileged libels; and I advise you to observe carefully both the law and the ordinary obligations of an honest scholar and gentleman.[58]

Charmian had no legal redress; she had signed her rights away. Yet her accusation of scandalmongering and sensationalism accurately anticipated the book's reception, and a certain moral—if not economic or legal—justice was done in the reviews of *Sailor on Horseback*.

Sailor on Horseback was serialized in the *Saturday Evening Post*, and before it was even released as a book, it met with a literary scandal uncannily mirroring the problems of its subject. Arnold Gingrich's "insider" magazine, *Ken*, was the first to notice the similarities between Stone's biography and London's *John Barleycorn*, originally serialized in the same magazine. *Ken* loudly proclaims: "Extra! Jack was a love-child, but Double Extra! Irving Stone's serial in the ubiquitous *Sat Eve Post* turns out to be rehash of London's own work, plus sentences and paragraphs in which pronoun is serialist's only contribution."[59] Below a graphic of parallel columns reminiscent of London's many plagiarism accusations, *Ken* quips,

> Irving Stone finds an easy way to write the biography of an author. Take the author's own words, and put "he" wherever the author said "I." Thus, the biographer can readily prove the authenticity of his material. He can also get some very nice prose written for him by this literal ghost-writing process.[60]

Ken makes much of the "literal" extensions of "ghost-writing" to argue the literary ethics of Stone's appropriations:

> Mere legality is not the sore spot, but the appropriation of a dead master's own words, without quoting, save indirectly and lamely in one instance, is a crime worse than illegality. It is robbing the dead of its laurels. It is a feast of ghouls.[61]

Interpreted literally, plagiarism as ghostwriting becomes a sort of literary cannibalism, a macabre feast on the "master's own words." *Ken* concludes, "Transposing the first person to the third does not constitute legitimate literary interpretation. It merely adds the face of the clown to the mask of the ghoul."[62] *Ken* thereby delegitimates Stone's exposé of London's illegitimacy.

This move has the significant consequence, though, of reinforcing the literary legitimacy of London himself as a classic author. Accusing Stone of plagiarism reinforces London's property in both his life and letters. In fact, before the publication of *Sailor on Horseback*, sales of London's books had been thin for at least a decade. Stone's sensational biography, advertised and reviewed extensively, spiked sales of London's books and renewed interest in the author himself as a romantic hero and literary professional along the Hemingway model. As Michael Szalay notes, "Jack London provided writers of the Depression era with an idealized image of the proletarian literary 'professional' who succeeds by virtue of a maniacal work ethic, by working at writing as if it were a physical discipline."[63] Stone's biography and the fiasco that followed on its publication helped establish London as a ballast for the masculinization of modernism in the 1930s.

And Charmian would get the last laugh when, instead of the project based on *Sailor on Horseback*, starring Clark Gable as London, Columbia Pictures released a film version of *Martin Eden*, with Glenn Ford in the title role. The autobiographical novel in which the author envisions his own suicide piggybacked on the publicity of the biographical novel that contended that the author really did commit suicide. London would have appreciated the irony.

4

Gertrude Stein's Money

"Alice B. Toklas did hers and now everybody will do theirs."[1] So opens Gertrude Stein's second major autobiographical work, *Everybody's Autobiography* (*EA*), published only four years after her first major autobiographical work, *The Autobiography of Alice B. Toklas* (*ABT*). In these four intervening years, Stein had witnessed herself transformed from relative obscurity to international celebrity, and much of her renown she knew to be based on the enormous popularity of *ABT*, in which she had adopted the persona and, to a certain degree, perspective of her lover and amanuensis in order to document her central role in the social life and aesthetic philosophy of Parisian expatriate modernism. This gossipy testimony to her own genius was eagerly devoured by the American public, and her ensuing triumphant return to the United States as a literary "lion" seemed to validate her stubborn confidence that she could write for and to an audience as big as the century—and country— she felt herself to represent.

Like *The Education of Henry Adams* and *The Americanization of Edward Bok*, *ABT* rhetorically strains the autobiographical pact in order to dwell more insistently on the named subject that ratifies that pact in the first place. By displacing the first-person pronoun onto Toklas, Stein pushes her own name—frequently written out fully as "Gertrude Stein"—resolutely into the foreground of the text. One critic has claimed that this "use of Stein's full name is clearly intended for humorous effect," but it also would appear to have the somewhat more serious consequence of placing its subject firmly into the objective unfolding of historical events.[2] As Stein herself remarks in her opening "message" to the *Selected Works* published shortly before her death: "I always wanted to be historical."[3] And the first selection in what has been since its publication the most familiar and available anthology of Stein's work is *ABT*. As with Henry Adams, the objectification of the autobiographical subject more effectively inserts that subject into a larger historical narrative—in Stein's case, the rise of modernism.

Unlike Adams, however, who renders a grand historical narrative in which he becomes a tragic onlooker, Stein's history is resolutely anecdotal, and she plays a key role in its unfolding. In fact, in its gossipy self-aggrandizement, *ABT* shares much with *The Americanization of Edward Bok*. *ABT* is a virtual feast of name-dropping insiderism, providing the larger public with an intimate view of a bohemian coterie that over the last two decades had moved to the forefront of high cultural production. Reviewers agreed that the book was "full of good gossip," that it was "witty, conversational and deals almost exclusively with the personalities grouped about Miss Stein."[4] Stein underscores what Bok and others had discovered a generation before: the cultural elite can enter into the mainstream U.S. public as personalities, as the subjects of anecdotal newspaper gossip and, eventually, chatty memoirs. *ABT* was only the first of a torrent of such memoirs to emerge from the cultural crucible of expatriate Paris in the 1920s, and it confirmed that Americans were vitally interested in the lives of these artists and bohemians, even if they were relatively uninterested in much of the art they produced.

Much as Stein participated in this popularization, she regretted some of its consequences. In *ABT*, she laments that

> she who is good friends with all the world and can know them and they can know her, has always been the admired of the precious. But she always says some day they, anybody, will find out that she is of interest to them, she and her writing.[5]

Once she became a celebrity, she discovered that she was, apparently, only half right. The great public was certainly interested in her, yet it continued to stubbornly resist all but her most accessible writing. Thus, in *EA* she admits that "it always did bother me that the American public were more interested in me than in my work" (50). After her celebrated lectures in the United States, she found that she was having her cake—she was now world famous and her work was finally being published—but she wasn't being allowed to eat it, too; her readers remained the "precious" few who had the patience and determination to work through her difficult writing.[6]

EA attempts, yet again, to explain why writing that is so apparently opaque and inaccessible is nevertheless intimately connected with the sensibilities of modern mass society, and therefore should be read by everybody. In this less-popular and less-acclaimed text, Stein tries to account for and intervene in the gradual process—partially enabled by the publication of *ABT* and her own consequent celebrity—whereby literary modernism, which had been developed in conscious resistance to commodification and the literary marketplace, itself became a commodity in that marketplace.[7] Although she had always desired publication and recognition, Stein understood that her newfound celebrity troubled the distinction between art and commerce, between symbolic and economic capital, between god and mammon, on which her original literary reputation was based. She realized that, now that she was famous, "what I did had a value that made people ready to pay, up to that time everything I did had a value because nobody was ready to pay" (*EA*, 45). In *EA*, Stein tries to forge a relation between these apparently incommensurable values.

Autobiography seemed the appropriate genre in which to forge this relation. It was a capitulation to the literary marketplace in which she could explore and critique her relation to that marketplace. It was a meditation on and expression of her famous personality in which she could further elaborate on and exemplify the writing that she felt made that personality famous. As Catherine Stimpson asserts, Stein's autobiographical writing in the 1930s works to undermine "the binary opposition that her reputation embodies."[8] Stimpson handily divides Stein's critical reputation into the "Good Stein," who the public liked, and the "Bad Stein," who the public hated. The Good Stein was introduced by the publication and popularity of *ABT*, while the Bad Stein persevered in the obscure and inaccessible texts that she continued stubbornly to publish. Stimpson further notes that "since the 1970s, a mélange of audiences has inverted Stein's reputations. The Old Good Stein is the New Bad Stein. She is too obedient to convention. The Old Bad Stein is the new Good Stein. Her transgressions are exemplary deeds."[9] Stimpson's thumbnail sketch of Stein's popular and critical reception provides a convenient illustration of how difficult it has been to relate the modernist author to the popular personality in anything but evaluative terms. In this analysis, I would like to make these evaluative terms the object, as opposed to the basis, of interpretation. I don't intend to either reduce the two Steins to one or multiply them into many; rather, I want to place them in a dialectical relation that accounts for the historical emergence and significance of the split.

Ultimately, *EA* reveals Stein exploiting the very category of the modernist genius to negotiate a relation between art and commerce that, in essence, enabled her simultaneously to sanctify and sell her writing. As Amy Kaplan convincingly argues of Theodore Dreiser, genius allows the writer to "imagine a way of entering the market while maintaining a distance from it."[10] In this chapter, I would like to chart out the autobiographical strategies with which Stein worked to render the literary genius as commercial celebrity in the 1930s, at the height of her fame. First, I will confront the issues of gender and sexuality, which since the 1970s have become central to academic studies of Stein. I intend to go somewhat against the grain here and argue that unlike with her male counterparts, sexuality was largely irrelevant to Stein's experience of celebrity. By the time she achieved fame, her sense of her sexuality and gender identity—and their relation to her public reception—were far less vexed than they were for her younger, male contemporaries. As a result, I contend, the problem of value precipitated by the complex engagement between modernism and mass culture emerges in her work with an unprecedented schematic clarity.

Recent critics have noted the degree to which Stein's "genius" accommodates modernism to mass culture. Susan Schultz observes that Stein's experimental writing "becomes a commodity through which Stein can buy the label of genius," while Bob Perelman maintains that "genius was Stein's trademark: what she wrote had to be 'Gertrude Stein,' unfathomable and glamorous as art but as immediately available as the sign of goods in a store window." More recently, Barbara Will has confirmed that *EA* "appears to resolve the conflictual relationship between 'the genius' and 'the masses' by restaging America of the 1930s as a space in which 'everybody' has the potential to be a 'successful one.'"[11] None of these critics, though, bother to anchor Stein's self-fashioning in the definitive event that marks its historical context: the Depression. In volatilizing the problem of value and throwing into doubt the significance of America's role in world history, the Depression deeply informed Stein's meditations on her own value and historical significance. In *EA*, as well as her other writings during the 1930s, both popular and obscure, I argue, Stein meditated on the problems of money and temporality in order to stabilize her literary reputation when a global economic collapse seemed to coincide with her own impending mortality.

The Gender of Genius

EA opens with a brief, but significant conversation between Stein and Dashiell Hammett. Stein shares with Hammett "something that is puzzling" her, something that applies to Hammett's writing and, implicitly, Hemingway's as well:

> In the nineteenth century the men when they were writing did invent all kinds and a great number of men. The women on the other hand never could invent women they always made the women be themselves seen splendidly or sadly or heroically or beautifully or despairingly or gently, and they never could make any other kind of women. From Charlotte Bronte to George Eliot and many years later this was true. Now in the twentieth century it is the men who do it. The men all write about themselves, they are always themselves as strong or weak or mysterious or passionate or drunk or controlled but always themselves as the women used to do in the nineteenth century. Now you yourself always do it now why is it. (5)

Hammett's answer legitimates, albeit obliquely, the authorial persona and narrative technique of the autobiography that follows. According to Stein, he replied,

> In the nineteenth century men were confident, the women were not but in the twentieth century the men have no confidence and so they have to make themselves as you say more beautiful more intriguing more everything and they cannot make any other man because they have to hold on to themselves not having any confidence. (5)

Hammett's response offers Stein's gender as a justification for her decision to write "everybody's" autobiography. If in the twentieth century, men can only write about themselves, it would have to fall to a woman to write about everybody.

This short exchange references a much larger and longer struggle in Stein's career with masculinity, sexuality, genius, and the nineteenth-century novel—a struggle that precipitated *The Making of Americans* (*MOA*). As Lisa Ruddick has affirmed, Stein wrote *MOA* under an overdetermined Oedipal shadow, condensing the specter of her real father and the figure of her brother Leo with male figures of intellectual authority such as William James. Ruddick sees *MOA* as an Oedipal attack not only on the stern, overbearing authority of her father and brother but on the entire bourgeois order of the nineteenth century and its conventional narrative forms.[12]

On the other hand, as Barbara Will has recently shown, the influence of Otto Weininger's *Sex and Character* on Stein during the composition of *MOA* rendered her own gender identity deeply ambiguous in this text as well as over the entire course of her career. In particular, Weininger's contention—rooted in nineteenth-century science and philosophy—that "genius is linked with manhood, that it represents an ideal masculinity in the highest form," profoundly informed Stein's sense of herself, leading her to speculate, in an oft-quoted notebook entry written while she was working on *MOA*, that "Picasso and Matisse have a maleness that belongs to genius. Moi aussi perhaps."[13]

As the names Pablo Picasso and Henri Matisse indicate, genius is not only male; it is modernist. Thus, as Will elsewhere states, "The notion of 'genius' for high modernism served as a key term in articulating an oppositional stance toward . . . the emergence of an enormous, literate mass that seemed to threaten the very conditions of possibility of modern art."[14] Stein, then, was caught in something of a double bind. The model of modernist creativity that she posed over and against the patriarchal authority of nineteenth-century narrative in *MOA* was also resolutely masculine.

Somewhat paradoxically, lesbianism would offer a resolution to this bind. As Shari Benstock explains, the model for Stein and Toklas's "marriage was a paternal and heterosexual one that duplicated the authority and submission patterns found . . . in the relationship of Stein's own parents."[15] And this marriage would become the anchor for Stein's literary experimentation. After *MOA*, she would embark on her most erotic and hermetic work, *Tender Buttons*, in which she would explore and celebrate her sexual relationship with Toklas as a conventional marriage in which she played the role of the husband. The two had settled into the intimate division of literary labor that would remain for the entire course of Stein's career, in which Stein would compose in the evening what Toklas would type in the morning. What was opaque for the public was most likely clear to Toklas, Stein's original private audience. Stein was beginning to discover that literary opacity and lesbian homoeroticism was a felicitous match.

Far from challenging the conflation of her sexual and literary identity, Parisian expatriate culture confirmed it. By the 1920s, when twenty-seven rue de Fleurus became a mecca for modernist writers and artists, Stein had settled comfortably into the androgyny of her literary authority. As the discussion with Hammett reveals, the feminization of the literary life did not provoke the same sort of strident psychosexual reaction from her as it would for male modernists such as Hemingway, who would feel the need to assert and affirm his male heterosexuality over and against an "effete" literary world in which sexual and literary experimentation were closely related.

Correlatively, Stein seems to have felt little need to leverage this relation into a challenge for the U.S. literary marketplace. Again in contrast to Hemingway, who repeatedly had to censor the more sexually explicit passages in his novels, Stein, not surprisingly, kept her sexuality private in the autobiographical work she did for popular consumption. Somewhat paradoxically, Stein's decision is more conventional in its maintenance of boundaries. Hence, Stein would tell her friend Samuel Steward that her homosexuality is "nobody's business," but that her more overtly lesbian work could be published after she was "dead and gone."[16]

As a celebrity, Stein's sexuality was sublimated into androgyny. Reporters claimed she had "the penetrating eyes of an aging statesman"; she sported a "masculine haircut"; she wore "a man's style topcoat."[17] In fact, it would be Stein's triumphant tour of the United States that would confirm the image of her sketched out by F. W. Dupree in his introduction to the selected works: "She seemed . . . at once female and male, Jew and non-Jew, American *pur sang* and European peasant, artist and public figure."[18]

As such, Catherine Stimpson's assertion that Stein's "modification of subversion into entertainment both follows and refines a homosexual method of seeking acceptance in modern heterosexual culture" actually confirms that sexuality is not the master key to understanding the anxieties precipitated by her celebrity.[19] The division between private homosexuality and public androgyny did not fundamentally challenge Stein's sense of her position in the modern cultural field. Stein's relationship with Toklas was more conventional and bourgeois than most heterosexual couples in the expatriate community. At the same time, her relationship with her audience was not antagonistic but solicitous. It is not surprising, then, that the psychosexual, erotic focus of her earlier work is absent from the writing she produced in the 1930s.

Funny Money

In other words, the dialectical engagement between modernism and mass culture did not pose the sort of psychosexual challenge for Stein that it would for male authors, who would feel the need to assert their masculinity over and against the twin threats of a feminized literary culture and feminizing mass marketplace. For this reason, the evaluative terms of this dialectic emerge in Stein's work in the 1930s with a felicitous schematic clarity. Contemplating the effect of the enormous popularity of *ABT*, she claims that

> what I did had a value that made people ready to pay, up to that time everything I did had a value because nobody was ready to pay. It is funny about money. It is funny about identity. You are you because your little dog knows you, but when your public knows you and does not want to pay for you and when your public knows you and does want to pay for you, you are not the same you. (*EA*, 45)

The apparently simple conferral of recognition by Stein's famous "little dog" fractures across the divide between a public who "does not want to pay" and one who now "does want to pay." Stein syntactically reproduces this historical fracturing in the last sentence, which begins with the reflexive affirmation "you are you" enabled by the knowledge of the little dog, and concludes with the reflexive negation "you are not the same you" generated by the transformation in the public's willingness to pay. This counterpoint between dog and public illuminates Stein's declaration, stated a few pages earlier, that money "is the difference between men and animals" (41). The recognition conferred by domestic animals is unchanging and unconditional, and therefore affirming; the recognition conferred by the public changes relative to the mediation of money.

Indeed, money volatilizes identity entirely as Stein alleges, echoing London's Martin Eden:

> If my writing was worth money then it was not what it had been, if it had always been worth money then it would have been used to being that thing but if anything changes then there is no identity and if it completely changed then there is no sense in its being what it has been (84).

What money introduces into the reflexive calculus of identity is, quite simply, change, which would seem to violate the very principle of sameness on which identity is based. And this volatility vexes author *and* text, both of which seem unable to maintain any continuity between before and after the public's willingness to pay. Thus, *EA* somewhat melodramatically stages the confrontation between symbolic and economic capital as a vertiginous historical rupture in the fabric of the self as well as the coherence of any text produced by that self.[20]

It is worth outlining Stein's personal relationship to money in this regard. Up until the 1930s, Stein and Toklas lived frugally on the fixed income dispersed to them by Stein's older brother, Michael, who had made a small fortune by consolidating the San Francisco streetcar lines. The concept of earning money through work would have been alien to Stein until the publication of *ABT*. Rather, spending, in particular on paintings, was their principal economic activity. In fact, the Steins—Gertrude, Leo, and Michael and his wife—became collectively known as the "Stein Corporation" in their organized, informed purchasing of work by Paul Cézanne, Picasso, Matisse, and other artists whose work would appreciate astronomically in the coming years. The enormous economic value of these paintings exacerbated Stein's anxieties about the purely symbolic value of her writings, for which she couldn't find a market. It is highly significant, in this regard, that Stein and Toklas financed their brief independent publishing venture, Plain Edition, by selling Picasso's *Woman with Bangs*. They were literally leveraging Stein's work into the marketplace with the economic value of Picasso's painting.

The publication of *ABT* changed all this, and Stein was initially overjoyed to make money by her writing. But she also, for the first time in her life, became unable to write. As she noted in an essay for *Vanity Fair*, "And Now," written in 1934 explaining the differences between *ABT* and *EA*:

> Well you see I did not know myself, I lost my personality. It has always been completely included in myself my personality as any personality naturally is, and here all of a sudden, I was not just I because so many people did know me. It was just the opposite of I am I because my little dog knows me. So many people knowing me I was I no longer and for the first time since I had begun to write I could not write.[21]

Nevertheless, Stein was enjoying spending the money she earned, until the stock market collapsed. As she continues, "I was spending my money as they had spent their money all the other painters and writers that I had blamed and condemned and here I was doing the same thing. And then the dollar fell and somehow I got frightened." And she concludes, "The fright has made me write" (64).

The significance of the Depression for Stein's writing in the 1930s has not been adequately appreciated. Here, she acknowledges that the volatilization of economic value precipitated by the Depression motivated her to write *EA*. It should not be surprising, then, that money and its meaning are central to that text. Stein contends that money is constitutive of the modern social world: "Money is money if you live together and as the world is now all covered over everybody has to live together and if you live together call it what you like it has to be money, and that is the way it is" (*EA*, 308). Money figures as a basic condition for living together in the "world," a world that Stein persistently considers in *EA* as "covered all over with people" (60). In fact, this "covering" of the world by people—another troubling revelation to result from her U.S. celebrity—expresses the abstraction of money in terms of population. Stein's sudden shift from the exclusive circles of expatriate modernism to the streets and hotels of urban America led her to envision the modern world as completely saturated with humanity. The world takes on the appearance of an enormous crowd in *EA*: "Anyway nobody can get lost any more because the Earth is all so covered with everybody and everybody is always moving around and you always see everybody and nevertheless very often you never see any of them again" (55–56).

This world crowd, like the money it needs to live together on earth, embodies an abstract principle of exchangeable anonymity that led Stein to reconsider her strategies of aesthetic representation, of writing. Thus, Stein wonders about the relevance of *The Making of Americans*, the text that until her celebrity, she had considered to be her magnum opus:

The Making of Americans is a very important thing and everybody ought to be reading at it or it, and now I am trying to do it again to say everything about everything only then I was wanting to write a history of every individual person who ever is or was or shall be living and I was convinced it could be done as I still am but now individual anything as related to every other individual is to me no longer interesting. At that time I did not realize that the earth is completely covered over with every one. In a way it was not then because every one was in a group and a group was separated from every other one, and so the character of every one was interesting because they were in relation but now since the earth is all covered over with every one there is really no relation between any one and so if this Everybody's Autobiography is to be the Autobiography of every one it is not to be of any connection between any one and any one because now there is none. (*EA*, 99)

Stein's discovery that the "earth is completely covered over with every one" dissolves the integrity of discrete groups—of expatriate artists in Paris in the 1920s or immigrant Jews in the nineteenth-century United States—into a basic democratic generality in which people can no longer be understood in relation to each other. This fundamental shift from a world populated by separate groups whose "interest" inheres in their relation to other groups to a world covered with people in which "anybody can know anybody" (*EA*, 101) mandates a basic change in the mode of writing through which one might represent modernity. From her small studio at twenty-seven rue de Fleurus, Stein had felt she could "write a history of every individual person who ever is or was or shall be living"; after mixing with the fans and crowds of the modern United States, she felt it was time to write "the Autobiography of every one."[22]

Like Howells a generation before, Stein had come to believe that autobiography was the mode of writing appropriate to modern democratic capitalism. Thus, "Autobiography is Easy like it or not autobiography is easy for any one and so this is to be everybody's autobiography" (*EA*, 6). But if autobiography is easy to write, and if it would seem to be the appropriate mode through which to represent the basic condition of international celebrity in an age of mass society, it does not resolve the problem of identity that precipitates it. In fact, it only confounds it:

And identity is funny being yourself is funny as you are never yourself to yourself except as you remember yourself and then of course you do not believe yourself. That is really the trouble with an autobiography you do not of course you do not really believe yourself why should you, you know so well so very well that it is not yourself, it could not be yourself because you cannot remember right and if you do remember right it does not sound right and of course it does not sound right because it is not right. (*EA*, 68)

Writing autobiography simply internalizes the identity crisis precipitated by recognition. When Stein wondered how, after her newfound celebrity, she could possibly be the same person she had been before, she situated the problem of identity in the inevitable shifts in external recognition that destabilize the continuity that might undergird the self. Autobiography recapitulates the same problem internally by constantly reminding you that you can never be who you remember yourself to be.

Yet writing everybody's autobiography collapses, at least rhetorically, the very opposition between interior and exterior, and thereby, somewhat paradoxically, would seem to resolve the problem of identity that the genre instantiates. For Stein, modern autobiography registers a basic shift in the source of personality—a shift that she associates with the ubiquity of "publicity" and death of that quintessentially nineteenth-century genre, the novel:

> And since there is so much publicity so many characters are being created every minute of every day that nobody is really interested in personality enough to dream about personalities. In the old days when they wrote novels they made up the personality of the things they had seen in people and the things that were the people as if they were a dream. But now well now how can you dream about a personality when it is always being created for you by a publicity, how can you believe what you make up when publicity makes them up to be so much realer than you can dream. And so autobiography is written which is in a way a way to say that publicity is right, they are as the public sees them. (*EA*, 69)

The source of personality is no longer internal; characters are no longer generated by the individual imaginative consciousness of the author. Rather, they are created by a publicity apparently exterior to any individual consciousness. This new source of personality is closely related to the ubiquity of money and saturation of the earth with people. In fact, publicity can be seen to enact a basic homology between people and money through rendering individuals as commodities in the mass public. Publicity, in a sense, is money dreaming about people. Autobiography, particularly celebrity autobiography, confirms publicity through acknowledging that "they are as the public sees them."

Stein's self-fashioning as a genius in her autobiographies can be understood as an attempt to confirm publicity in this way. Stein persistently exploited and encouraged the process whereby the obscurity of the literary genius can become the popularity of celebrity. Indeed, *EA* is centrally engaged with the alchemy whereby the literary resistance to exchange value can generate exchange value. Stein thus claims that "this extraordinary welcome that I am having does not come from the books of mine that they do understand like the Autobiography but the books of mine that they did not understand" (8). And further on she reflects:

> They ask me to tell why an author like myself can become popular. It is very Easy everybody keeps saying and writing what anybody feels that they are understanding and so they get tired of that, anybody can get tired of anything everybody can get tired of something and so they do not know it but they get tired of feeling they are understanding and so they take pleasure in having something that they feel they are not understanding. (122)

Stein realizes quite lucidly the close relation between modernist and mass cultural valorizations of the new, both of which can be understood as responses to boredom, to getting "tired" of what you feel you understand. In this way, obscurity can become a form of advertisement since, as Stein knew, "the biggest publicity comes from the realest poetry and the realest poetry has a small audience not a big one, but it is really exciting and therefore it has the biggest publicity" (284).[23]

Publicity doesn't only generate recognition; it makes money. As I have already noted, it was the connection between popular recognition and money that led Stein to conclude that her identity had changed. Elsewhere in *EA*, she describes this fracturing of identity as a process of being turned inside out:

> The thing is like this, it is all the question of identity. It is all a question of the outside being outside and the inside being inside. As long as the outside does not put a value on you it remains outside but when it does put a value on you then it gets inside or rather if the outside puts a value on you then all your inside gets to be outside. (47)

Here, the temporal rupture of identity is conceived of spatially as a violation of the boundaries of the interior consciousness. Catherine Parke cites this passage in support of her contention that "we should fear having our talent turned into a commodity, as we should fear the valuing of human nature over the human mind," and certainly this is one of Stein's more vivid and resonant depictions of the psychic violence of success.[24] And yet, it is right after this passage that Stein continues, "But there was the spending of money and there is no doubt about it there is no pleasure like it, the sudden splendid spending of money and we spent it" (*EA*, 47). Stein's anxieties about the external valuation of her insides must be understood alongside this refreshingly frank exuberance in "sudden splendid spending." Stein and Toklas used the money from *ABT* to modernize their already-comfortable lives. They had a bathroom and an electric cooker installed in their summer home at Bilignin; they had telephones installed in both their Bilignin and Paris residences; and they bought a new, eight-cylinder Ford.[25] In a sense, they used the money to upgrade the technologies mediating outside and inside. Both the telephone and automobile connect the interior domestic space to the outer public world. Stein may have worried that money turns you inside out, but she used it to help bring the outside in.

Stein herself would claim that "the style in the autobiographies is what I call my moneymaking style. But the other one is the main one, the really creative one."[26] Critics have followed her lead by looking for the deeper meaning behind the relatively blithe characterizations of her success in *EA* in the less-accessible writings she produced during the same era. Susan Schultz turns to *Stanzas in Meditation* in order to show how Stein can "buy the label of genius," while Parke cites *The Geographical History of America* as proof of "the condition of our minds' independence, the fact of their radical separateness one from another which must, like universal suffrage, be respected and protected."[27] Both Schultz and Parke link Stein's popular and obscure writing in terms of her attempt to render the immediate process of thinking, to externalize the autonomous human consciousness at work, and their readings consequently remain firmly grounded in the critical tradition—established by such pioneering Stein scholars as Donald Sutherland and Allegra Stewart—of interpreting Stein's specific version of modernism in terms of temporal transcendence. This fundamental tenet that Stein's writing expresses the immediate present of an interior consciousness has oriented a whole ongoing tradition of interpretation of her work, and a way of linking the difficult writing to the accessible autobiographies.[28]

Few critics, however, have noted how Stein grew to associate this autonomous interiority with that most exterior of human productions: money. In fact, Stein's meditations on money provide a less-appreciated conceptual bridge between the "easy" writings, which made some money, and the "difficult" ones, which did not. Stein's conceptual struggles with money also help us historicize her persistent desire to de-historicize the "human mind." Throughout *The Geographical History of America* (*GHA*), Stein insists that "money has something to do with the human mind."[29] She draws a number of interesting correlations between money and the mind—correlations that reveal her striving to integrate the agency behind the crisis of value precipitated by her success into the center of her writing process. Stein meditates on money in order to calibrate the internal workings of modern consciousness to the external unfolding of historical modernity. In the end, she discovers money to be a sort of objective correlative to the elemental abstraction of her specifically American genius.

In *EA*, Stein states her belief, so persistently challenged by her own experiences with the literary marketplace, that "there should be a buyer for every seller" (65). In *GHA*, she elevates this from a subjunctive imperative to a foundational condition: "The human mind can live does live by anybody being able to sell something to somebody. That is what money is" (398). Here, money is no longer an external measure imposed on the mind of the writer; rather, it is a basic condition on which that mind works. Money reduces things and persons to the sheer generality of exchange relations not unlike the categorical abstractions of human thought. The human mind requires that money objectively confirm the abstraction through which it conceives relations between people.

And, like thought, money remains constitutively outside the relations it determines. Thus, "money can be alone and at its best it is alone money is alone and the human mind and the universe" (*GHA*, 448). The basic abstractness of money means that like the mind and universe, it can't be reduced to the terms it establishes for relations in the world. Money has no value because it is value. And as "there is no identity and no time in a masterpiece nor in the human mind" (451), "money has no time and identity" either (462). Like the mind, masterpiece, and genius, money simply is; it doesn't remember or forget.

Stein's desire to affirm in language a conceptual homology between money and the mind illuminates the reactionary naïveté with which she approached economic issues in the United States. During the time she was writing *EA*, Stein contributed five brief meditations on money to the *Saturday Evening Post* that, as Bryce Conrad maintains, reveal her difficulty understanding the economics of corporate capital and the emerging welfare state.[30] There can be little doubt that Stein's critique of the New Deal in these short articles indicates a fundamental misconception of economics, and even some confusion as to the cultural logic of her U.S. celebrity, but they also provide some clues to the role of money as a transcendent signifier in Stein's writing during this period. It is therefore interesting to note that the question with which Stein opens almost perfectly inverts the question of identity in *EA*:

> Everybody now just has to make up their mind. Is money money or isn't money money. Everybody who earns it and spends it every day in order to live knows that money is money, anybody who votes it to be gathered in as taxes knows money is not money. That is what makes everybody go crazy.[31]

If money, in *EA*, brought about a shift from the reflexive "you are you" to the negative "you are not you," here money itself undergoes the same split precipitated by the difference between "everybody who earns it and spends it" and "anybody who votes it." Money causes Stein to realize that "anybody" is not reducible to "everybody," and that this inadequation stems from the difference between the private household economy and public circulation of value. As such, Stein attempts to reinscribe her own subjective schizophrenic experience of fame into the objective structure of the world economy.

But in the end, the elemental abstraction that conceptually links money and the mind gets complicated by the medium in which it must be expressed. If money is outside and the mind is inside, then language, and particularly writing, represents the materialization of their meeting. It is the danger of inadequation at this crucial location where exterior and interior meet that generates an anxiety that, I believe, illuminates some of the primary obsessions of both Stein's writing and her authorial self-fashioning as a genius.[32] In fact, I would argue that the problem presented by the possibility that language does not adequately translate money to the mind is what generates writing in the first place. Stein writes:

> Money is what words are.
> Words are what money is.
> Is money what words are.
> Are words what money is. (*GHA*, 422)

This tiny stanza conveniently illustrates how the apparently easy homology between money and the mind breaks down at the very point where it should find its signal expression. By expressing the relation of equivalence in all its syntactic permutations, Stein finds the mode shifting from statement to question. As long as subject and object sandwich the verb, the statement remains affirmative; when the relation between subject and verb is inverted, the mode shifts from indicative to interrogative. The organizing syntactic principle of the stanza reflects an attempt to have language replicate the basic equivalence enabled by money: by placing the words in all their possible syntactic relations, their basic conceptual congruence should be affirmed. But this is not what happens. Rather, the interrogatory relations expressed in the last two lines undermine the indicative relations expressed in the first two. Instead of equating money and the mind, syntax, the inevitable temporality of language, intervenes between them. And consequently, writing must continue as an ongoing attempt to calibrate the internal relations of thought to the external relations of money.

The Death of Genius

Stein's struggles with the relation between writing and value deeply informed her theories of narration and temporality, not only in terms of narrative modes but also in terms of public reception. Stein's celebrity resulted not so much from a reevaluation on the part of a single public as from a shift in recognition from an elite public of avant-garde writers and artists to a bourgeois public of middlebrow U.S. readers, college students, and mainstream intellectuals. As James Agee so eloquently remarks in his review of *ABT*, "At one long deferred bound she has moved from the legendary borders of literature into the very market-place, to face in person a large audience of men-in-the-street."[33] She had moved, in other words, from Bourdieu's "autonomous field" of the avant-garde, where the symbolic value of art is seen to derive from its resistance to economic value, to the "heteronomous field" of bourgeois culture, where the intimate relation between symbolic and economic capital is no longer disavowed.[34] By neglecting to specify this crucial shift from one public to another, Stein renders its consequences as an absolute historical rupture.

In fact, by considering the cultural contours and consequences of this shift, we can more effectively unpack *why* it would be both experienced and represented as a historical rupture precipitating both an identity crisis and writer's block, followed by a return to writing increasingly preoccupied with death and posthumous reputation. The avant-garde and bourgeois fields of culture, as Bourdieu confirms, involve different audiences and temporalities, different "life-cycles" of both author and work.[35] The bourgeois field mandates investment and marketing strategies based on the immediate popularity of a work that almost inevitably and rapidly wanes; the avant-garde field mandates, on the contrary, the initial unpopularity of the work, whose prestige as a classic must develop gradually, frequently only coming to fruition after the author or artist's death.

Up until the publication of *ABT* by Harcourt, Brace, all of Stein's earlier work had fallen into this latter temporality. She had been published by tiny presses like Grafton, which originally published *Three Lives*; Claire Marie, which published *Tender Buttons*; and Payson and Clarke, which published *Useful Knowledge*. And she had regularly contributed to the little magazines of the avant-garde such as *transition*, *Broom*, and *Little Review*. The people associated with these publishing houses and editorial boards were resolutely not interested in making a quick buck. Indeed, their objective was not to be popular and not to make money, and thereby to trade on the prestige of this refusal.

The publication of *ABT* in the *Atlantic Monthly*, in which she had always wanted to appear, catapulted Stein into the bourgeois field of culture, where her name came to represent an investment in the sales of the book. In fact, she was partly encouraged to come to the United States in order to promote the sales of the other work that Bennett Cerf, on the recommendation of Carl Van Vechten, had promised to publish with Random House.[36] Thus, Stein's interior experience of temporal rupture corresponds to a shift in the investment strategies that dictate the entry of her work into the cultural marketplace.

This shift in investment strategies corresponds to a shift in the value and meaning of the authorial life cycle. Thus, Stein observes in *EA*, "I was getting older when I wrote the Autobiography, not that it makes much difference how old you are because the only thing that is any different is the historical fact that you are older or younger." She explains that "the only thing that does make anybody older is that they cannot be surprised," and then goes on to say that the continual surprise of her visit to the United States proves that it doesn't "make much difference how old you are" (39). Once again, Stein disingenuously reduces a specific relation between cultural fields to a general philosophical truth. According to Bourdieu, the field of restricted cultural production has a relatively autonomous history that

> arises from the struggle between the established figures and the young challengers. The ageing of authors, schools, and works is far from being the product of a mechanical, chronological, slide into the past; it results from a struggle between those who have made their mark. . . and those who cannot make their own mark without pushing into the past those who have an interest in stopping the clock.[37]

By the time she wrote *ABT*, Stein's position in the history of the field of modernism had seemed undebatable. She was widely acknowledged as having centrally participated in the "discovery" of modernism in painting, she had been the adviser to a generation of younger writers in the 1920s, and her own writing was recognized, even by its detractors, as having been a key influence on modernist poetry and prose. She had "made her mark." But over the course of the 1920s, she had been gradually pushed to the margins of the world of painting: The new painters she patronized never became acclaimed or well known. And the generation whose writing she influenced had now resolutely come of age, their own fame frequently exceeding hers. She could probably feel herself being pushed "into the past" before she had fully enjoyed her reputation in the present, or established her legacy for the future. Her sudden fame seemed an opportunity to stop the clock.

But the surprising immediacy of U.S. fame did not mesh with the gradualism of European reputation. After the publication of *ABT*, Stein's acceptance into the field of U.S. bourgeois culture quickly precipitated her rejection by much of the European avant-garde, as the notorious "Testimony against Gertrude Stein," published in *transition* in 1935, dramatically established. The signatories to this document—Georges Braque, Eugene and Maria Jolas, Matisse, Andre Salmon, and Tristan Tzara—bitterly complained that Stein "had no understanding of what really was happening around her. . . . [T]he mutation of ideas beneath the surface of the more obvious contacts and clashes of personalities during that period escaped her entirely."[38] Astonishingly, the document that follows is almost entirely taken up with nitpicky corrections of specific details from

ABT. And yet the vehemence behind these details reveals that by popularizing the avant-garde's history and placing herself at the center of it, Stein had violated the autonomy by which the history of the field was understood to operate. By doing so, she had, in a sense, refused to grow old.

Stein achieved the international recognition she desired, but apparently at the expense of much of the prestige she had been gradually accruing among the modernist elite, most of who resented their portrayals in *ABT.* Her challenge was to reconcile the temporalities of these two opposed segments of the cultural field, to prove that her greatness straddled the divide between avant-garde and middlebrow.

I would argue that for Stein, the specific temporality of genius emerges in the dissonance between the temporalities of the restricted and general fields of cultural production. In "How Writing Is Written," one of her final lectures in the United States, Stein reiterated her philosophy that everybody, including the artist, "is contemporary with his period."[39] But most people don't recognize the contemporariness of the artist because "in the things concerning art and literature they don't have to live contemporarily, because it doesn't make any difference; and they live about forty years behind their time" (151). The contemporariness of the artist is disjunct from the contemporariness of the audience, resulting in a delayed or syncopated recognition. Stein therefore maintains that "thirty years from now I shall be accepted" (152). To an audience of high school students representative of her future U.S. public, Stein describes her work in the temporality of the restricted field of cultural production, whereby symbolic value is accrued through the delayed acceptance of the artist, creating an illusion that she is ahead of her time, when really she is resolutely of her time.

Contemporariness, however, is not simply the inevitability of being in and of your time; it is also a matter of being attuned to the specific "time-sense" that defines that time as a time (152). And for Stein, the twentieth century—the American century, her century—has replaced "the feeling of beginning at one end and ending at another" with "the conception of assembling the whole thing out of its parts" (152). Stein felt that her own method of "present immediacy" corresponded to and reflected this twentieth-century temporality. Stein's aesthetic of transcending time is simultaneously a way of being of her time. Her claim in *EA* that "genius is the existing without any internal recognition of time" (243) is paradoxically a resolutely historical claim in that it establishes a correlation between genius and modernity.

In other words, to be contemporary and have no recognition of time are, for Stein in the twentieth century, the same thing, and this convergence emerges out of the dissonance between modernist artist and mass audience. *EA* unfolds in this peculiar narrative space where the subject's attempt to transcend temporality is simultaneously an attempt to be of her time, and where her effort to be of her time is simultaneously a guarantee that she won't be recognized by it.

This clash of temporalities inevitably led to meditations on death since Stein was trying to import her posthumous reputation as a genius into her contemporary experience as a celebrity. As she argues in *EA*, "The only novels possible these days are detective stories, where the only person of any importance is dead" (102). The combination of sudden fame and advancing age gradually led her to think of her own writing as in some sense a detective story about her own death, a meditation on how the iconicity of celebrity functions as a harbinger of death. She thereby alleged that *GHA* was "a detective story of how to write" (409), opening with the fact that she, George Washington, and Abraham Lincoln were born in the same month, and then following with "let us not talk about disease but about death" (367). Celebrity taught Stein how little one's public image really depends on one's private existence. The detective story becomes the genre in which one can repetitively dwell on the readerly conventions of this afterlife, where the dead person is the orienting object of the narrative.[40]

If the dead person at the center of the detective story allows Stein to anticipate her own death in the persistence of her public image as the subject of writing, the criminal in the news reveals the U.S. public sphere as, in essence, a land of the undead. It is worth remembering that Stein's celebrity coincided with the worldwide publicity around the Lindbergh kidnapping and the enormous popularity of glamorous criminals like John Dillinger. It was also the period of Hollywood's classic gangster films, in which U.S. capitalism and chic criminality were both implicitly and explicitly compared. Thus when Stein and Toklas were in Chicago, they spent one evening driving in a police squad car. There was no crime that night, but they did see an event that precipitated one of Stein's more revealing meditations on celebrity in the United States written, significantly, for the *New York Herald Tribune*:

When we went around in that squad car and when there was no crime in Chicago they took us to see a walking Marathon. I had never seen any such thing and it was a strange a very strange thing to be seeing. As they went moving around a state of sleeping they were young things and they were asleep and they kept moving, it meant anything and nothing that they fell asleep and young and touch-touching and that they were asleep and that they kept moving, and they were there to be anything that is to say they were existing as they would be to any one looking at them and of course it was not a crime that they were doing what they were doing but it might have been, it would have been they would have been the same if it was a crime for them to do as they were doing. Do you see what I mean when I say anybody in America can be a public one, and anybody in America being able to be a public one it has something to do with the hero crime and so many people are always doing this thing doing the hero crime it gets into anybody who can have his picture where it is to be seen by anybody.[41]

The spectral vision of "young things" sleepwalking and "touch-touch-ing" through the streets of Chicago becomes an unsettling allegory of America's democracy of publicity, in which anybody can be a "public one." And although sleepwalking through the streets is not a crime, Stein uses the spectacle to draw a connection between publicity and criminal-ity.

It was through the public image of both the hero and victim of crime that Stein was able tentatively to come to terms with her own mortality. In another article she wrote for the *Herald Tribune*, on U.S. newspapers, she noted that the impossible task of the press was "to make the things that happened yesterday happen today."[42] Usually the big city papers fail in this temporal sleight of hand, but occasionally some item of news is ex-citing enough actually to achieve a sort of historical leapfrog:

> Dillinger and Lindbergh were and are exciting in that way and that is not because the story their story is exciting it is exciting their story but what is really exciting is that they are exciting and that is the reason that what happens to them yesterday is still what happens to them to-day be-cause they are existing every day and exciting every day and every day they are existing they are exciting and so any day any newspaper tells anything about them it makes it like to-day and so be exciting. (90–91)

For some people, to exist and excite converge, and these people are mirac-ulously able to carry yesterday over into today, to cheat mortality and finitude much in the same way that the genius exists without any internal sense of time. For Stein, the ongoing challenge was to forge a working relationship between existing, being exciting, and writing. Stein's crime was that she was able to be exciting precisely by writing as if she were dead, as if her critical reputation were already established, thereby autobiographically enfolding the temporality of the avant-garde into that of the mainstream.

5

Being Ernest

No study of authorial celebrity in the modern United States would be complete without a consideration of the career of Ernest Hemingway. To a great extent, Hemingway paradigmatically condenses the key anxieties and conflicts previously examined in the careers of Twain, London, and Stein. Like Stein, Hemingway experienced the classic career arc from European modernist little magazine cachet in the 1920s to U.S. mass cultural celebrity in the 1930s. Like Twain, he was obsessed with death, particularly in its relations to literary celebrity. Like Twain and London, he was widely impersonated. As with Twain, there is a Hemingway Foundation that owns his copyrights, and continues to issue and profit from work compiled by editors and scholars in his name. Like all three previously considered authors, his life became as important as his work, and the principal challenge to Hemingway critics has always been located in the vexed relation between literary biography and literary criticism. And with Hemingway, we witness the full force of the institutional mediations—publishers, editors, critics, and academics—that would form on the boundary between the restricted and general fields of cultural production, both enabling and policing the passage between them.

Furthermore, Hemingway's career represents the apex of a development that was only emerging with London: the modernist author as a model of masculinity simultaneously within and against the marketplace. The terse minimalism that originally established Hemingway's literary reputation has been widely understood as a specifically masculine response to feminine genteel literary conventions, a way of making literature safe for real men. And of course, his worldwide public image as "Papa," the indestructible U.S. sportsman and aficionado, became a veritable paradigm of masculinity in the American cultural imaginary.

Traditionally, however, these two categories—the literary style and public persona—have been analyzed and evaluated separately. In many ways, the critical tradition on Hemingway has been built on trivializing the latter while sacralizing the former. Hemingway's fame, in other words, has ironically become analytically dislodged from the stylistic innovations that enabled it in the first place.

In general, the public personality that Hemingway developed in the 1930s has been an embarrassment for literary critics. Edmund Wilson, in his influential *Atlantic Monthly* article of 1939, "Ernest Hemingway: Gauge of Morale," laments that after the publication of *Death in the Afternoon*, the author "passes into a phase where he is occupied with building his public personality. . . . [T]he opportunity soon presents itself to exploit this personality for profit: he is soon turning out regular articles for well-paying and trashy magazines." As far as Wilson is concerned, "This department of Hemingway's writing there is no point in discussing in detail."[1] Wilson can only provocatively conclude that Hemingway's public personality "is certainly his own worst-invented character."[2] The terms of Wilson's critical analysis are clear: personality and the profit gained thereof are not only opposed to but destructive of the literary innovations that originally put Hemingway on the literary map. In the 1930s, Hemingway found himself straddling a divide between modernism and mass culture that literary critics would understand as an almost-heroic struggle between the ascetic demands of the "style" and the worldly temptations of the "personality."

Surprisingly enough, this conceptual and evaluative split, constitutive of modernism as such, seems to have persisted into our own contemporary era when it comes to Hemingway. John Raeburn's fine study *Fame Became of Him: Hemingway as a Public Writer*, confirms that the "disparity between his literary reputation and his public reputation . . . was one of the most arresting aspects of Hemingway's career. . . . Nearly everything he published after 1930 reflected this awareness."[3] And yet, Raeburn opens his groundbreaking consideration of Hemingway's fame with the caveat that "Hemingway's literary achievement is tangential to understanding [his] public fame," and concludes by conceding that "there seems to have been an inverse relationship between the growth of Hemingway's celebrity and the quality and even quantity of his fiction."[4] Leonard Leff's equally informative study *Hemingway and His Conspirators: Hollywood, Scribner's, and the Making of American Celebrity Culture*, similarly concludes that long before the last years of his life, he had understood that he could no longer supply the vast audience of the twentieth century with work that was quick, honest, and controlled, work as powerful or as enduring as *In Our Time, The Sun Also Rises,* and *A Farewell to Arms.* He could supply the audience only with himself, Ernest Hemingway the Professional Writer, Ernest Hemingway the husk.[5]

The story remains one of the heroic modernist author whose skills are corroded by mass cultural celebrity; style and personality are still the evaluative poles along which Hemingway's literary career is oriented.

And yet, the irony persists that it was precisely the personality, the life story of Hemingway, that was the model for the male characters in all the major writing, and thus biographical considerations inevitably obtrude into any critical accounting of Hemingway's work. The most fascinating, and most informative, versions of these considerations have been psychoanalytic and, significantly, tend to be couched in the same critical caveats characteristic of studies of Hemingway's fame. This psychoanalytic strand of Hemingway criticism can conveniently be traced to Philip Young's pioneering study *Ernest Hemingway: A Reconsideration,* in which Young essentially codified the theory of the traumatic foundational wound as constitutive of both Hemingway's heroes and Hemingway the man. Nevertheless, Young makes sure to remind us that

> the attempt has simply been to show how certain theories—of "trauma," of the "repetition compulsion" and of its function, of the "primitivation" of personality which is the price of readjustment, of vicarious dying and the implications of a preoccupation with violent death—throw a good deal of light on Hemingway and his work. They do not illuminate everything.[6]

Clearly nervous that he will be accused of being reductive, and most likely still anxious over his fascinating struggle with the author himself over the legitimacy of his critical claims, Young assures his readers that "it is not the trauma but the use to which he put it which counts; he harnessed it, and transformed it to art" (171). Young hopes to affirm that the cultural category of "art" can be separated from the interpretative category of "trauma"; the artist becomes the man who is capable of dealing with the trauma in an aesthetic way. We can therefore have our artist and read him, too.

Yet Young goes right ahead and reduces Hemingway's style to his psychoanalytic rubric. He observes in the very next chapter that

> the style was developed and perfected in precisely the same period when Hemingway was grimly reorganizing his whole personality after the scattering of his forces in Italy. The fact that the two efforts came together chronologically has nothing to do with coincidence: they came together because they were inseparable aspects of one effort. (209)

Essentially undermining his earlier claim, Young argues that "his style . . . was, like a great deal else in Hemingway, a direct result of trauma. And this, finally, is the message the style has to give." Young then collapses the two categories he had earlier contrasted by concluding that "the style *is* the man" (210).

As with recent critical considerations of Hemingway's fame, the psychoanalytic understanding of Hemingway has persisted with this contradictory dichotomy intact. This is particularly surprising considering the new license on critical life that Hemingway received with the posthumous publication of *The Garden of Eden*, which inspired a veritable school of reconsiderations of gender and sexuality in Hemingway's work. Carl Eby, in his recent study *Hemingway's Fetishism: Psychoanalysis and the Mirror of Manhood*, contends that Hemingway "can no longer be seen as the simple male chauvinist pig of much early feminist criticism," and that, on a broader level, "Hemingway's art should remind us that there *is* no such thing as an entirely monovocal masculinity."[7] Nevertheless, Eby prefaces his study with the familiar caveat: "Hemingway's position in American literature surely owes more to his contribution as a literary stylist and technical innovator than it does to his expression of psychosexual issues."[8]

Even more sophisticated poststructuralist accounts of the post-*Garden* Hemingway feel compelled to dismiss the "myth." Debra Moddelmog's "queering" of Hemingway, *Reading Desire: In Pursuit of Ernest Hemingway*, asserts that Jenks's edition of *The Garden of Eden* is "based on the popular, commodified Hemingway and his work," and consequently occludes the queer Hemingway she is attempting to construct.[9] The bifurcation between personality and art has persisted through a variety of critical and historical transformations of our understanding of Hemingway, despite the fact that it seems perpetually undermined by the intimate connections between them.

In this chapter, I will argue that Hemingway's innovative literary style and his mass cultural persona embody two poles of a specifically American dialectic of masculinity that emerges from the configuration of the cultural field in the modern United States. I will start by considering Hemingway's persistent feminization of his audience, both mass cultural and modernist, in what one critic describes as his "so-called celebrity text," *Death in the Afternoon*.[10] In this text, we can see Hemingway's characteristic hypermasculinity emerging explicitly in response to the fission of his marketplace. Next, I will maintain that the potentially homoerotic extensions of this hypermasculinity in turn generate the complex homophobia that pervades Hemingway's work. In particular, I will reexamine his vexed relation to Stein and Fitzgerald as agons in a model of homoerotic authorship in which writing becomes a struggle, frequently to the death, between men. Then, I will explore Hemingway's desperate struggles with academic critics and biographers later in his life, especially his remarkable series of exchanges with Philip Young over the publication of Young's psychoanalytic study. Here, I will emphasize the degree to which Hemingway equated biographical criticism with murder, revealing how modern authorial celebrity folds the temporality of posthumous reputation onto the present, rendering fame as a form of death. Finally, I want to look at the resuscitation of Hemingway's literary reputation in the critical wake of the publication of *The Garden of Eden*, particularly in relation to that text's obsession with androgyny, which has led to a wholesale reconsideration of gender and sexuality in Hemingway's life and work. In the end, I hope to show that Hemingway's struggles with gender identity were tightly stitched into his struggles with celebrity, and that both these struggles undermine our continued attempts to separate the life from the art.

The Author versus the Audience (Misogyny)

All the critics agree that it was with *Death in the Afternoon*, ostensibly a sort of ethnographic analysis of bullfighting in Spain, that Hemingway began to establish the hypermasculine public persona that he would present to the international public sphere for the rest of his life. In fact, most contemporaneous criticism acknowledged that the book would have little interest aside from its elaboration of Hemingway's authorial persona. Thus, Granville Hicks, writing for the *Nation*, affirmed that "if anyone

else had written the book, there would be little more to say. . . . [F]ortu-
nately the author, fully aware of the interest in his personality, has made
a vigorous effort to put as much of himself as possible into his book."[11]
And Robert Coates, writing for the *New Yorker*, agreed that most readers will "pay more attention to Mr. Hemingway than to the bull."[12] However, it would be Max Eastman's famous quip, in his *New Republic* review titled "Bull in the Afternoon," that Hemingway was developing "a
literary style . . . of wearing false hair on the chest," that would echo loud-
est and longest through the critical corridors.[13]

Other reviewers acutely recognized that Hemingway's stylized masculinity corresponded to an exaggerated feminization of his audience,
particularly in the character of the "Old Lady" with whom he converses
through much of the book. H. L. Mencken noted that "the reader he
seems to keep in his mind's eye is a sort of common denominator of all
the Ladies' Aid Societies in his native Oak Park, Ill."[14] Coates realized the
metaphoric scope of this common denominator by affirming that "he creates in your image a mythical Old Lady," and provocatively concluded
that *Death in the Afternoon* "seems almost a suicidal book in its deliberate flouting of reader and critic alike."[15] Hence we can see, as Leff remarks, that

> *Death in the Afternoon* was not about matadors and bulls but (as re-
> viewers sensed) about author and audience. Hemingway had had as his
> goal "the holding of his purity of line through the maximum of expo-
> sure" and the desire "never to write a phony line." The tone and content
> of the "bullfighting book," though, along with the publicity it occa-
> sioned and the culture of celebrity that *Time* and others reinforced, had
> now fully drawn the Hemingway persona.[16]

Death in the Afternoon, then, established bullfighting as an allegory for
Hemingway's relationship to his audience. What Leff neglects to emphasize here is the degree to which this choice of allegory also revealed the intimate relationship between Hemingway's gender identity and the structure of his literary marketplace.

For it is crucial to recognize that Hemingway had not one audience at
this point but two, and that he conflates them in many ways in this text.
As I noted above, Hemingway originally established his literary reputation with the international modernist set in the 1920s. He circulated in
the restricted field of cultural production, publishing in little magazines

such as the *Double Dealer* and Ford Madox Ford's *Transatlantic Review* (which he also coedited); his first books were published by Bill Bird's Three Mountains Press and Robert McAlmon's Contact Editions. Needless to say, he made little money from these publications. After the enormous success of *The Sun Also Rises* and *A Farewell to Arms*, though, Hemingway had become an international celebrity whose works made much money in the general field of cultural production. As Raeburn succinctly observes, "The audience which gives a writer literary reputation is an elite; the audience which gives him public reputation is larger and more heterogeneous."[17]

But Raeburn neglects to consider a crucial institutional mediation that had emerged between these audiences: a loosely bound community of editors and publishers became responsible for shepherding authors from the elite to the general field in the 1920s and 1930s. Alfred Knopf, Horace Liveright, Bennett Cerf, and a host of lesser-known figures straddled these fields during the period, and developed strategies for leveraging modernist cachet into mainstream sales. The key figure for Hemingway in this regard, as all biographies acknowledge, was Scribner's editor Maxwell Perkins, who wrote to Fitzgerald that Scribner's should get Hemingway

> because we are absolutely true to our authors and support them loyally in the face of losses for a long time when we believe in their qualities and in them. It is that kind of publisher Hemingway probably needs . . . because I hardly think he would come into a large public immediately. He ought to be published by one who believes in him and is prepared to lose money for a period in enlarging his market.[18]

Perkins operated on the cusp between the literary elite and cultural mainstream, and he understood that prestige in the former could leverage popularity in the latter, but only with a patience and fidelity that, arguably, was specific to publishers of the modern era. Hemingway could rely on Perkins to respect his reputation in both fields, manage the relays between them, and in a sense, provide a masculine preserve autonomous from feminizing audiences.

At first, it would seem that Hemingway's Old Lady, who keeps pushing him for "conversation" and "dialogue," who wants to hear about the "love life" of bulls, who longs for something "amusing yet instructive," represents Hemingway's caricature of the mainstream audience, members of what he called the "litero-menstrual clubs."[19] And this interpretation jibes with the more general cultural history of how audiences were gendered in the twentieth-century United States. *Death in the Afternoon* quite clearly corresponds to Andreas Huyssen's foundational assertion that in modernist literature, "woman . . . is positioned as reader of inferior literature—while man . . . emerges as writer of genuine, authentic literature." Hemingway's macho posturing and dismissive hostility toward his mass readership in this text can be understood as an instance of what Huyssen identifies as a "powerful masculinist mystique" in much literary modernism.[20] That *Death in the Afternoon* in its very genre resists the mass cultural popularity of his earlier novels further supports this claim.

In truth, the situation is more complicated since Hemingway's exchanges with the Old Lady leverage his attacks on many of his fellow modernists—attacks that are also deeply gendered. Hemingway concludes his chapter on the bulls with the comment:

> But, you say, there is very little conversation in this book. Why isn't there more dialogue? What we want in a book by this citizen is people talking; that is all he knows how to do and now he doesn't do it. The fellow is no philosopher, no savant, an incompetent zoologist, he drinks too much and cannot punctuate readily and now he has stopped writing dialogue. Citizen, perhaps you are right.[21]

Referencing the near-unanimous praise he received for his dialogue in *The Sun Also Rises* and *A Farewell to Arms*, Hemingway begins to reveal that his gendered disdain for his audience is adequately matched by his disdain for his critics and colleagues, who he knew would be skeptical of his decision to follow up on these critical successes with a nonfictional book on bullfighting.

Furthermore, this flippant aside provides an opening for Hemingway to reflect on the sex life of bulls in a way that illuminates their allegorical relation to his understanding of the literary life. Responding to the Old Lady's request to hear about the love life of bulls, Hemingway declares, "Madame, their love lives are tremendous" (120). Hemingway then proceeds to reflect on the mating habit of bulls in a manner clearly reflecting his own experience:

> The bull is polygamous as an animal, but occasionally an individual is found that is monogamous. Sometimes a bull on the range will come to so care for one of the fifty cows that he is with that he will make no case

of all the others and will only have to do with her and she will refuse to leave his side on the range. When this occurs they take the cow from the herd and if the bull does not then return to polygamy he is sent with the other bulls that are for the ring. (122)

When the Old Lady replies that this is a "sad story," Hemingway engages in an oft-quoted meditation on love and death:

> Madame, all stories, if continued far enough, end in death, and he is no true-story teller who would keep that from you. Especially do all stories of monogamy end in death. . . . There is no lonelier man in death, except the suicide, than that man who has lived many years with a good wife and then outlived her. (122)

As critics note, this pessimistic appraisal of love emerges from Hemingway's recent break with his first wife, Hadley, and rapid second marriage to Pauline Pfeiffer. Less-commonly remarked is that this meditation emerges out of a discussion of the mating habits of bulls.

In fact, the allegorical role of bulls in this text has frequently been occluded by critics who focus on the more obvious correspondence between writer and matador.[22] Nevertheless, as this chapter on bulls affirms, Hemingway related at least as closely to the bulls in the ring. This chapter, unsurprisingly, is concerned with illuminating the difference between male and female bulls, and Hemingway clarifies the stakes of his argument by obliquely framing it as a response to Virginia Woolf's scathing review of his work for the *New York Herald Tribune*. In that review, Woolf condemned Hemingway's short story collection *Men without Women* with the allegation that

> any emphasis laid upon sex is dangerous. Tell a man that this is a woman's book, or a woman that this is a man's, and you have brought into play sympathies and antipathies which have nothing to do with art. The greatest writers lay no stress upon sex one way or the other.[23]

Hemingway was enraged by Woolf's criticism, and he answers her in this text by way of a complex allegory of sexual difference in the world of bulls.

He achieves his allegory by uncharacteristically shifting the axis of sexual difference from the biological to the social, opening with the claim that "it is in the female of the fighting bull that you see most plainly the difference between the savage and domestic animal" (106). Hemingway contends that the difference between male and female bulls is a matter of training, not biology, and he explicitly establishes this view as a response to Woolf: "The females that are used in amateur fights almost invariably make for the man rather than the cape . . . but they do this not because of any innate superior intelligence in the female, as Virginia Woolf might suppose" (106). Indeed, in this chapter, Hemingway maintains that the male bulls that are used for professional bullfighting are deliberately kept stupid:

> The bullfight has been so developed and organized that the bull has just time enough, coming in to the ring completely unfamiliar with dismounted men, to learn to distrust all their artifices and reach the summit of his danger at the moment of killing. The bull learns so rapidly in the ring that if the bullfight drags . . . he becomes almost unkillable by the means prescribed in the rules of the spectacle. It is for this reason that bullfighters always practice and train with female calves which, after a few sessions, become so educated . . . that they can talk Greek and Latin. (107)

The tongue-in-cheek reference to Woolf here, only a page after mentioning her by name, is clear. On the one hand, Hemingway acknowledges that, in essence, there is no difference between male and female bulls. On the other hand, he argues that differences in training account for differences in intelligence that, in turn, enable him to use female bulls as a metaphor for cultural critics like Woolf and, more broadly, the feminization of culture itself under the conditions of modernity.

In fact, it becomes quite apparent in this chapter that Hemingway is using the world of bulls as an allegory for the complex triangulation of masculinity, modernism, and mass culture that defines his career. Thus he continues:

> The maneuvering of fighting bulls is made possible by the operation of the herd instinct which makes it possible to drive bulls in groups of six or more where one bull, if detached from the herd, will charge instantly and repeatedly anything, man, horse, or any moving object, vehicle or otherwise, until he is killed. (107)

Hemingway then narrates an example of this "detachment" from the herd that, since he modulates it into his famous definition of "nobility" in bulls, is worth quoting in full:

> One year when we were in Spain this happened before the last house of a little village outside of Valencia. The bull stumbled and went to his knees and the others were past when he got to his feet. The first thing he saw was an open door with a man standing in it. He charged at once, lifted the man clear out of the door, and swung him back over his head. Inside the house he saw no one and went straight through. In the bedroom a woman sat in a rocking chair. She was old and had not heard the commotion. The bull demolished the chair and killed the old woman. The man who had been tossed in the doorway came in with a shotgun to protect his wife who was already lying where the bull had tossed her into the corner of the room. He fired point blank at the bull but only tore up his shoulder. The bull caught the man, killed him, saw a mirror, charged that, charged and smashed a tall, old-fashioned armoire and then went out into the street. He went a little way down the road, met a horse and cart, charged and killed the horse and over-turned the cart. The driver stayed inside it. The herders by this time were coming back down the road, their galloping horses raising a great dust. They drove out two steers that picked the bull up and, as soon as there was a steer on each side of him, his crest lowered, he dropped his head and trotted, between the two steers, back to the herd. (108–9)

It is hard to miss the thinly veiled allegory of the male individual in mass society here. He breaks free from the herd, at which point his killer instinct is unleashed on the entire world; he can only be reincorporated into the herd by being placed between two castrated males. Almost perversely, Hemingway translates the intensity of this instinct into bravery, concluding the above anecdote with the assertion that "a truly brave bull fears nothing and, to me, is the finest of all animals to watch in action and repose" (109). Bravery, in other words, designates the hysterical death instinct unleashed when the male individual, raw and untrained, is detached from the herd.

If the allegory here is still unconvincing, Hemingway continues with a string of such stories, all derived from "a book, now out of print in Spain, called *Toros Celebres*, which chronicles, alphabetically by the names the breeders gave them, the manner of dying and the feats of some three hundred and twenty-two pages of celebrated bulls" (110). It is in his discussion of these celebrity bulls that Hemingway explains that "the best of all fighting bulls have a quality, called nobility by the Spaniard, which is the most extraordinary part of the whole business" (113). For those in need of clarification, Hemingway defines "noble" in his glossary as a "bull that is frank in its charges, brave, simple and easily deceived" (426). And of course, bulls that lack this quality are "certified for castration and the meat market" (116).

The broad allegorical significance of this disquisition can be further confirmed through an examination of Hemingway's struggles with Perkins over censorship issues in *The Sun Also Rises*. As with all of Hemingway's texts, Perkins was concerned about the frank dialogue, and the two men had a series of delicate epistolary exchanges about deleting some of the more offensive terms. At one point, Hemingway wrote Perkins, "I have thought of one place where Mike when drunk and wanting to insult the bullfighter keeps saying—tell him bulls have no balls. That can be changed—and I believe with no appreciable loss—to bulls have no horns."[24] Undoubtedly, this seemed acceptable to Hemingway because horns had enough of a phallic resonance to maintain a metaphoric association with masculinity. Nevertheless, this particular voluntary instance of censorship took on a broader meaning for him. The very next month he wrote Perkins that "we've . . . unfitted the bulls for a reproductive function."[25] Already the complexity of the censorship is evident: Hemingway has *metaphorically* castrated the bulls by excising a phrase in which they are *literally* designated as such. In other words, the castration is really of the text, not the bulls, as would become clear when, in negotiations over later texts, Hemingway would refer to censorship as a form of emasculation.

Hemingway would more explicitly associate this emasculation with his *image* in the marketplace in a letter to Perkins after the publication of *The Sun Also Rises*:

> Thanks so much for sending the reviews and advertisements. The portrait, Bloomshield's drawing, looks much as I had imagined Jake Barnes; it looks very much like a writer who had been saddened by the loss or atrophy of certain non replaceable parts. It is a pity it couldn't have been Barnes instead of Hemingway.[26]

The bulls have dropped out here, but they still resonate as a third figure for the "writer who had been saddened by the loss or atrophy of certain non replaceable parts" insofar as their balls have explicitly been removed in concession to the gentility of the U.S. literary marketplace. As such, we can see that the dialectic between virility and emasculation so central to Hemingway's heroes can be understood as a complex figuration of his relation to a feminized, castrating literary marketplace in which both middlebrow book clubs and highbrow critics vie to keep the lonely author safely in the herd.

The Author versus Himself (Homophobia)

In the same letter in which Hemingway expressed a willingness to replace "balls" with "horns," he held his ground on another term: "But in the matter of the use of the word *Bitch* by Brett—I have never once used this word ornamentally nor except when it was absolutely necessary."[27] If Hemingway is willing to euphemize the object of castration, he draws the line at its agent. Yet he was willing to relent on this one when it came to *Green Hills of Africa*, in which he chose to respond to Stein's caricature of him in *The Autobiography of Alice B. Toklas*:

> About the Stein thing—I was just trying to be completely honest. I don't mention her name and what proves it is Gertrude? What would you like me to put in place of bitch? Fat bitch? Lousy bitch? Old Bitch? Lesbian Bitch? . . . I'll change it to fat female or just female. That's better. That will make her angrier than bitch, will please you by not calling a lady a bitch, will make it seem that I care less about her lying about me, and will please everyone but me who cares only about honesty.[28]

Hemingway was, of course, enraged at Stein's representation of him in her best-selling memoir, and his responses all reveal the extent to which sexuality and the literary marketplace had become deeply entangled for him. First of all, it is worth remembering that Stein's principal critique of her most famous "pupil" involved the developing contradictions between his public and private personae:

> What a book . . . would be the real story of Hemingway, not those he writes but the confessions of the real Ernest Hemingway. It would be for

another audience than the audience Hemingway now has but it would be very wonderful . . . what a story that of the real Hem, and one he should tell himself but alas he never will. After all, as he himself once murmured, there is the career, the career.[29]

In an autobiography that famously developed an artificial public persona that in turn jump-started a literary career, this accusation takes on rich layers of ironic identification that Hemingway was loath to appreciate.

Before their break, Hemingway had written to Sherwood Anderson that "Gertrude Stein and me are just like brothers." When Hemingway arrived in Paris, in fact, he had already been using the nickname "Hemingstein," and even "Stein"—a coincidence whose significance expands given the numerous and complex literary and psychosexual affinities between the two.[30] In many ways, Stein's development of a public persona that screened out her private sexuality in *The Autobiography* was not all that different from Hemingway's own construction of a tough-guy alter ego in the 1930s. Both were calculated strategies for success in the U.S. literary marketplace, and interestingly, both were predicated on distancing the author from the experimentation with sexuality and gender boundaries characteristic of bohemian Paris in the 1920s.

Hemingway persistently reduced his break with Stein to matters of sexuality meant to uphold the differences between them. As he wrote to Janet Flanner:

> I never cared a damn about what she did in or out of bed and I liked her very damned much and she liked me. But when the menopause hit her she got awfully damned patriotic about sex. The first stage was that nobody was any good that wasn't that way. The second was that anybody that was that way was good. The third was that anybody that was any good must be that way. . . . The only way, I suppose, is to find out what women are going to write memoirs and try to get them with child.[31]

Hemingway stages his break with Stein as an affirmation of sexual differences in terms of both gender and preference. From the original fraternal relation emerges a menopausal lesbian and a heterosexual male.

This difference, finally, translated into a literary one whereby Hemingway sought to distance his own work from the gossipy memoirs emerging in the wake of the golden age of Montparnasse. Hemingway's most vicious attack on Stein occurred in the introduction he wrote to *This*

Must Be the Place: Memoirs of Montparnasse by Jimmie "the Barman" Charters. Hemingway begins with the claim, "Once a woman has opened a salon it is certain that she will write her memoirs. If you go to the salon you will be in her memoirs; that is, you will be if your name ever becomes known enough that its use, or abuse, will help the sale of the woman's book."[32] He continues:

> The memoir writer will usually prove that a lady's brain may still be be-
> tween her thighs . . . and will treat you in her memoirs exactly as any girl
> around the Dome or the Select would; imputing you this, denying you
> that and only withholding the Billingsgate because it would fit illy in the
> pantheon of her own glory that every self-made legendary woman hopes
> to erect with her memoirs. (2)

Here, Hemingway explicitly relates his sexual difference from Stein to the genre of the "memoir" and its intimate connections to the gossipy world of self-promotion and loose sexual relations associated with bohemian Montparnasse. Indeed, the genre and social milieu are linked by gossip, the tactical exposure of private lives to public light.

Significantly, Hemingway contrasts this world of the salon, in which the boundaries between public and private seem systematically violated, with a saloon. As he states, "You should expect to go into a saloon or bar and pay for your drinks without appearing in the bartenders' memoirs" (2). The salon and the saloon were, arguably, the two central social institutions of bohemian Paris, and Hemingway chooses to contrast them not only in terms of their relations to the public/private axis but in terms of the gender of their proprietors. Salons were almost invariably run by women; saloons were almost invariably run by men.

It would be more along the model of the reticent barman, of course, that Hemingway would develop his authorial persona in the 1930s, but it was an image always haunted by the bohemian world in which he served his literary apprenticeship. We can at least partly understand the former as a homophobic reaction to the latter. The genesis of "Papa" in the 1930s achieves considerably more depth if we understand Stein's assertion of a "real Hem" beneath the public facade on both a psychosexual and sociological level. Like Stein herself, Hemingway screened out the psychosexual realities of his private life in order to manufacture an image acceptable to the U.S. mass public. Lost-generation biographer James Mellow affirms that in the late 1920s, "Hemingway set about creating a new persona and a new program for himself as a professional writer. He plainly did not want to be considered an aesthete."[33] And Raeburn confirms, "He fashioned [his public personality] partly to keep the private man unseen, to disguise who he really was."[34]

Raeburn argues that it was in the nonfictional materials of the 1930s, especially *Death in the Afternoon*, in which Hemingway self-consciously "formulated his public personality," and he echoes the critics in asserting that the text offers bullfighting as "a metaphor or model for the artist's way."[35] Understanding Hemingway's art in terms of "the holding of his purity of line through the maximum of exposure" has become something of an interpretative credo in Hemingway criticism.[36] And undoubtedly, Hemingway idealized—even fetishized—the aesthetic appeal of the bullfight. It is worth acknowledging, however, that this appeal was also homoerotic, and that Hemingway's descriptions of the bullfight in *Death in the Afternoon* allow him somewhat obliquely to explore some of the psychosexual anxieties underpinning his developing masculine image.

Nancy Comley and Robert Scholes, in their considerably uneven study *Hemingway's Genders*, note "an extraordinary interest in homoeroticism" in *Death in the Afternoon*.[37] Of course, most of this interest takes the form of an almost hysterical homophobia, as in Hemingway's assertion that El Greco believed

> in life after death and death after life and in fairies. If he was one he should redeem, for the tribe, the prissy exhibitionistic, aunt-like, withered old maid moral arrogance of a Gide; the lazy, conceited debauchery of a Wilde who betrayed a generation; the nasty, sentimental pawing of humanity of a Whitman and all the mincing gentry. (205)

But the violent homophobia here only partly masks Hemingway's anxieties that the "tribe" of which he speaks could as easily refer to modernist writers as to male homosexuals.

Indeed, Hemingway's vexed relationship with Fitzgerald during the 1930s usefully illuminates these anxieties. Both Robert McAlmon and Zelda Fitzgerald circulated rumors that Hemingway and Fitzgerald were homosexual lovers, and both writers were in the habit of referring to each other in homoerotic terms. Thus, Hemingway inscribed one photo to Fitzgerald with "To Scott, from his old bedfellow, Richard Halliburton," referring to a homosexual schoolmate of Fitzgerald's from his days at Princeton.[38] Whereas Fitzgerald, in a letter deprecating Hemingway's criticism of *Tender Is the Night*, plays off McAlmon's accusation with "Did that ever happen to you in your days with MacCallagan or McKisco, Sweetie?" Fitzgerald himself conceded, in an oft-quoted notebook entry, "I really loved him, but of course it wore out like a love affair. The fairies spoiled all that."[39]

The nigh sadomasochistic, homoerotic relationship between Hemingway and Fitzgerald, where "Hemingway felt a compulsion to dominate, to lord it over others, and Fitzgerald had a complementary need to be dominated," has been noted by many biographers and critics, but it is worth underscoring the degree to which their psychosexual engagement was linked to their contrasting positions in the literary marketplace.[40] Fitzgerald's career started out with a middlebrow best seller. After the publication of *The Great Gatsby*, he had been frantically publishing Jazz Age short stories in high-paying, mainstream, commercial magazines such as the *Saturday Evening Post* in order to repay advances to Scribner's for *Tender Is the Night*; he never achieved the high cultural cachet that Hemingway did in the 1920s. In the 1930s, Hemingway had rocketed to celebrity status, while Fitzgerald was having trouble getting published anywhere. As one biographer of their friendship puts it, "As Fitzgerald's fortunes declined, Hemingway's prospered."[41]

The contrast was starkly played out in the pages of *Esquire*, a magazine whose surprising success at the height of the Depression indicates the complex confluence of modernism, mass culture, and masculinity in the cultural field of the 1930s. Developed by David Smart and Arnold Gingrich out of a menswear catalog called *Apparel Arts*, *Esquire* used its association with Hemingway to, as Gingrich describes it, "deodorize the lavender whiff coming from the mere presence of fashion pages."[42] Gingrich, who was both a collector of Hemingway first editions and an advertising copywriter, would become a key figure in reconciling high cultural cachet and mass cultural popularity through slick appeals to masculine sophistication.

In his memoirs of his days at *Esquire*, Gingrich calls the 1930s "the Hemingway-Fitzgerald" years since both authors appeared so frequently in the pages of the magazine in that inaugural decade, and for much less pay than either was accustomed to receive.[43] Thus, Fitzgerald's "Crack-Up" essays would be featured alongside Hemingway's "letters" on hunting and fishing. The crucial crossover would occur in the August 1936 issue, when Fitzgerald's "Afternoon of an Author" would appear alongside Hemingway's "The Snows of Kilimanjaro," in which Hemingway lamented "poor Scott Fitzgerald" for his fascination with the rich.[44] At Fitzgerald's request, Hemingway reluctantly took his name out of future printings, but the anecdote survives.

Indeed, it becomes clear from Hemingway's correspondence that he was in the process of negotiating, both publicly and privately, the literary and psychosexual legacy of his relationship with Fitzgerald (and Stein as well). In a 1936 letter to Perkins, he says of Fitzgerald:

> Work would help him; noncommercial, honest work—a paragraph at a time. But he judged a paragraph by how much money it made him and ditched his juice into that channel because he got an instant satisfaction. . . . It was a terrible thing for him to love youth so much that he jumped straight from youth to senility without going through manhood.[45]

Characteristically, Hemingway renders literary labor in sexual terms, affirming that noncommercial work emerges from sublimating the easy release of commercial publication. On the other hand, Hemingway repeatedly insisted during these years that Fitzgerald was stalled on *Tender Is the Night* because of his obsession with writing a high cultural masterpiece; clearly referencing Parisian expatriate life, if not Stein herself, Hemingway wrote Fitzgerald, "Nobody but Fairies ever writes . . . Masterpieces."[46] For Hemingway, the masculine discipline of "noncommercial, honest work" allows the writer to delicately straddle the rail between the fields of mass cultural popularity and high cultural prestige.

Over the course of the next two decades, Hemingway would continue these attacks on Fitzgerald, as well as Stein and many others, conflating literary and psychosexual inadequacy. And he addressed these attacks to the very men—Perkins, Wilson, Malcolm Cowley, and Arthur Mizener—who would midwife the "Fitzgerald revival" (as part of the more general canonization of U.S. literary history) that occurred after his death in 1940, when all of his books combined sold seventy-two copies.[47] Indeed, by carefully circulating gossip that would later be published posthumously in *A Moveable Feast*, Hemingway was strategically managing Fitzgerald's passage from ephemeral anecdote to canonized literary history. As Matthew Bruccoli explains, "Hemingway is the only source for some of the most widely circulated anecdotes about Fitzgerald that have become enshrined as literary history."[48]

The most celebrated and astonishing anecdote in this regard concerns Fitzgerald's anxiety about the size of his penis—an anecdote published posthumously in *A Moveable Feast*. Hemingway had already circulated the anecdote in private letters to both Mizener (Fitzgerald's first biographer) and *New York Times* Book Review editor Harvey Breit; once published, it was responded to by both Gingrich and Sheila Graham.[49] In *A Moveable Feast*, published shortly after Hemingway's death and the first book to be copyrighted to "Ernest Hemingway Ltd.," Hemingway tells Fitzgerald that Zelda has attacked his masculinity in order to put him "out of business."[50] He then concludes with a later discussion between himself and a bartender at the Ritz who claims not to remember Fitzgerald. The bartender tells him "you write about him as you remember him and then if he came here I will remember him" (193), thereby indicating that Hemingway will become custodian of Fitzgerald's memory. Literary history and psychosexual anxiety were linked for Hemingway, as he struggled to shape the reception of his friendship with Fitzgerald in such a way as to shield himself from the feminizing forces of the cultural field.

In fact, I would like to argue that *Death in the Afternoon* is partly an attempt to represent the homoeroticism of the aesthetic experience in such a way as not to threaten the almost hysterical heterosexuality of Hemingway's public persona. Here is one of his more celebrated descriptions of the aesthetic value of the bullfight: "The beauty of the moment of killing is that flash when man and bull form one figure as the sword goes all the way in, the man leaning after it, death uniting the two figures in the emotional, aesthetic and artistic climax of the fight" (247). The climactic penetration of the bull by the man, both arguably models for the male modernist, takes an undeniably erotic form; it enables Hemingway to bring these two projections of his own masculinity together in a deadly embrace.

Hemingway confirms the violent homoeroticism of the bullfight in his brief appendix on his friend Sidney Franklin, the only U.S. matador of any renown at the time. According to Hemingway, "He ran into bad luck on his second fight early in March of 1930, when he was gored by a bull he had turned his back to after having put the sword in and received a tremendous wound that perforated the rectum, sphincter muscle and large intestine" (475). Here, we see a quite explicit homoerotic correlative to Jake's war wound, in which the male artist, instead of being castrated, figures as a victim of symbolic homosexual rape. And once again,

I would maintain that this confrontation, for Hemingway, figures narcissistically as a death struggle between male artist and his animal double, between the male individual and the horrifying specter of his own homoerotic desire.

Once he became firmly established in the literary canon, Hemingway came to understand authorship itself as a homoerotic struggle, a sort of macho version of Eliot's "Tradition and the Individual Talent." Thus, in a 1949 letter to Charles Scribner, he summarizes his place in the canon:

> For your information I started out trying to beat dead writers that I knew how good they were. . . . I tried for Mr. Turgenieff first and it wasn't too hard. Tried for Mr. Maupassant (won't concede him the de) and it took four of the best stories to beat him. He's beaten and if he was around he would know it. Then I tried for another guy (am getting embarrassed or embare-assed now from bragging; or stateing [*sic*]) and I think I fought a draw with him. This other dead character. Mr. Henry James I would just thumb him once the first time he grabbed and then hit him once where he had no balls and ask the referee to stop it.[51]

This concluding mention of James—who like the bulls, has no balls (another anecdote he helped canonize)—along with Hemingway's parenthetical concern that he is "embare-assing" himself, clearly indexes the homoerotic extensions of this battle for literary preeminence. In his desperate attempts to discount the feminized mass audience that made him famous, Hemingway constructs modernist authorship as a macabre blend of narcissism, homoeroticism, and necrophilia.

The Author versus the Biographers (Death)

Of course, it has become a basic axiom of Hemingway criticism that he was preoccupied with death, both his own and others. Given his wounding in World War I, his father's suicide, and then his own suicide, death provides one of the principal axes for relating his biography to his writing, or even for explaining why he became a writer in the first place. As Leff asserts, "Death. . . affected not only the content of his work but the very fact that he was an author, since, finally, he wrote to deny the void."[52] And the psychoanalytic underpinnings of this theory were articulated in Young's important claim in *Ernest Hemingway: A Reconsider-*

ation, that Hemingway's writing is motivated by the Freudian death drive:

> Suffering from the wounds and shock crucially sustained in the First World War, Hemingway, in terms of Freud's analysis, was continually in his prose disregarding the pleasure principle, and returning compulsively to the scenes of his injuries. (166)

Young's study established the "wound" as an interpretative crux for a whole series of later studies of Hemingway's work. As Michael Szalay has recently observed, Young inaugurated an entire tradition of reading "Hemingway's writing through the wounding he received in World War I." Szalay wishes to challenge the essentially therapeutic method that he believes emerges from this precedent:

> In this model writing is significant as an activity or labor that reflects and expresses anxieties and neuroses that are always elsewhere and never specific to the text in question. But although it is true that the wound remains a central category in Hemingway's writing, the wound is a threat that writing is meant to alleviate as a surrogate identity, not as an endless process that metonymically extends the failings of human identity.[53]

Szalay reminds us that Hemingway's writings cannot be simply assumed to be symptomatic expressions of the psychic injuries of their author, but he seems too eager to buy into the autonomy of the "surrogate identity" they establish (or indeed, to assume that "alleviation" is no less symptomatic than "extension"). The biographical studies that began to emerge late in Hemingway's life precisely exposed the degree to which textual and human identities become conflated in the phenomena of celebrity, as well as the degree to which this conflation is usefully susceptible to psychoanalytic inquiry.

Indeed, Young's pioneering work is not only significant for its interpretative claims; his study, written before Hemingway's death, precipitated a struggle between critic and author that is equally revealing. The aging author felt deeply violated by Young's argument, and in turn, Young ended up feeling partly responsible for Hemingway's suicide, which seemed to confirm his argument. Throughout his life, Hemingway violently opposed biographically oriented criticism of his work, which he

felt should be reserved for authors already dead. But is it possible to allege that biographical criticism *literally* killed him?

I don't quite intend to make that claim here, but I do want to argue for
a close relationship between the psychoanalytic assumption that public
texts are intelligible in terms of private obsessions and the modern experience of celebrity as an invasion of privacy. And for Hemingway, insofar
as the psychoanalytic theory of the traumatic wound grounds his writing
in the death drive while the biographical exposure of that wound is understood as a form of murder, death, as a troubling location where figurative and literal collapse, also becomes the location where psychoanalysis and celebrity meet. This location is particularly important because it
confirms the *public* extensions of psychoanalytic critical method. The interesting issue, in other words, lies not in a psychoanalytic unpacking of
Hemingway as a private individual but in the way that private symptoms
come to figure in the public subject of Hemingway as a celebrity author
canonized by both academic critics and the mainstream media.

Wounding and celebrity for Hemingway were linked from the beginning since the first publicity he received was for his wounding in Italy. At
the time, he wrote to his parents, "It's the next best thing to getting killed
and reading your own obituary."[54] The blithe cleverness of this assertion,
however, is belied by his more sober assessment for one of the men he met
in Italy: "You know and I know that all the real heroes are dead. If I had
been a really game guy I would have gotten myself killed off."[55] From the
start, we see Hemingway's ambivalence about the intimate cultural linkages between the private experience and public circulation of this wounding. For Hemingway, celebrity precipitated a temporal disjunction, a feeling of uncannily witnessing a posthumous existence. This temporal disjunction in turn generates a deep subjective dissonance, a certainty that
public hero and private self do not converge. The publicity around Hemingway's wound, in other words, was as foundational for his career as the
wounding itself.

In fact, for Hemingway, contemporaneous publicity became a form of
wounding. In his negotiations with Perkins concerning the mention of
James's "obscure hurt" in *The Sun Also Rises*, the young author declares:

> Henry James is dead and left no descendants to be hurt, nor any wife,
> and therefore I feel that he is as dead as he will ever be. I wish I had the
> ms. here to see exactly what it said. If Henry James never had an acci-
> dent of that sort I should think it would be libelous to say he had no

matter now long he were dead. But if he did I do not see how it can affect him—now he is dead.[56]

If James were alive, public mention of his hurt would "hurt" him; but the death of the author opens up a temporal gap between the wound and its public exposure—a gap that ensures that the author can no longer be hurt by a discussion of his hurt. Death is the ultimate shield against wounding.

Of course, Hemingway did hurt a lot of less well-known people with *The Sun Also Rises*, precisely by making them notorious. The text achieved its initial notoriety as a roman à clef, and as Carlos Baker explains, "The international guessing game of who was who . . . assisted with the word of mouth promotion of the book." Yet it is noteworthy that Baker, in the end, must dismiss the book's initial success:

> The question with any such novel is always whether it has the power to survive the immediate moment when its possible real-life origins are being gossiped about. Unless the *clef* of a *roman à clef* is finally irrelevant, the novel can have no more just claim on the interest of posterity than the society pages or racing forms from last year's newspaper. The *succes de scandale* of 1926 could not possibly explain the rapidity and assurance with which *The Sun Also Rises* became, as it remained, one of the genuine classics of modern American fiction.[57]

Few paragraphs more economically compress Hemingway's contradictory overlap of modernist and mass cultural cachet than this apparently simple evaluative contrast. In cleanly dividing the novel's contemporary success from its critical reputation, Baker willfully disregards the extent to which they were conflated for Hemingway himself. After all, it could only be in the mass cultural context that novels could become "classics" with such "rapidity" that the author would still be alive and working on their entry into the canon. Nevertheless, Baker's neat separation of modernism and mass culture here helps illuminate Hemingway's nervousness about biographical criticism, which served as a perpetual reminder of their complex coordination.

This was a difficult task for a writer who based all of his work, both practically and theoretically, on his own personal experiences. Once he became famous, it became a full-time job for Hemingway to combat promotional or critical attempts to draw the obvious parallels between his art and life, especially regarding his experiences during the war. During negotiations over the promotion of *A Farewell to Arms*, he wrote to Perkins, "Really though I would rather not have any biography and let the readers and the critics make up their own lies."[58] And five days later he elaborated:

> I know I should have given you some sort of biographical material but the only reason I didn't was because I hate all that so that I thought if I didn't furnish it there would not be any. . . . Of course the whole thing that is wrong is this damned clipping system. No living person should read as much stuff about themselves as they get through those cursed clippings.[59]

Hemingway's comment that "no living person" should receive such clippings echoes the earlier experience of reading his own obituary. And the sheer volume of the clippings reminds him that publicity is self-generating; his own reticence will not stave off speculation about the biographical parallels between his art and life. The experience with *A Farewell to Arms*, a text so obviously based on his own experiences during the war, forced Hemingway to acknowledge that it was impossible either to suppress or ignore public speculation about his private life. Thus, when promotion began for the film version, he asked Perkins to circulate the following statement:

> Mr. Ernest Hemingway has asked his publishers to disclaim the romantic and false military and personal career imputed to him in a recent film publicity release. Mr. H., who is a writer of fiction, states that if he was in Italy during a small part of the late war it was only because a man was notoriously less liable to be killed there than in France. He drove, or attempted to drive, an ambulance and engaged in minor camp following activities and was never involved in heroic actions of any sort. . . . While Mr. H. appreciates the publicity attempt to build him into a glamorous personality like Floyd Gibbons or Tom Mix's horse Tony he deprecates it and asks the motion picture people to leave his private life alone.[60]

By the time the film version of *A Farewell to Arms* was released with Gary Cooper as Lieutenant Frederick Henry, however, Hemingway had precisely become "a glamorous personality," one that he now began to participate actively in constructing.

As Raeburn notes, Hemingway's self-generated public persona represented an attempt to "keep the private man unseen," to build a sort of prophylactic buffer designed to deflect the more embarrassing speculations about his personal life. Raeburn further claims that Hemingway formulated this public persona in his nonfictional work of the 1930s, most important *Death in the Afternoon*, which he calls "a portrait of the author as he wished to appear." Raeburn then follows the now well-established dictum that "bullfighting was Hemingway's metaphor or model for the artist's way."[61] Still, *Death in the Afternoon*, in my opinion, dwells as extensively on the *differences* between these métiers as it does on their similarities, and these differences, significantly, dwell on the relations between death and celebrity.

Hemingway's famous opening renders death as a crucial element of aesthetic theory with the contention that "I was trying to learn to write, commencing with the simplest things, and one of the simplest things of all and the most fundamental is violent death" (2). If Hemingway opens by positing death as a point of contact between writing and bullfighting, though, he also ends up using it as a criteria for contrasting them. Hence he maintains of bullfighting:

> If it were permanent it could be one of the major arts, but it is not and so it finishes with whoever makes it, while a major art cannot even be judged until the unimportant physical rottenness of whoever made it is well buried. It is an art that deals with death and death wipes it out. (99)

Once again we see that the analogy between author and matador is a poor one. The aesthetic value of the bullfight can only be appreciated at the moment of the death that forms its central objective; writing, on the other hand, can only be valued *after* the death of author. Hemingway continues:

> Suppose a painter's canvases disappeared with him and a writer's books were automatically destroyed at his death and only existed in the memory of those that read them. That is what happens in bullfighting. The art, the methods, the improvements of doing, the discoveries remain; but the individual whose doing made them, who was the touchstone, the original, disappears and until another individual, as great, comes, the things, by being imitated, with the original gone, soon distort, lengthen,

shorten, weaken and lose all reference to the original. All art is only done by the individual. (99)

Clearly writing poses temporal difficulties that are entirely absent from the practice of bullfighting. Literary history unfolds by a completely different temporal logic. Writing persists, and thus it constitutively maintains a far more attenuated relation with the original, individual writer.

The permanence of the "major arts" in the modern world therefore poses an evaluative conundrum completely absent from the practice of bullfighting. For what happens when writing starts to be judged, like bullfighting, before "the unimportant physical rottenness of whoever made it is well buried"? And what if this value, again like bullfighting, is appraised precisely in reference to that physical rottenness, the writer's body and private experience? It is here that we can begin concretely to understand why modern celebrity can be experienced as death. Hemingway's contemporaneous celebrity enfolds the temporality of posthumous reputation onto the present. Once he became a celebrity, he started to feel, like Twain, as if he were witnessing his own posthumous existence. Thus, we can more clearly understand why Hemingway was so upset when he received the galleys for *Death in the Afternoon*, every page of which was headed "Hemingway's Death": "But listen Max could you *bawl out* please or raise hell with the son of a bitch who slugged all those galleys Hemingway's Death? You know I am superstitious and it is a hell of a damn dirty business to stare at that a thousand times."[62] In seeing the words "Hemingway's Death" repeated "a thousand times," the author witnesses precisely the mass cultural conflation of his art and life that this text was designed to deflect.

Hemingway's almost hysterical resistance to biographical criticism, then, was not simply a matter of theoretical disagreement over the meanings of texts; rather, it was about the *temporality* of authorial reception and reputation. Biographical criticism composed before the death of the author reminded Hemingway of the uncomfortable overlap, in the U.S. literary marketplace, between posthumous fame and contemporaneous celebrity. Mellow notes that in the wake of his fame, "Hemingway was besieged by biographers, future biographers, and critics seeking information on his personal life or his relationships with the Lost Generation writers." Mellow concludes, "In his early fifties . . . he was a man negotiating his role in literary history, the broker of his past and private life." According to Mellow, Hemingway found this role acutely uncomfortable because "for him biography was an obstruction, an invasion of privacy."[63] It would be in his tragicomic negotiations with Young that Hemingway would imply that such an invasion was tantamount to murder. Young was almost convinced.

In the lengthy forward to the second edition of his now-classic study, Young details these negotiations along with the anxieties they still provoke in him. When Hemingway committed suicide, Young received numerous letters congratulating him on his accurate "prediction" of exactly such an act. These letters forced Young to reconsider the relationship between his text and Hemingway's life, and these reconsiderations resulted in this amusing and provocative forward. He opens with a question: "If a diagnosis implies a prognosis can the diagnosis operate so as to induce the prognosis?" (4). Did his study of Hemingway's suicide actually help provoke the author to kill himself? And if so, what does this say about the relationship between biography and its subject?

In order to respond to these troubling questions, Young goes back over the fascinating composition and publication history of his text, placing his own career as a writer in a revealing juxtaposition to Hemingway's. Indeed, with Young (along with Charles Fenton [author of *The Apprenticeship of Ernest Hemingway*], Carlos Baker, and numerous others who benefited from the postwar expansion of the U.S. university), we witness the final institutional mediation of not only Hemingway's fame but also modern celebrity authorship more generally: academia. If in the 1920s and 1930s the passage from high cultural to mass cultural appeal was mediated by publishers, editors, and critics, in the 1940s and 1950s academic careers begin to be built on both policing and negotiating this passage through academic publication and disseminating the canon as a pedagogical tool for English teachers. *Ernest Hemingway: A Reconsideration* started as a dissertation that was "supposed to pass and be forgotten with the rest" (60). Young got his PhD (from the University of Iowa) and had moved to New York as an adjunct professor at New York University, at which time he was "conned by some generous and well-intentioned people into a tedious interchange with a couple of university presses" (6). Though his negotiations with these presses went nowhere, the manuscript did end up in the hands of Rinehart and Company's Thomas Bledsoe, who expressed an interest in publishing it. The manuscript was sent to Malcolm Cowley as an outside reader, who in turn notified Hemingway.

Young quickly discovered that the author "was absolutely determined that no biography of him was going to appear while he was alive to stop it" (7). Hemingway wrote to Bledsoe: "A critic has no right to write about your private life while you are alive. I am speaking about moral rights; not legal rights. . . . Public psycho-analyzing of liveing [*sic*] writers is most certainly an invasion of privacy."[64] As Hemingway stressed in all his correspondence concerning this text, the issue was not so much substance as timing. Biography and biographical criticism, particularly of the psychoanalytic variety, is only wrong if practiced while the author is alive. He had hoped to prevent publication of the book by refusing to allow Young to quote from his works, thereby preventing the critic from citing the evidence necessary to prove his thesis. But in the terms of this letter, we see his nascent realization that he has little recourse in literary property law here. As Young avers, "If a case came to court in which a critic had without permission quoted for legitimate purposes and was not trying to sell the author's work as his own, the court would almost certainly find for the critic" (11). Thus, Hemingway emphasizes that the issue is moral, not legal, a matter of privacy more than property. Young correlatively asked himself:

> At what point can criticism become an invasion of an author's privacy? And how much privacy can a writer expect when he has allowed himself to become an internationally public figure, or even, according to some, had worked very hard at promoting the image? (10)

Young is, of course, correct in noting the irony, if not hypocrisy, in Hemingway's attempting to suppress a critical analysis of the relationship between his art and life that he himself had been instrumental in promoting. How can an author forbid a critic from analyzing a life that the author himself has so carefully fashioned in the public sphere?

Yet as Young gradually realized, it wasn't so much his biographical substance as his psychoanalytic method that was the problem. As Hemingway made clear in a letter to Scribner's editor Wallace Meyer:

> I am opposed to writing about the private lives of liveing authors and psychoanalysing them while they are alive. Criticism is getting all mixed up with a combination of the Junior F.B.I.-men, discards from Freud and Jung and a sort of Columnist peep-hole and missing laundry list school. . . . [E]very young English professor sees gold in them dirty sheets now.[65]

The terms of Hemingway's anxieties are revealing here. Nowhere does he claim that psychoanalytic criticism is necessarily wrong or illegitimate. When practiced while the author is still alive, however, it has the effect of getting cultural fields "all mixed up" by submitting highbrow texts, meant to be autonomous from the personality of the author, to mass cultural "peep-hole"–type analyses.

Such criticism is wrong because it interferes precisely with the author's ability to produce more highbrow texts. When Young finally did hear from Hemingway directly, he was shocked at the trouble he had apparently caused:

> It seems to me, truly, that there are enough dead writers to deal with to allow the living to work in peace. From my own stand point, as writer, I have so far had worry, annoyance and severe interruption of my work from this book. . . . No part of this is good for some one who is trying to keep his peace of mind and work well with, in one year, the death of his first grand-son in Berlin . . . ; the death of his mother; serious illness of his father-in-law with cancer; death of his former wife and mother of two of his sons; suicide of the maidservant in this house . . . then last the death of my last old friend in Africa and then the death of my very dear friend and publisher Charlie Scribner. All this time I have tried to work steadily and well and this mystery about your book and now the neurosis or neuroses at Detroit have been of little help.[66]

Even if biographical criticism doesn't literally kill the author, it can effectively do so by impeding his ability to work, particularly since his work seems precisely to be a method of dealing with death. The equation between psychoanalytic criticism and death could not be more clearly delineated. It is not surprising that Young states that "the effect of seeing myself in the company of such events was nearly catatonic" (20).

At this point, Young seriously considered dropping the project. Career pressures intervened, though, as he discovered that "as an untenured instructor in 1951 who had not published anything breathtaking I was perishing fast" (21). On hearing of this, Hemingway relented:

> I have made my stand on this thing throughout as a matter of principle and have explained it to you and Mr. Bledsoe at some length. He wants to get a book out and you say that whether you and your wife

eat depends on it. I would maintain my stand with Mr. Bledsoe forever. But I feel damned badly at your work, however mistaken I believe it to be, being held up and you yourself being thwarted and your living imperilled [*sic*].[67]

Hemingway concludes by offering to loan Young two hundred dollars. The book was published in 1953 to near-universal critical acclaim, and Young became one of the first academic authorities on the life and work of Hemingway. Hemingway, on the other hand, did not publish another book during his lifetime. He became increasingly depressed and paranoid, killing himself on Sunday, July 2, 1961.

Young's study did not, of course, kill Hemingway, but its publication during Hemingway's lifetime did reveal the extent to which psychoanalytic criticism, based as it is on the constitutive relations between private life and public texts, can undermine the logic of literary reputations in a way that looks very much like murder. For psychoanalysis violates the autonomy of the modernist text by stitching it to the biographical personality of the author, thereby potentially degrading a permanent work of art to the ephemeral level of gossip. In this sense, psychoanalysis and authorial celebrity commit the same sin of sullying the dividing line between the restricted and general field of cultural production. Both expose the degree to which high cultural texts cannot avoid circulating in the mass cultural field by way of the author's marketable personality. If for Hemingway, however, celebrity could function as something of a buffer, shielding the real traumatic sources of his art, psychoanalytic criticism works in the reverse direction of exposing those very sources.

The Author Reborn? (Androgyny)

Hemingway's death did not end his relations with Young. In fact, in a felicitous irony of literary fate, Hemingway's widow would choose Young over Baker, Hemingway's "official" biographer, as the first scholar to examine the materials that would eventually become the Hemingway Archives, now housed at the JFK Library in Boston, Massachusetts. Among these voluminous materials, Young found "a very long and tedious novel called *The Garden of Eden*" that when edited and published a decade and a half later, would resuscitate Hemingway's career and rekindle critical consideration of his work.[68]

If *The Garden of Eden* hadn't been written, it would have been necessary to invent it, at least if we wanted to keep Hemingway's critical heritage alive for a postfeminist, postmodern world. Publication of this unfinished text precipitated a resurgence of interest in Hemingway, which has led to a wholesale reconsideration of the role of gender and sexuality in his writing. As Kenneth Lynn, whose widely publicized biography came out only a year after *The Garden of Eden*, puts it:

> The transexual fantasies that inform *The Garden of Eden* have compelled reluctant recognition of the possibility that he was not the writer, or the man, he was thought to be, and that he has been misread and misinterpreted by enthusiasts and detractors alike.[69]

And this recognition, almost invariably, complicates both the masculine image Hemingway worked so hard to construct and the conventionalized relations between the sexes he seemed to prefer for his novels. Given this, Comley and Scholes, in the preface to their study *Hemingway's Genders*, admonish their readers: "To all who have read him in one way, as an embodiment of monolithic masculinity—and to all those who have resisted him on those grounds—we ask simply that you try reading him our way."[70] Eby, in his psychoanalytic study *Hemingway's Fetishism*, agrees that Hemingway "can no longer be seen as the simple male chauvinist pig of much early feminist criticism."[71]

The most provocative participant in this ongoing reevaluation, though, is Mark Spilka, whose study *Hemingway's Quarrel with Androgyny* takes Young's theory of the wound and, using *Garden of Eden* as its central evidence, updates it for a postfeminist critical environment. In fact, for Spilka, androgyny *is* the wound:

> Androgyny seems to have been a childhood condition that initially promised great happiness to Hemingway but was soon resisted and repressed; a wounding condition, then, that could be overcome only through strenuous male activities, athletic and creative, as with his active or vicarious devotion to a variety of manly sports and his serious dedication to writing as to an athletic discipline.

Spilka concludes: "Androgyny might after all be the wound against which he had always drawn his masculine bow."[72]

Hemingway's celebrity is somewhat tangential to all these studies, which is unfortunate since without it, *The Garden of Eden* would certainly never have been published. Indeed, its publication was widely perceived as a product of the "Hemingway industry" that was incorporated as the Hemingway Foundation by surviving family members and, according to *Time* magazine, "will market the family name for use on such items as fishing rods and safari clothes."[73] Hemingway's continuing cachet as a celebrity author is a fundamental condition of possibility for the above reconsiderations, and therefore it is crucial in fully understanding the critical and cultural stakes involved. Furthermore, in their rush to reconsider Hemingway in light of the fascinating scenes of cross-dressing and transgender identification in the text, these critics have, for the most part, neglected to recognize that *The Garden of Eden* is also about authorial celebrity.

The Garden of Eden unfolds along a private-public axis that determines the primary poles of David Bourne's writerly practice and literary career. The main narrative as published concerns the intimate sexual life of Bourne and his new wife, Catherine, in which the wife initiates a series of transgender experiments that threaten her husband's masculine identity. These experiments, which have been linked to both Hemingway's childhood when his mother dressed him as a girl and his series of marriages to boyish, short-haired women, have formed the core of recent criticism revising Hemingway's gender politics and sexuality. The character of Catherine Bourne not only allows critics to revise Hemingway's treatment of women, it also opens up a whole new field of biographical sources for reconsidering his entire oeuvre.[74]

Still, in identifying David and Catherine Bourne's sexual relations as the biographical key to Hemingway's treatment of gender and sexuality throughout his novels, critics have tended to overlook the degree to which their private world unfolds in dialectical tension with Bourne's increasing public acclaim as an author. Throughout the narrative, David regularly hears from his publisher about how well his first novel is doing, and he is therefore constantly reminded that another identity is being generated for him in a public world over which he has little control. Early in the novel, he receives "three letters from his publishers and two of them were fat with clippings and the proofs of advertisements. . . . Sentences had been underlined in the reviews that would probably be used in the future advertisements."[75]

As the source of "future advertisements" that will promote David's reputation, these clippings come to represent the public pole against which Catherine constructs their private life. She asks him: "How can we be us and have the things we have and do what we do and you be this that's in the clippings?" (24). The journal that David keeps of their sexual life becomes for Catherine the private "us" intended to stave off the incursions of this public "you." She originally intends not to publish it: "I'm so proud of it already and we won't have any copies for sale and none for reviewers and then there'll never be clippings and you'll never be self conscious and we'll always have it just for us" (78). David's journal, then, becomes an ideal model of the modernist text unsusceptible to market exigencies. In this sense, it is also a model for *The Garden of Eden* itself, which covers the same narrative terrain and which Hemingway never completed or published during his lifetime.[76]

But David's public notoriety continues to proliferate, until Catherine explicitly perceives it as a sexual threat. Later in the novel, she complains that

> there were hundreds of them and every one, almost, has his picture and they were all the same pictures. It's worse than carrying around obscene postcards really. I think he reads them by himself and is unfaithful to me with them. In a wastebasket probably. (215)

Catherine constructs David's fame as an obscene caricature of the author masturbating into the wastebasket as he contemplates hundreds of identical pictures of himself. For Catherine, then, David's public persona generates a narcissistic onanism that threatens the fragile androgynous reciprocity she has constructed for them in their marriage.

But Catherine is not only threatened by David's growing fame; she also resents the other writing on which he is working. J. Gerald Kennedy affirms that "Hemingway depicts David's inner conflict between the pull of androgyny and his instinct for masculine self-preservation through two types of writing in which he engages."[77] The writing that expresses David's "instinct for masculine self-preservation" is an African story in which he explores his relationship with his father. For Catherine, this story, which represents the kind of writing for which David is achieving such public renown, is equally threatening to the private world unfolding in the journals:

Can't you see? Jumping back and forth trying to write stories when all
you had to do was keep on with the narrative that meant so much to all
of us. It was going so well too and we were just coming to the most exciting parts. Someone has to show you that the stories are just your way
of escaping your duty. (190)

Both the stories and fame represent, to Catherine, a masculine world that
she cannot enter. In fact, it is the dialectical relation between David's masculine writing and his public image as a male writer that excludes her and
the androgynous world represented in David's private journals.

There is a tragic irony in her gradual discovery that the only way to intervene in this dialectic is to publish the journals. She begins to shift the
scene of her interventions from their private life to his public career:
"First we have to start seeing about getting the book out. I'm going to
have to have the manuscript typed up to where it is now and see about
getting illustrations. I have to see artists and make the arrangements"
(188). Finally, Catherine is compelled to destroy David's other writings,
as well as his clippings, in order to ensure that her version of him decon-
structs the dialectic between masculine writing and public renown that
sustains his career. Catherine's transgressions of gender identity and heterosexual normativity must be understood in terms of this parallel trans-
gression of the boundary between private experience and public expression. For although Hemingway represents the couple's sexual experimentation as risky and threatening, it is really Catherine's decision to publish
David's writings about them that destroys the relationship. The practices
themselves are, in the end, less threatening than the possibility that the
public would find out about them.

For *The Garden of Eden* does not so much expose the secret truth beneath Hemingway's writing and self-image as it reveals the gradual disintegration of the dialectic that sustained the relationship between them.
Hemingway constructed his career around the tension between the ostensibly autonomous practice of modernist writing and the frantically
heteronomous experience of mass cultural celebrity. *The Garden of Eden*
reveals how delicately and deeply the writer's gender identity inheres in
this fragile dialectical engagement between modernism and mass culture,
and further envisions how the revision of this identity also portends the
disintegration of this dialectic.

Thus, the timing of the text's publication is as significant as the substance it relates. *The Garden of Eden* could only emerge as a postmodern

coda to Hemingway's career, well after his writerly craft and public image have receded from both academic and popular attention. We are not so much witnessing the truth of what Hemingway was; we are constructing the truth of what he himself was realizing he would inevitably become after the decay of modernism.

In this sense, it is deeply ironic that Tom Jenks, the editor of the published version of *The Garden of Eden*, chose to conclude the text with Bourne's miraculous and sudden ability to reconstruct the texts that Catherine had destroyed. According to Robert E. Fleming, "In the handling of the ending, Jenks altered the novel so that it runs counter to the pattern of tragedy Hemingway had been preparing."[78] Whatever Hemingway's original intentions, and they are far less clear than Fleming claims, it is apparent that Jenks's ending serves to resuscitate a model of modernist authorship that is deeply vexed within the narrative itself. Hence, in Jenks's choice of an ending, we see the literary marketplace's continuing investment in Hemingway as a modernist—an identity he himself was increasingly unable to occupy late in life. *The Garden of Eden* resurrects a model of authorship whose historical conditions of possibility have vanished. And it is this continuing critical and popular investment, I would argue, in Hemingway's particular brand of masculine modernism that has foreclosed any close consideration of the obvious relations between his art and celebrated life.

6

The Norman Conquest

> What joy might be found in a world which
> would have no hope of a Hemingway?
> —Norman Mailer, *Of a Fire on the Moon*

When Norman Mailer decided to organize *The Time of Our Time*, his retrospective collection, chronologically by the historical period he had been writing about, he was conveniently able to open with his retelling of the famous anecdote about Hemingway's boxing match with Morley Callaghan in Paris. This choice not only confirms the long-standing critical truism that Mailer modeled his public persona—if not his writing style—on Hemingway but it also foregrounds the crucial differences between the two authors—differences that reveal how Mailer could surpass the older author's celebrity without ever truly achieving his literary stature.[1]

It would be in *Advertisements for Myself* (1959), Mailer's eloquent adolescent cry for recognition after the critical and commercial failure of *Barbary Shore* (1951) as well as the censorship controversies over *The Deer Park* (1955), that Mailer would begin to meditate explicitly on the Hemingway model. The first advertisement establishes his "great sympathy for The Master's irrepressible tantrum that he is the champion writer of this time, and of all time."[2] In particular, Mailer was impressed with Hemingway's dexterous straddling of the divide between mass cultural celebrity and modernist cachet, his uncanny ability to use his personal popularity to ballast his literary reputation. Thus, Mailer concedes that *Advertisements* is, in essence, a ghostwritten writer's guide to precisely such a strategy:

> An author's personality can help or hurt the attention readers give to his books, and it is sometimes fatal to one's talent not to have a public with a clear public recognition of one's size. The way to save your work and reach more readers is to advertise your self, steal your own favorite page out of Hemingway's unwritten *Notes from Pap on How the Working Novelist Can Get Ahead.* (5)

On the one hand, such a deliberate entanglement of personality and work scuttles the evaluative capacities of your critics. As Leo Braudy would remark in his introduction to one of the first collections of critical essays on Mailer, he "has so concertedly placed his personal character and beliefs at the center of his work that the disentangling of work and man, a process that seems so important to our current definition of lasting literary value, becomes an almost impossible task."[3]

On the other hand, the model of Hemingway indicated that the definition of lasting literary value might inhere precisely in the masculine character of the author. Mailer's most recent biographer, Mary Dearborn, notes that "Hemingway's was the life of the writer as public spectacle, as performance; his example could not have been lost on Mailer. Being a writer, very early on, meant cultivating an image, an image of a man of action, tough-minded and masculine."[4] Mailer himself, discussing his early war stories in *Advertisements*, agreed that "it is more attractive to conceive of oneself as (and so to write about) a hero who is tall, strong, and excruciatingly wounded" (9). Yet he could never be "excruciatingly wounded" in the same way as Hemingway, which reveals why he would open his retrospective anthology in 1929, when Hemingway was beginning to manufacture his macho public image, rather than a decade earlier, when the trauma that formed the kernel of that image occurred. Without the war wound to justify the fragility of his masculine ego, Hemingway's public squabble with Fitzgerald and Callaghan would be trivial and ridiculous, unworthy of the kind of recognition Mailer's anthology affords it.

But Mailer's early life was disappointingly without trauma; he suffered no injuries in World War II, and his generation gradually realized that the Second World War would not resonate in the literary world with the same magnitude as the first one.[5] Indeed, the literary world itself had changed; modernism had become entirely canonical, fully assimilated into the academy and presided over by a well-established intellectual elite. Mailer's ingenious solution to this problem would be to transform what in Hemingway's career had been *signifiers* of personal trauma into the trauma itself. Hemingway's celebrity, his gargantuan public image, was a sign of his internal turmoil that deflected public attention from the turmoil itself (unless you were a psychoanalytic critic). For Mailer, celebrity itself was the trauma. Thus his claim in *Advertisements*: "Success has been a lobotomy of my past" (72). Famous but without a war wound to generate literary material, Mailer discovers that

> there was nothing left in the first twenty-four years of my life to write about; one way or another, my life seemed to have been mined and melted into the long reaches of the book. And so I was prominent and empty, and I had to begin life again; from now on, people who knew me would never be able to react to me as a person whom they liked or disliked in small ways, *for myself alone* (the inevitable phrase of all tear-filled confessions); no, I was a node in a new electronic landscape of celebrity, personality and status (71)

Mailer's genius was to render the very experience of celebrity as a psychic trauma generating an authorial persona that in its symptomatic richness far exceeded Hemingway's one-dimensional Papa. In choosing to focus his literary energies on this "alienated" condition, on this "new electronic landscape of celebrity, personality and status," Mailer was also conceding that the ultimate literary objective of Hemingway's career—the Great American Novel—might be forever beyond his reach.

In this chapter, I make a case for Mailer as the last celebrity author; he ballasted his mass cultural fame in a model of masculine modernist genius that was, by the post–World War II era, clearly residual.[6] First, I show how Mailer responded to his inability to produce a successful follow-up to *The Naked and the Dead* by deliberately manufacturing a public authorial persona based on the Hemingway model. He would then use this model as an armature for entering the postmodern mass marketplace while maintaining a sense of himself as a modern novelist. I then track how Mailer's third-person persona over the course of the 1960s gradually shifts from the embattled engagement of Hemingway to the cranky detachment of Henry Adams. It would be as an Adams-like figure—an elderly man struggling against his own anachronism—that Mailer would confront the force that would destroy him: women's liberation. Kate Millet's book *Sexual Politics* exposed the masculine mystique that ballasted Mailer's dialectical understanding of himself as both authorial genius and media personality. After Millet's attack, Mailer would gradually retire the third-person voice that made him famous. Mailer's career thus exposes crucial linkages between second-wave feminism and postmodernism; the former dismantled the masculine ethos of literary genius, while the latter eliminated the cultural field in which genius was recognized. Ironically, Mailer would start to produce encyclopedic novels at precisely this point, when the marketplace that might make them classic works of genius no longer existed.

Declaration: First among Equals

It all happened backward for Mailer. Instead of establishing himself in the restricted field of cultural production before catapulting into the general field, like Hemingway or Stein, he exploded onto the scene with a middlebrow blockbuster, like Fitzgerald, and had to work his way painfully backward through a series of failures only to discover that the modernist coterie that could establish avant-garde credentials no longer existed. After the celebratory reception of *The Naked and the Dead* (1948), Mailer attempted to model himself in the modernist mold of the private artist. In an interview with the *New Yorker*, he claimed,

> I think it's much better when people who read your book don't know anything about you, even what you look like. I have refused to let *Life* magazine photograph me. Getting your mug in the papers is one of the shameful ways of making a living, but there aren't many ways of making a living that aren't shameful.[7]

Nevertheless, the very success of *The Naked and the Dead* seemed to jeopardize the critical ballast necessary to support this self-image. As Norman Podhoretz would later maintain, the New York intellectuals who controlled literary reputations at this time "thought Mailer was merely a middlebrow—a term used a lot those days—who wasn't in the same league as Faulkner, Hemingway, or Fitzgerald."[8] *The Barbary Shore*, as Mailer confirms, was intended precisely to please those "best literary critics" who were crucial to the reputation he desired. The total failure of this sophomore effort showed Mailer that he was not in tune with the critical establishment. Then, after *The Deer Park*, his Hollywood novel, was rejected by seven major publishing houses, Mailer realized that he was not in tune with the publishing industry either.[9]

Advertisements for Myself would turn these failures into successes. In this unusual text, Mailer would begin to manufacture a career through anachronistically importing a modernist sense of the restricted field into what he knew to be an emergent postmodern order. On the one hand, he felt forced to concede in *Advertisements* that "there was no room for the old literary idea of oneself as a major writer, a figure in the landscape. One had become a set of relations and equations, most flourishing when most incorporated, for then one's literary stock was ready for merger" (202–3). On the other hand, he argued, in the forum of the *Partisan Review*, "Is there nothing to remind us that the writer does not need to be integrated into his society, and often works best in opposition to it?" (162). The irony of a young postwar novelist feeling compelled to remind his modernist elders of their youthful oppositional stance was not lost on Mailer. It accounts for his conviction, throughout his career, of being temporally eccentric, of being somehow both in and out of his time. As he asserts in the opening of *Advertisements*, "Defeat has left my nature divided, my sense of timing is eccentric, and I contain within myself the bitter exhaustions of an old man, and the cocky arguments of a bright boy" (1). It would be this very eccentricity that would free Mailer up to circulate his public personality in the mass media while simultaneously maintaining a residual modernist sense of being apart from or above it all.[10]

Mailer also expressed this asynchronous sensibility in spatial terms, averring that the willful development of a protean public personality enabled him to occupy vantage points both inside and outside his private subjectivity. This double consciousness accounts for the vertiginous oscillation between arrogance and humility in Mailer's prose, as well as his sustained attention to dialectical method. Hence, he can see himself from the outside as simply "another vain, empty, and bullying body of our time" while on the same page asserting in *Advertisements* that he "will settle for nothing less than making a revolution in the consciousness of our time" (1). Mailer reveals in a later interview that it would be in these years that "I started smoking pot and seeing myself from the inside and the outside both. The inside and the outside: I could go back and forth every five or ten seconds in my head."[11] This would also be the period when Mailer began recording himself speaking in different accents, listening to them repeatedly not only to perfect his various personae but also to double as his own auditor, to be literally inside and outside his own head.[12]

This willed schizophrenia was, at least in part, a response to the changing structure of the literary marketplace, an accommodation to a new postwar scene in which, according to Mailer in *Advertisements*, "your reputation is uncertain, your name is locked in the elevators of publicity and public fashion, and so your meetings with every man and woman around become charged and overcharged" (4). As the *Partisan Review* symposium alleged, intellectuals no longer perceived of themselves in opposition to the establishment; therefore, they couldn't possibly forge a critical reputation for an oppositional artist. Correlatively, as Mailer's first biographer, Hillary Mills, observes, the publishing world was starting "to undergo its postwar change from a gentleman's occupation to a profit-oriented corporate industry."[13] Mailer rode to fame on a wave of expansion and consolidation that publishing historian John Tebbel calls the "Great Change" when "the viewpoints of the corporate boardroom had been brought into a business that had, from the beginning, functioned as a small community."[14] Without a clear elite field to recede into, Mailer, as he puts it in *Advertisements*, had no choice but to "become an actor, a quick-change artist, as if I believe I can trap the Prince of Truth in the act of switching a style" (2). And Mailer was not only switching styles; he was switching publishers, helping to inaugurate a new era in which loyalty to a single house was supplanted by going to the highest bidder. Indeed, Mailer was one of the first authors to benefit from the age of huge advances based on competitive bidding managed by agents, not editors. He in turn forged the vertiginous uncertainty of the mass marketplace into the basis of his talent and structure of his career.

Seen in this context, Mailer's "quick and expensive comments on the talent in the room" (424), the seemingly offhand and irresponsible critiques of his fellow novelists that so damaged his relations with many of them, are really more a critique of the market conditions in which authors operated. Mailer concludes his vicious little series of hatchet jobs in *Advertisements* with an attack on the U.S. field of cultural production. Willfully echoing Hemingway, he asserts that

> America is a cruel soil for talent. It stunts it, blights it, uproots it, overheats it with cheap fertilizer. And our literary gardeners, our publishers, editors, reviewers and general flunkeys, are drunks, cowards, respectables, prose couturiers, fashion-mongers, old maids, time servers and

part-time pimps on the Avenue of the President Madison. The audiences are not much better—they seem to consist in nine parts of the tense tasteless victims of a mass-media culture, incapable of confronting a book unless it is successful. The other part, that developed reader in ten with education, literary desire, a library, and a set of acquired prejudices is worse, for he lacks the power to read with a naked eye. His opinion depends on the sluggish and culturally vested taste of the quarterlies, and since these magazines are all too often managed by men of large knowledge and small daring, the writers they admire are invariably minor, overcultivated, and too literary (435)

Resurrecting yet again Van Wyck Brook's cri de coeur against a U.S. commercial culture incapable of sustaining artistic talent, Mailer simultaneously tries to lay the groundwork for the cultivation of his own.

But Mailer would have to establish the roots of this talent in the infertile soil of a promise he arguably would never be able to keep: to write the Great American Novel that would both wow the critics and appeal to the masses. In the concluding pages of *Advertisements*, he introduces this bifurcated audience to a "prologue to a long novel":

If some of you will understand immediately what I mean, I still must think of the others who are to take the trip with me: that mob of readers whose experience of life is as narrow as it is poor. . . . [T]hey are picking up this book because they have heard it is good for the bathroom and so may palliate their depression. (470)

Mailer follows this somewhat-clumsy caveat—addressed to an elite audience, yet clearly more deeply concerned with a mass audience—with another, this time about the changing nature of authorship. Attempting to sustain the cryptic, characterless narrative voices of Mikey Lovett from *Barbary Shore* and Sergius O'Shaugnessy from *The Deer Park*, Mailer writes,

The mark of a philosopher is that he puts his name to his work. . . . So, properly, I should introduce myself here, and indeed I would, if I were able, but my name eludes me and at present would slip by without meaning to you—I am virtually married to Time unless she has already divorced me . . . and so my name alters as Time turns away from me. (470–71)

Ironically, this stalled effort marks the end of any anonymity—posed or real—that Mailer might maintain as a novelist. His ambitious, eight-part novel would never be written; it was barely ever begun. Nevertheless, the anachronistic promise of a great novel in the modernist tradition would sustain the name Mailer made for himself as an artist through the next decade.

As the gender of "Time" in the above passage indicates, *Advertisements* also confirmed that Mailer's asynchronic sense of his literary career was entangled with the frequently retrograde theories of sexuality he would develop over the next decade. In the most controversial story in the collection, "The Time of Her Time," he returns to O'Shaugnessy, the narrator of *The Deer Park*, who has now opened a bullfighting school in the village. The story details his violent seduction of a frigid Jewish coed, who he manages to bring to orgasm through anal sex, but who leaves with the devastating comment, "You do nothing but run away from the homosexual that is you" (463). And the narrator concludes, "She it was who proved stronger than me, she the he to me silly she" (459). Mailer here is able to acknowledge explicitly what his Master Hemingway only implied: masculinity must be repeatedly established in desperate opposition to both femininity and homosexuality. This struggle informs not only the authorial persona and novelistic character but indeed the very narrative structure itself. Thus, Richard Poirier cryptically glosses this story with the remark, "The connection between writing and time in Mailer is the same as the connection between fucking and creation."[15] This similitude, I would argue, emerges from Mailer's sense that both his novelistic ambitions and masculine postures are out of synch with the emerging historical order; thus, both are characterized by a kind of embattled desperation. Mailer, then, forges a crucial link between the residual protocols of modernist authorship and the emergent crisis in post–World War II American masculinity. Historians of sexuality tend to agree that the postwar era—with its combination of weakening job security, the rise of second-wave feminism, and the crisis of Vietnam—is characterized by the increasing fragility of patriarchal authority, which generates the sorts of strident masculine response we see in writers like Mailer.[16]

In this regard, Mailer can stand in for a generation of embattled autobiographical novelists, from Jack Kerouac to Frederick Exley, who emerged in the shadow of Hemingway. The Beats, whose collective ethos Mailer so effectively championed in "The White Negro," were briefly able to resurrect both the career arc—from bohemian coterie to mass marketability—and masculine pose of the modern era. However, they also inaugurate the disintegration of a stable relation between masculinity and high cultural cachet. More so than with Mailer, the implicit masochism of the Hemingway persona with the Beats becomes explicit and public. In a sense, the rigor of their autobiographical mandate exposed the very realms of infantilism, femininity, and homosexuality that the Hemingway persona was designed to repress. As the dramatic self-destruction of Kerouac after the publication of *On the Road* attests, masculinity no longer can function as a protection against the vagaries of mass cultural celebrity.[17]

Engagement: The Third Man

Far less confessional than Kerouac, Mailer would also avoid his fate. Stalled as a novelist, he gradually discovered that the asynchronous and offset armature of personality that he formulated in *Advertisements* would end up being much more effective as a ballast for his public career as a journalist. Journalism would become the public outside from which Mailer could maintain a perspective on the private inside of his own determination to be a great novelist. It could provide him with a rich, risky arena in which to deploy the many personae he was developing. And it would supply him with a broad cultural perspective from which to contemplate what emerged for him as the trauma of his age: the death of Hemingway. If the trauma of his own fame precipitated the search for a self that culminated in *Advertisements*, then Hemingway's suicide would help generate the emphatically masculine third-person voice of Mailer's classic journalistic texts of the 1960s and early 1970s: *Armies of the Night, Miami and the Siege of Chicago, Of a Fire on the Moon, The Prisoner of Sex, St. George and the Godfather,* and *The Fight.* As Mailer would aver in *The Presidential Papers:* "Ernest, so proud of his reputation. So fierce about it. His death was awful. It was the most difficult death in America since Roosevelt. One has still not recovered from Hemingway's death. One may never." In fact, Mailer would "wonder if it is possible Ernest Hemingway was not a suicide. It may be said he took his life, but I wonder if the deed were not more like a reconnaissance from which he did not come back."[18] The oddly objectified tough-guy persona that Mailer established in the 1960s can be seen as a willed resurrection of Hemingway, an erasure of the cowardliness of his suicide, an obsessive

184 | *The Norman Conquest*

repetition of the confrontation with death that in the end, Hemingway apparently lost.[19]

Mailer would admit, in the widely acclaimed *Armies of the Night*, that "for want of a live Hemingway, he would be expected to serve as a poor man's Papa."[20] It was partly as an ersatz ghost of Hemingway that Mailer would enter onto the cultural battlefield of the antiwar movement, in which his principal adversary was neither the urban intellectuals who opposed the war—and who made up his primary audience—nor the mainstream middle Americans who supported it—and who made up the general readership on which he always had an eye—but the mass media that reported on it. As with the Beats, Mailer's main adversary was *Time* magazine (and the Luce media empire more generally), with whose account of his appearance on the night before the "March on the Pentagon" he begins his own, far-more-lengthy narrative. By starting with a mass-mediated version of himself, Mailer can frame his own text as a modernist alternative, justifying his repeated references to himself as the "Novelist." Buttressed in his ego by Hemingway's ghost, Mailer drags the disintegrating dialectic of modernism and mass culture into the emerging postmodern moment as a "novel metaphor," proclaiming in *Armies of the Night* that

> the mass media which surrounded the March on the Pentagon created a forest of inaccuracy which would blind the efforts of an historian; our novel has provided us with the possibility, no, even the instrument to view our facts and conceivably study them in that field of light a labor of lens-grinding has produced. (219)

Armies of the Night has to be a novel for Mailer because that is the genre most culturally apposite to the magazine article with which the text opens. It provides a depth and complexity model of cultural vision in dialectical opposition to the superficial monochrome of *Time*. As Philip Beidler confirms of this classic 1960s' text, "Existential claims to the contrary, Mailer was a nostalgic modernist, a philosopher even, above all an author."[21]

Mailer's modernist opposition to the mass media also provided him with the appropriate metaphoric armature to exploit his celebrity image without having to take full responsibility for it. And that metaphor, not surprisingly, was death. Thus, after quoting the *Time* article in which he is called an "anti-star" and a "publicity hound," Mailer informs us in *Armies of the Night* that he had "learned to live in the sarcophagus of his image" (5). Mailer extends the metaphor brilliantly:

> At night, in his sleep, he might dart out, and paint improvements on the sarcophagus. During the day, while he was helpless, newspapermen and other assorted bravos of the media and the literary world would carve ugly pictures on the living tomb of his legend. Of necessity, part of Mailer's remaining funds of sensitivity went right into the war of supporting his image and working for it. (5–6)

In figuring the generation and maintenance of his public image in terms of both death and war, Mailer underscores the continuity with the Hemingway persona. It is as if Mailer's descent into the mass media fray is the continuation of Hemingway's reconnaissance with death.

Armies of the Night was Mailer's most critically acclaimed text of the 1960s; it established his literary credentials at a time when he was beginning to be seen as more of a journalist and media personality. The *Nation* called it "a permanent contribution to our literature."[22] The *Saturday Review* proclaimed, "The real promise of this book lies in its importance as literature."[23] It won both the Pulitzer Prize and National Book Award. Yet as Beidler points out, Mailer was "increasingly at odds with the desires of an audience seeking to submerge the egocentric political implications of literary authorship and authority into the communitarian experience of the text."[24] As Beidler indicates, reading and the reader, both in the popular and academic sphere, were displacing writing and the writer as a mode for the authoritative interpretation of texts (Stanley Fish's "Literature and the Reader: Affective Stylistics" would appear in 1970). It is not surprising, then, that this would be the first text in which Mailer's style and approach began to be compared with that classic figure of anachronism: Henry Adams.

Mailer's gradual sea change from Hemingway to Adams illustrates the increasing fragility of his masculine persona, and foreshadows its eventual disappearance in the 1970s. Significantly, while Hemingway was always a conscious model, Mailer claims that he was unaware of the strong similarity between his third-person narration in *Armies* and Adams's *Education*. In an interview with Barbara Probst Solomon in 1981, Mailer declares,

I never wrote about Adams, never thought about him particularly, would never have mentioned his name as one of the writers that were important to me, and yet in *Armies*, one starts reading it, and immediately one says—even I said—"My God, this is pure Henry Adams." What the hell is going on here? It's an absolute take-off, as if I were the great-grandson of Henry Adams.

Mailer concludes: "Adams was stuck in my unconscious as a possibility."[25] And Solomon agrees, "You do seem more like Henry Adams's great-grandson at this moment than you do Hemingway's son."[26]

Over the next few crucial years in Mailer's career, this "unconscious" model of Adams would gradually supplant the conscious one of Hemingway as a reference point for Mailer's own deteriorating masculine modernist persona. Nowhere was this clearer than in the book that came out a year after *Armies*, *Of a Fire on the Moon*, which opens, characteristically, with yet another lament over Hemingway's suicide. This time, however, Mailer couches the trauma in meditations on his own mortality. Thus he opens, "Hemingway's suicide left him wedded to horror. It is possible that in the eight years since, he never had a day which was completely free of thoughts of death."[27] Yet we see that like Adams, Mailer's death is more cultural than natural; it figures as a premonition of his own developing irrelevance.

As Gordon Taylor would argue five years later, *Of a Fire on the Moon* has much in common with *The Education of Henry Adams*.[28] Like Adams, Mailer contends in *Fire* that "he has little to do with the spirit of the time" (10). Like Adams, he poses as a tired old man, no longer certain of his significance: "He was weary of his own voice, own face, person, persona, will, ideas, speeches, and general sense of importance" (11). In fact, he claims he is beginning "to live without his ego" (55). Nevertheless, again like Adams, he compensates for this loss by coordinating it with the more general historical passing away of an era, deciding to name himself "Aquarius" and infuse the book with a generalized fin de siècle melancholy, affirming that "the century was done—it had ended in the summer of 1969" (381). Mailer lines up his "loss of ego" with the end of an era, simultaneously diminishing and exalting the importance of the persona he had been developing over the course of the decade.

Unlike Adams, Mailer made a lot of money on *Of a Fire on the Moon*. In fact, Mailer's large advances from the publishing industry were starting to damage his oppositional stance. Rumors that he was getting a million dollars for *Fire* slowed contributions to his failed campaign for mayor of New York City. More significantly, he was now actually working for Time, Inc., the very company that had represented the totalitarian cultural menace in all of his previous journalistic work. Reluctantly yet inevitably, he was being forced to abandon his sense of himself as a modernist genius pitched in dialectical battle with the mass marketplace. He was selling out.

And he was selling out at least partly in order to pay alimony and child support. Mailer had already justified his controversial installment contract for *An American Dream* by asserting that

> since I'd been married four times, I was quite justifiably paying for my past. I had to earn a lot of money in a year. That meant I had to do a novel, and I knew the only way I could write a novel in a year was as a serial. Otherwise I'd work it over too much, never get it done.[29]

Mailer acknowledges not only that the economic logic of his career emerges from the structure of his domestic life but that this logic has, in turn, come to dictate the narrative strategies of his writing. By the time of *Fire*, Mailer's fourth marriage was failing, he was growing weary of his journalistic persona, and he was beginning to realize that transformations in gender relations were rendering his masculine authorial pose less and less feasible as a position of cultural authority. He was, both literally and figuratively, paying for his past in order to finance an increasingly precarious present.

Defeat: The Second Sex

If, as we saw in the case of Adams and Bok, the first wave of feminism in the later nineteenth century helped usher in a cultural order that would link U.S. masculinity to U.S. modernism, second-wave feminism, as Mailer's example reveals, would permanently sever that link. It is appropriate, then, that it was Gloria Steinem who would most cogently encapsulate the transcendent function of masculinity for Mailer:

> What unites his public and private personas is his idea of what a man should be, which, in a larger, anthropological sense, dictates that men should be aggressive, take chances, father many children. It's an

exaggeration of a patriarchal idea that in and of itself is impossible to achieve and has enormous penalties, more so for women but also for men, who are under stress, have heart attacks, then go off to war, get killed, do a whole lot of destructive stuff to live up to this code. For Norman the division between his public and private selves is minor compared to the compulsion to live up to this masculine image.[30]

Steinem here accounts for why Mailer would be so deeply traumatized by Kate Millett's critique of him in her groundbreaking study *Sexual Politics*, and why feminism would come to figure for him as the final triumphant wedge of the totalitarian menace. Since for Mailer, the heroic individual who confronted totalitarianism was always implicitly or explicitly male, he could only perceive an attack on the protocols of modern masculinity as an attack on individuality itself. As such, Mailer's desperate and hysterical engagement with feminism in *The Prisoner of Sex* would reveal retrospectively how crucial this model of masculinity was to sustaining the sense of an opposition between modernism and mass culture in the United States. Indeed, it would only be in the wake of the disintegration of this model that the deep dialectical interpenetration between them would become retrospectively exposed.

The article that grew into *The Prisoner of Sex* generated the biggest-selling single issue in the history of *Harper's* magazine, and it thrust Mailer firmly and forcefully into the media spotlight being cast on women's liberation in the late 1960s and early 1970s. Nevertheless, it marked the beginning of the end of "Norman Mailer" as a public figure in the U.S. field of cultural production. After the dust settled from this strangely staged "battle of the sexes," Mailer would retire his third-person public persona for good.

Millett had accused Mailer of being a "prisoner of the virility cult," and it would be Mailer's brilliance to appropriate and exploit this metaphor by exposing its necessary relationship to his own celebrity.[31] He opens *The Prisoner of Sex* with the rumor, which later proved false, that he was going to win the Nobel Prize. In fact, he was not even up for the prize (it went to Samuel Beckett). But Mailer claims he hadn't wanted it in the first place since, given his own experience of fame, "the Nobel Prize would have incarcerated him into a larger paralysis."[32] Offering his own celebrity as a kind of imprisonment, Mailer exploits the dialectical tension between the near homonyms "prisoner" and "prizewinner" throughout the rest of the book.

It is a tension, as Steinem knew, ballasted by masculinity. When Mailer decides to call himself "the PW" for this book, he wonders:

> Prisoner or Prizewinner? They were polar concepts to be regarded at opposite ends of his ego—so they provided a base for his reactions whenever that equivalent of a phallus, that ghost-phallus of the mentality, firm strong-tongued ego, had wandered onto unfamiliar scenes. (12)

The "polar concepts" of prisoner and prizewinner, final avatars of the modern opposition between genius and celebrity, are necessarily linked (like testicles?) by the "ghost-phallus" that stands, firm yet increasingly fragile, between them. In a characteristic combination of candor and canniness, Mailer concedes that his particular brand of dialectical thinking offers a sort of emotional armature for his masculine ego. Without dialectical concepts to provide a "base for his reactions," he would be naked and exposed whenever he "wandered onto unfamiliar scenes." And women's liberation was an unfamiliar scene; Mailer had become famous partly for so accurately prophesying and then presiding over the cultural and political transformations of the 1960s, but he hadn't seen this one coming.

It is not surprising, then, that he tries to frame it with the same conceptual apparatus that had served him so well in the past. Like *Armies of the Night*, *The Prisoner of Sex* opens in dialectical counterpoint to *Time* magazine, whose editor has proposed to do a cover story on Mailer's reactions to women's liberation. Having "become cordial yet wary" (16) with the magazine that he once despised, Mailer admits he is tempted:

> To be the center of any situation was, he sometimes thought, the real marrow of his bone—better to expire as a devil in the fire than an angel in the wings. His genius was to mobilize on the instant. Eight bright and razor-edged remarks leaped to his tongue at the thought of what he could say about the ladies of the Liberation, and yet the tired literary gentleman in himself curbed the studhorse of this quick impulse. Only a fool would throw serious remarks into the hopper at *Time*. (17)

Equivocating between Hemingway's "studhorse" and Adams's "tired literary gentleman," Mailer opts for the latter and refuses to do the story; six weeks later, Millett appears on the cover of *Time*. Correlatively, *The Prisoner of Sex* can appear as a more measured male modernist response to this latest, and most threatening, incursion of totalitarian logic into the existential mysteries of the individual.

For Mailer is sure that Millett is simply, as he notes in *The Prisoner of Sex*, the "mouthpiece for a corporate body of ideas" (83). He had constructed his own vision of the 1960s, and indeed of the twentieth century, as a battleground between the heroic individual and corporate state. Millett, as a critic of the cult of masculinity that underpinned the heroic individual, represented an unwitting soldier of the corporate state:

> She had all the technological power of the century in her veins, she was the point of advance for those intellectual forces vastly larger than herself which might look to the liberation of women as the first weapon in the ongoing incarceration of the romantic idea of men—the prose of future prisons was in her tongue, for she saw the differences between men and women as nonessential. (161)

Thus, Millett forces Mailer to concede that his political and aesthetic opposition to corporate power in the United States is, in the final analysis, based on "the differences between men and women."

But Mailer was no simple essentialist. Rather, male and female are the ultimate dialectical poles that undergird his oppositional identity as a writer. Though *Prisoner* is peppered with quasi-Darwinian meditations about the mysteries of reproduction, Mailer couches this apparent biological determinism in a key concession to performativity: "humans-with-phalluses, hardly men at birth, must work to become men" and "humans-with-vaginas, not necessarily devoted from the beginning to maternity, must deepen into a condition which was not female automatically, must take a creative leap into becoming women" (121). Being a man, or being a woman, does not come naturally; it takes work. Correlatively, abandoning gender identity is, in a peculiar sense, simply lazy:

> Men and women were, after all, equally the inheritors of a male and female personage in their individual psyche, their father and mother no less, and so it might be more comfortable to develop into some middling mix of both sexes. Indeed, in a technological time when the tendency was to homogenize the work-and-leisure patterns of men and women (because that made it easier to design the world's oncoming social machine) so a time might arrive which would be relatively free of cultural conditioning, and then males and females might virtually cease to exist. (121)

Anatomy is explicitly not destiny for Mailer. Becoming a man or woman means struggling against a natural tendency toward androgyny buttressed by a historical tendency toward homogeneity. All Mailer's seemingly adolescent fulminations about the essential difference between the sexes must be understood in this fundamentally dialectical frame: masculine and feminine are conceptual objectives, the pursuit of which legitimates individual identities in a homogenized world.

Nevertheless, the pursuit, in Mailer's view, would seem to be different for men and women. If men are involved in a struggle that is heroic and martial, women, apparently, must simply strive to become mothers, to assume "the mysterious advantage and burden of her womb" (48). As Michael Glenday affirms, Mailer's "main offence in the sex wars of the early 1970s was to insist on an existentialist definition of the male and an essentialist principle for the female, whose ultimate expression would always be through the womb."[33] But *The Prisoner of Sex*, I would argue, is confused on this point. Mailer knew what it meant to work to become a man—after all, he had the inimitable example of Hemingway—but women's liberation did reveal to him that he had far less understanding of the nature of the "creative leap into becoming women." Mailer's ironic endorsement at the end of *Prisoner*—that "women must have their rights to a life which would allow them to look for a mate. And there would be no free search until they were liberated" (168)—was ultimately an unsatisfactory resolution to the issues raised by the text. It is therefore not surprising that Mailer's next major work would explore the relationship between femininity and fame.

They are intimately linked, as Mailer would discover with *Marilyn: A Biography by Norman Mailer*, published one year after *The Prisoner of Sex* to considerable media fanfare but little critical acclaim. It put Mailer on the cover of *Time*, but only in a black-and-white effigy formally subordinated to the color photograph of Marilyn Monroe. The text trumpets: "Two Myth's Converge: NM discovers MM." The composition of *Time*'s cover neatly indicates the peculiar cross-gender identifications enacted in the book itself. By going back to the woman whose celebrity coincided with his own—he later claimed in an interview that if he had been a woman, he "would have been a little bit like Marilyn Monroe"—Mailer attempts to outflank the feminist criticism of his historical significance.[34]

If Mailer opened the 1960s by attempting to resurrect Hemingway, he would close them by retrospectively resurrecting Monroe, whose apparent suicide marked the end of the same era. The two had always been linked in Mailer's mind. In the *Presidential Papers*, he warns: "Hemingway and Monroe. Pass lightly over their names. They were two of the people in America most beautiful to us" (103). And in *Cannibals and Christians*, he worries that "some process of derailment, begun with Hemingway's death and the death of Marilyn Monroe, had been racing on now through the months."[35] However, the significance of Monroe's death was never as clear to Mailer as Hemingway's. He opens his "Novel Biography" with the claim: "Her death was covered over with ambiguity even as Hemingway's was exploded into horror."[36] *Marilyn* attempts to clarify this ambiguity through a willed identification between author and subject.

The vaguely homonymic similarity between their names was convenient in this regard. Mailer knew that celebrity inhered in the iconic significance of names, and he knew that as a project, *Marilyn* relied on the nominal juxtaposition of author and subject. Thus he notes that "it was a fair and engraved coincidence that the letters in Marilyn Monroe (if the 'a' were used twice and the 'o' but once) would spell his own name leaving only the 'y' for excess" (20). Unwittingly anticipating the academic feminism to come, Mailer concedes that something in Monroe, something in her femininity, would exceed his powers of representation. He is able to relate to the basic narcissism of Monroe's fame, averring that "her love affair would necessarily be with herself" (38), that "she is her career and her career is herself" (102), but in the end Monroe can only figure as the object of his desire; as a subject she eludes him (which explains why he would later attempt to write a mock autobiography of her).

In fact, he admits at the beginning that it had always been his "secret ambition . . . to steal Marilyn" from her third husband, Arthur Miller, with whose name, and whose fame, Mailer has as much in common. In contemplating Monroe's life, in considering the fame of a cinematic sex symbol, Mailer can only perceive an evacuation of identity: "If you think to stand in the world for all to see, then give up your piece of identity" (63). Correlatively, it is the marriage to Miller that potentially redeems this sacrifice: "He is the first man she has met upon whom she can found an identity, be Marilyn Monroe, the wife of Arthur Miller" (167). In openly stating his desire to "steal Marilyn" from Miller, Mailer reveals that he can supply an identity for her, but he can never fully identify with her. In the end, as Pauline Kael observed in calling *Marilyn* Mailer's "whammy to Arthur Miller," the book is as much about male mimetic desire as female identity.[37]

Marilyn confirms the constitutive difference between authorial and cinematic celebrity, and further reveals how this difference, ultimately, is inextricably implicated in gender difference. In retaining agency over their work, authors can anchor their public persona in their private identity; in losing that very agency, film stars risk becoming completely evacuated of identity. Therefore, in his later mock autobiography of Monroe, Mailer would have her say, "I guess I have no personality of my own."[38] In characterizing Monroe in this way, Mailer indicates that there is something feminizing about fame insofar as it robs the individual of control of the most basic resources of identity. Masculine authorship functions as a counterbalance to this vertiginous loss of agency.

The *Marilyn* project, however, showed the degree to which these differences were dissolving, as Mailer increasingly lost agency in the uses to which his public persona and literary credentials were put. He told *Time* that he wrote the book "as a way of making money."[39] In fact, almost every project he had worked on in the last decade had been under deadline, and partly out of financial necessity. More crucially, the idea for the project was not originally his. As *Time* magazine affirms, the "project was assembled by the Barnum of still photography, Larry Schiller."[40] Schiller, whose nude photographs of Monroe had leveraged his career as a buyer of "rights to people's lives," had originally simply wanted a preface to introduce the pictures.[41] The text has no Mailer copyright; his name doesn't appear on the cover; the flyleaf claims it was "produced by Lawrence Schiller and designed by Allen Hurlburt." Mailer's closing acknowledgments read:

> The writer contracted for a preface and discovered after reading Fred Lawrence Guiles' book *Norma Jean* that he wished to do a biography. . . . In a polluted and nihilistic world, one clings to professionalism, so the work was done with the private injunction to finish a text in the allotted time. (257)

The writing, in the end, was supplemental to a project that was "assembled" and "produced" by others. Mailer can cling to "professionalism," but he can't truly retain authorship. He is part of the title, but the text is not his literary property. Ironically, then, the form of the book brings him closer to Monroe than the substance of his biography; he is simply part of a marketing plan.

Furthermore, and equally symptomatic, Mailer was accused of plagiarism for this text. He had written it in such haste that he hadn't noticed the similarities to the biographies he used as references. Guiles had given Mailer permission to quote from his book, but since it is the publisher, not the writer, who controls such rights, a highly public controversy ensued. The publishers settled and the media attention only helped spike sales for the book, yet the controversy also confirmed that *Marilyn* jeopardized Mailer's identity as a modernist author whose works are marked by originality and creative control.

It is thus not surprising that Michael Glenday uses *Marilyn* to mark the end of Mailer's "middle period" (which had begun with *Advertisements*).[42] Mailer's confrontation with women's liberation had severed the link between his status as a celebrity and stature as an author; he could no longer be sure that his public persona emerged from his own authorial agency. Feminism had shown him that he was not fully in control of his historical significance; *Marilyn* had shown him that he had become part of an investment strategy. He was, of course, still famous, but his fame had none of the dialectical dynamic of his career in the 1960s. "Norman Mailer" was just another, increasingly minor, media personality; he was no longer interesting as the orienting consciousness of literary narrative.

Executing the Author

As if hoping to have a graceful exit after the confrontation with feminism, Mailer gradually retired his public persona. After a grumpy reappearance as "Aquarius" in *St. George and the Godfather*, where he continued to muse that "Women's Liberation might be a totalitarian movement," he would make his last appearance in *The Fight*, an account of the Muhammad Ali–George Foreman bout in Zaire.[43] It would be a deliberately elegiac appearance, in which he would contemplate not only the increasing illegitimacy of his third-person narrative technique but also the looming possibility of his own physical death. Deciding, almost helplessly, to simply call himself "Norman" this time, he admits, "He was no longer so pleased with his presence. His daily reactions bored him. They were becoming like everyone else's."[44] His public persona, divested of its modernist resistance to the mainstream, no longer provides any dialectical distance from his subject matter.

Mailer comes to this conclusion in a chapter titled "The Millionaire," and he quite clearly perceives the connection between his fading relevance and his wealth:

> Months ago, a story had gotten into the newspapers about a novel he was going to write. His publishers were going to pay him a million dollars sight unseen for the book. If his candles had been burning low in the literary cathedral these last few years, the news story went its way to hastening their extinction. He knew that his much publicized novel (still nine-tenths to be written) would now have to be twice as good as before to overcome such financial news. Good literary men were not supposed to pick up *sums*. (34)

Mailer's million-dollar contract with Little, Brown for the book that would become *Ancient Evenings* indicates the ironic belatedness of his novelistic ambitions. The industry that would finally enable him to complete it could also no longer sustain the type of reputation that would make it a classic. Bottom lines and six-figure advances had come to dominate publishing, and there was no longer an avant-garde literary refuge from which a novelist could establish a critical stance.

As such, it is entirely appropriate that Mailer, in Africa, would have a vision of his own death and its effect on his reputation. Having gone for an early morning run with Ali, with whom he can't keep up, he's walking home when he hears a lion roar. He speculates, "To be eaten by a lion on the banks of the Congo—who could fail to notice that it was Hemingway's own lion waiting down these years for the flesh of Ernest until an appropriate substitute had at last arrived?" (92). And he concludes, "What a perfect way to go. His place in American literature would be forever secure" (92). Not only would such a dramatic death redeem Hemingway's far-more-embarrassing suicide, it would confirm the classic emplotment of literary careers: reputations are only established posthumously. Mailer's retirement of his public persona in this text takes on an almost ritualistic significance as a sort of rehearsal of the death of the author.

It would be a crowning irony that *The Executioner's Song*, a project once again conceived by Schiller and based on his obtaining legal rights to the life of Gary Gilmore (executed by firing squad in Utah in 1977) and everyone related to him, would be hailed by many as Mailer's novelistic masterpiece. And what all the critics unanimously lauded was the absence of Mailer's authorial persona. Finally, Mailer seemed to have achieved the Flaubertian ideal of being like God in creation, invisible and all-powerful behind and beyond the world he had created.

But the world of *Executioner's Song* is, in the end, not the literary world of Gustave Flaubert or James Joyce, and it is appropriate that one critic called the book "an act of literary suicide."[45] The world of *Song* is one where personalities have become entirely fungible as commodities; behind the story of Gilmore is the story of Schiller, the man who already had rights to the lives of Jack Ruby and Manson-killer Susan Atkins, and who would later produce books on the O. J. Simpson trial and JonBenet Ramsey murder case, eagerly obtaining signatures from anyone and everyone related to the story, so that Mailer can then appropriate them into his narrative. The absence of Mailer's own personality is partly an attempt to shield him from the process that enabled the project in the first place.

Executioner's Song, as well as *Ancient Evenings* and *Harlot's Ghost*, reveals that, as Sean McCann has recently observed, Mailer's "literary ambitions seem neither plausible nor desirable" in the contemporary world.[46] Mailer finally got around to writing encyclopedic novels during a period when, as a novelist, he no longer really mattered, when, in fact, novels no longer mattered as they did during the modern era. For a time, Mailer managed to leverage this anachronism into a journalistic career based on a residual novelistic promise. But the promise, which anchored his celebrity persona to his authorial genius, was more important than its fulfillment, which only reveals that the whole idea of literary genius has lost the cultural capital it once had. Mailer's work can now, at best, achieve middlebrow respectability; the dialectical engagement between modernism and mass culture that might have made his novels "masterpieces" has dissolved in a postmodern world of fragmented cultural fields that offer neither the continuity for authorial celebrity nor the refuge for authorial genius.

Coda
Nothing Personal

In 1991, Don DeLillo published *Mao II*, the story of Bill Gray, a famous author-recluse who, after living in seclusion for many years during which he has refused to publish anything new, decides to get his picture taken. Inspired by a photograph of J. D. Salinger that appeared on the front page of the *New York Post* in 1988, and named after an Andy Warhol silkscreen series, *Mao II* quickly became a seminal statement on the problems of authorial celebrity in the postmodern era. Thus, it is not surprising that DeLillo and his novel enjoy pride of place in Joe Moran's recent study, *Star Authors*, which focuses on contemporary literary celebrity. For Moran, DeLillo's celebrity derives from "the efforts of publishing houses in the 1980s to exploit the potential of serious, intellectually complex fiction as a consumer product."[1] And yet, Moran is forced to concede that DeLillo's model of authorship in this text is resolutely residual, such that *Mao II* foregrounds "the figure of the author as romantic individualist while precluding any meaningful social role for him."[2] Furthermore, he admits that DeLillo's novels are "very far from being crypto-autobiography."[3]

Indeed, after he analyzes *Mao II* in some detail, Moran's discussion of DeLillo's own "semi-conversion to public life in the 1980s and 1990s" is notably brief, underscoring that his career illustrates the diminished scale and scope of literary celebrity in the postmodern age. DeLillo's career is clearly based on a residual modernist model of "the writer in opposition, the novelist who writes against power, who writes against the corporation or the state or the whole apparatus of assimilation."[4] The relative modesty of his celebrity compared to London, Hemingway, or Mailer testifies to the diminished cultural authority of this model. And the primary symptom of this diminishment is the author-recluse of which DeLillo writes.

Moran notes "the apparently paradoxical fascination with author-recluses in celebrity culture," offering them as "perhaps the most obvious example of [the] symbolic struggle between the restricted and large-scale fields."[5] And yet, it would seem more accurate to say that the public reticence of figures such as Salinger and Thomas Pynchon, and DeLillo as well, represent a crucial alteration in the terms of this struggle. Such seclusion would seem to indicate that the restricted field no longer exists as a semiautonomous socioeconomic space in which authors can professionally ballast their public personae. Salinger's gradual inability to tolerate first promotion and then publication itself of his deeply autobiographical works is quite clearly a symptom of this shift. Lacking any modernist coterie into which he could retreat, he withdrew entirely into his own private consciousness, claiming, in 1970, that he writes "just for myself and my own pleasure."[6]

Pynchon, on the other hand, whose sustained encyclopedic literary output contrasts almost too conveniently with Salinger's refusal to publish anything, indicates the degree to which postmodern literature has abandoned the autobiographical mandate that informed so much modernist prose. As one critic affirms, the self-consciousness of postmodern fiction "generally reflects itself in the self-effacement of the author as *personality*. While the author may constantly intrude, *qua* author, it is rarely in an autobiographical or confessional manner."[7] The rise of postmodernity, in other words, has witnessed a greatly diminished interest in the personal lives and styles of literary figures. DeLillo may be a minor celebrity, but readers and critics alike are generally uninterested in his private experience, which is widely acknowledged as unhelpful for the interpretation of his texts. A biography of him is unlikely to be written, and if one is, it is unlikely to be popular.

Biographies of Salinger, on the other hand, are doing a somewhat brisk business: four have been published over the last two decades. But Salinger is resolutely not the same sort of author as DeLillo. The interest in his life is generated not simply by his refusal to reveal anything about it but, more significantly, by the clearly autobiographical nature of his fiction, particularly after he returned from World War II, during which he suffered trauma, the nature of which can only be read symptomatically through the prose he produced afterward. Indeed, the later works on the Glass family can be read as an autobiographical epitaph on the modernist author, Seymour, the "true artist-seer" who has committed suicide and whose poems his Brother Buddy, a sellout to academia and the publishing world, refuses to quote.[8] Salinger, in other words, represents the afterlife of the celebrity author of the modern type, whose personality generates biographical interest because it seems to offer a master key for the interpretations of his texts.

On the other hand, these recent studies are not strictly biographies. Ian Hamilton's *In Search of J. D. Salinger* is, as the title implies, more about the biographer's failed attempts to flesh out the scant biographical details already known about his subject. Notably, Hamilton schizophrenically objectifies his "sleuthing other self," referring to the "biographer" in the third person, and thereby tries, like Bok, to distance himself from his immersion in the journalistic world.[9] As such, it is interesting to note that the principal drama of Hamilton's book emerges from his ongoing efforts to obtain the right to print excerpts from Salinger's letters—an effort in which he ultimately fails. Hamilton's legal struggle with Salinger resurrects the terms of Edith Wharton's "Copy," based as it is on the assumption that the private letters provide a crucial key to the published texts.

It is further noteworthy, in this regard, that two of the more recent "biographies" of Salinger are really autobiographies of women whose lives were damaged by him. Joyce Maynard's *At Home in the World* and Margaret Salinger's *Dream Catcher* both narrate the harm that Salinger's obsession with privacy caused for the women who participated in his private life. Maynard, who was initially seduced by Salinger through epistolary correspondence that she herself cannot quote, concludes that "Jerry Salinger has sought his protection in privacy and silence. I have come to believe that my protection comes in self-disclosure."[10] And Margaret Salinger affirms, "Behind every good, enlightened man, Christ figure, Teddy, or Seymour in my father's writing, there's a damnation or a demonization of womanhood."[11] Second-wave feminism's dictum that the personal is political thus trumps modernism's mandate of masculine autonomy. As with Mailer, the cultural authority of Salinger's authorial celebrity has been undermined by the revelation of its sexism.

Celebrity, of course, remains a crucial ingredient in the marketing of books, but like publishing itself, it has become almost entirely absorbed into the protocols of the general field of cultural production. Hence, when André Schiffrin, in his important reflection on the conditions of contemporary publishing, complains that "celebrity books are the titles that will make or break firms," he is referring to figures such as Harold Robbins and Jackie Collins, who make no claims to literary distinction. Schiffrin concludes that "books today have become mere adjuncts to the world of mass media."[12] This decline-and-fall tone is familiar, and it is tempting to identify it as just another panicky jeremiad against the "commercialization of literature"; and yet, it is worth crediting the historical accuracy of his assertion that "until quite recently, publishing houses were for the most part family owned and small, content with modest profits that came from a business that still saw itself as linked to intellectual and cultural life."[13] The age of mergers and acquisitions that began with Random House's purchase of Knopf in 1960 and reached a certain apotheosis with Bertelsmann's takeover of Random House in 1998 may not quite signify the end of "intellectual and cultural life," but it does indicate that with the increasing postmodern interpenetration of the cultural and economic, the restricted field of cultural production no longer commands the same leverage in the publishing world.

Indeed, the bohemias that nourished the literary personalities of the early and mid–twentieth century no longer exist. The sort of dissident experimental apprenticeship that determined the careers of Hemingway or Kerouac no longer centrally informs the work of contemporary authors. Little magazines and small, independent houses continue to publish, but since the Beats, they neither speak for a coherent class fragment nor attract the attention of the mass media. Nor, since the heyday of the New York intellectuals, does a coherent class of cultural critics continue to arbitrate literary distinction in such a way as to get the attention of the culture industries.

Literary celebrity as a historically specific articulation of the dialectical tension between modern consciousness and public subjectivity persists only as a residual model of authorship. It no longer commands the cultural authority it did in the modern era; and it never will again.

Notes

NOTES TO THE INTRODUCTION

1. Gertrude Stein, *Everybody's Autobiography* (New York: Vintage Books, 1937), 45.

2. Gertrude Stein, *The Making of Americans* (Normal, IL: Dalkey Archive Press, 1995), 289.

3. See Daniel Borus, *Writing Realism: Howells, James, and Norris in the Mass Market* (Chapel Hill: University of North Carolina Press, 1989); Amy Kaplan, *The Social Construction of American Realism* (Chicago: University of Chicago Press, 1988); Thomas Strychacz, *Modernism, Mass Culture, and Professionalism* (New York: Cambridge University Press, 1993); Jennifer Wicke, *Advertising Fictions: Literature, Advertising, and Social Reading* (New York: Columbia University Press, 1988), 54–119; and Christopher Wilson, *Labor of Words: Literary Professionalism in the Progressive Era* (Athens: University of Georgia Press, 1985). See also Kevin J. H. Dettmar and Stephen Watt, eds., *Marketing Modernisms: Self-Promotion, Canonization, Rereading* (Ann Arbor: University of Michigan Press, 1996). One of the few scholars to confirm the importance of authorial celebrity is John Cawelti, in his brief essay, "The Writer as Celebrity: Some Aspects of American Literature as Popular Culture," *Studies in American Fiction* 5, no. 1 (Spring 1977): 161–74.

4. P. David Marshall, *Celebrity and Power: Fame in Contemporary Culture* (Minneapolis: University of Minnesota Press, 1997), 56.

5. Ibid., 57.

6. Richard Dyer, *Stars* (London: British Film Institute, 1979). See also his *Heavenly Bodies: Film Stars and Society* (New York: St. Martin's, 1986). Although Dyer focuses almost exclusively on cinematic celebrity, his lucid summary of the various methods of accounting for celebrity and his pioneering courage in taking celebrity seriously continue to shape this new field of cultural studies. For a good cross-section of contemporary celebrity criticism, see Christine Gledhill, ed., *Stardom: Industry of Desire* (New York: Routledge, 1991). Other recent studies of celebrity include Joshua Gamson, *Claims to Fame: Celebrity in Contemporary America* (Berkeley: University of California Press,

1994); Leo Braudy, *The Frenzy of Renown: Fame and Its History* (New York: Vintage, 1986); Richard Schickel, *Intimate Strangers: The Culture of Celebrity* (New York: Doubleday, 1985); Charles L. Ponce de Leon, *Self-Exposure: Human Interest Journalism and the Emergence of Celebrity in America* (Chapel Hill: University of North Carolina Press, 2002); and Jeffrey Louis Decker, *Made in America: Self-Styled Success from Horatio Alger to Oprah Winfrey* (Minneapolis: University of Minnesota Press, 1997).

7. Marshall, *Celebrity and Power*, 4.

8. Ibid., 57.

9. Roland Barthes, "The Death of the Author," in *Image, Music, Text*, ed. Stephen Heath (New York: Hill and Wang, 1977), 143. Michel Foucault, "What Is an Author?" in *The Foucault Reader*, ed. Paul Rabinow (New York: Pantheon, 1984), 102. For an excellent selection of the scholarship on authorship to which these essays are central, see Martha Woodmansee and Peter Jaszi, eds., *The Construction of Authorship: Textual Appropriation in Law and Literature* (Durham, NC: Duke University Press, 1994).

10. Seán Burke, *The Death and Return of the Author: Criticism and Subjectivity in Barthes, Foucault, and Derrida* (Edinburgh: Edinburgh University Press, 1998), 178.

11. Indeed, as Fredric Jameson affirms, literary theorists seem to have replaced modernist writers in enacting this paradoxical form of celebrity: "The waning of the modern . . . was not merely marked by the slow disappearance of all the great *auteurs* who signed modernism in its grandest period from 1910 to 1955; it was also accompanied by the emergence of those now equally famous names from Levi-Strauss to Lacan, from Barthes to Derrida and Baudrillard, that adorn the heroic age of Theory itself" (*The Cultural Turn: Selected Writings on the Postmodern, 1983–1998* [New York: Verso, 1998], 85). I would disagree only with the claim that they are "equally famous"; Derrida never commanded the mainstream cultural cachet of, for instance, Ernest Hemingway.

12. T. S. Eliot, "Tradition and the Individual Talent," *Selected Essays* (New York: Harcourt, Brace, 1960), 10.

13. James Joyce, *A Portrait of the Artist as a Young Man* (New York: Modern Library, 1928), 252.

14. In addition to *The Autobiography of Alice B. Toklas*, a short list of these memoirs would have to include Robert McCalmon's *Being Geniuses Together*, Ernest Hemingway's *A Moveable Feast*, Malcolm Cowley's *Exile's Return*, Maurice Sterne's *Shadow and Light*, Sylvia Beach's *Shakespeare and Company*, Clive Bell's *Old Friends*, Louis Bromfield's *Pleasant Valley*, Morley Callaghan's *That Summer in Paris*, Robert Coates's *The View from Here*, Jo Davidson's *Between Sittings*, John Glassco's *Memoirs of Montparnasse*, Hutchins Hapgood's *A Victorian in the Modern World*, Bravig Imbs's *Confessions of Another Young Man*, Matthew Josephson's *Life among the Surrealists*, Mabel Dodge Luhan's *Intimate*

Memories, Samuel Putnam's *Paris Was Our Mistress*, Francis Rose's *Saying Life*, Edith Sitwell's *Take Care Of*, and Ambrose Vollard's *Memoirs of a Picture Dealer*. If you were in Paris in the 1920s and had anything to do with the art world, it was almost a cultural imperative to write memoirs about it—not to mention the countless references in magazines and newspapers from *Vanity Fair* to the *New York Herald Tribune*.

15. Eliot, "Tradition and the Individual Talent," 11.

16. Roland Barthes, *Writing Degree Zero*, trans. Annette Lavers and Colin Smith (New York: Noonday, 1953), 10.

17. Pierre Bourdieu, *The Field of Cultural Production: Essays on Art and Literature*, ed. Randal Johnson (New York: Columbia University Press, 1993), 40.

18. Ibid., 115.

19. Mutlu Konuk Blasing, *The Art of Life: Studies in American Autobiographical Literature* (Austin: University of Texas Press, 1977), xv. Although authorial celebrity has been somewhat neglected as a literary critical field, there is a well-established postwar tradition of studies in American authorial autobiography. See, for example, Robert F. Sayre, *The Examined Self: Benjamin Franklin, Henry Adams, Henry James* (Princeton, NJ: Princeton University Press, 1964); Albert Stone, *Autobiographical Occasions and Original Acts: Versions of American Identity from Henry Adams to Nate Shaw* (Philadelphia: University of Pennsylvania Press, 1982); Thomas Cooley, *Educated Lives: The Rise of Modern Autobiography in America* (Columbus: Ohio State University Press, 1976); Herbert Leibowitz, *Fabricating Lives: Explorations in American Autobiography* (New York: Knopf, 1989); G. Thomas Couser, *American Autobiography: The Prophetic Mode* (Amherst: University of Massachusetts Press, 1979); A. Robert Lee, ed., *First Person Singular: Studies in American Autobiography* (New York: St. Martin's, 1988); Timothy Dow Adams, *Telling Lies in Modern American Autobiography* (Chapel Hill: University of North Carolina Press, 1990); and John Paul Eakin, ed., *American Autobiography: Retrospect and Prospect* (Madison: University of Wisconsin Press, 1991).

20. Philippe Lejeune, *On Autobiography*, trans. Katherine Leary (Minneapolis: University of Minnesota Press, 1989), 5.

21. John Paul Eakin, *Touching the World: Reference in Autobiography* (Princeton, NJ: Princeton University Press, 1992), 27. For an earlier criticism of Lejeune, see Paul de Man, "Autobiography as De-facement," *Modern Language Notes* 94, no. 5 (December 1979): 919–30.

22. Eakin, *Touching the World*, 3.

23. Ibid., 23.

24. Warren Susman, *Culture as History: The Transformation of American Society in the Twentieth Century* (New York: Pantheon, 1984), 277.

25. Ibid., 283.

26. Ibid., 273.

27. Samuel D. Warren and Louis D. Brandeis, "The Right to Privacy," *Harvard Law Review* 4, no. 5 (December 15, 1890): 195. For some examples of the debate this article sparked, see "Law and Privacy," *Scribner's* 9, no. 2 (February 1891): 261; "The Right to Privacy," *Nation* 51 (December 25, 1890): 496–97; John Gilmer Speed, "The Right of Privacy," *North American Review* 158 (July 1896): 64–74; and Elbridge Adams, "The Law of Privacy," *North American Review* 175 (September 1902): 361–69. For further discussion of the foundational role of Warren and Brandeis's article, see Don R. Pember, *Privacy and the Press: The Law, the Mass Media, and the First Amendment* (Seattle: University of Washington Press, 1972), 33–58; and Darien A. McWhirter and Jon D. Bible, *Privacy as a Constitutional Right* (New York: Quorum Books, 1992), 75–91. For a comprehensive review of the legal debates over this article, see James H. Barron, "Warren and Brandeis, *The Right to Privacy*: Demystifying a Landmark Citation," *Suffolk University Law Review* 13, no. 4 (Summer 1979): 875–922. Barron claims that the actual effect of the article on privacy law has been negligible, and that the piece's reasoning has been overrated. Yet the pervasive persistence of Warren and Brandeis's logic in evaluations of the modern media indicates that the article remains a cultural, if not a legal, landmark. On the significance of this article for literary realism in the United States, see Brook Thomas, *American Literary Realism and the Failed Promise of Contract* (Berkeley: University of California Press, 1997), 53–88. On how this right to privacy gradually developed into a right of publicity—that is, a right of the individual over his or her public image—see Jane Gaines, *Contested Culture: The Image, the Voice, and the Law* (Chapel Hill: University of North Carolina Press, 1991), 175–208.

28. Warren and Brandeis, "The Right to Privacy," 196.

29. Ibid., 207.

30. Ibid., 193, 205.

31. Ibid., 193.

32. Ibid., 198.

33. Ibid., 200.

34. Ibid., 204.

35. Ibid., 205.

36. Mark Rose, *Authors and Owners: The Invention of Copyright* (Cambridge, MA: Harvard University Press, 1993), 140. See also Bruce Bugbee, *Genesis of American Patent and Copyright Law* (Washington, DC: Public Affairs Press, 1967); Lyman Ray Patterson, *Copyright in Historical Perspective* (Nashville, TN: Vanderbilt University Press, 1968); and Rosemary J. Coombe, *The Cultural Life of Intellectual Properties: Authorship, Appropriation, and the Law* (Durham, NC: Duke University Press, 1998), 166–71. The classic text from the period is R. R. Bowker, *Copyright: Its History and Its Law* (Boston:

Houghton Mifflin, 1912). On copyright in the nineteenth-century United States, see Michael Newbury, *Figuring Authorship in Antebellum America* (Stanford, CA: Stanford University Press, 1997), 158–201; Meredith McGill, "The Matter of the Text: Commerce, Print Culture, and the Authority of the State in American Copyright Law," *American Literary History* 9, no. 1 (Spring 1997): 21–59; and Wilson, *Labor of Words*, 63–92.

37. For an excellent discussion of these developments, see Phillip Fisher, "Appearing and Disappearing in Public: Social Space in Late-Nineteenth-Century Literature and Culture," in *Reconstructing American Literary History*, ed. Sacvan Bercovitch (Cambridge, MA: Harvard University Press, 1986), 155–88.

38. Henry Dwight Sedgewick, "The Mob Spirit in Literature," *Atlantic Monthly* 96 (July 1905): 9. See also Brian Hooker, "Reputation and Popularity," *North American Review* 195 (March 1912): 404–13; Helen Marshall North, "What Americans Read," *North American Review* 150 (April 1890): 533–35; Brander Matthews, "On Pleasing the Taste of the Public," *Forum* 21 (April 1896): 219–27; Bliss Perry, "On Catering for the Public," *Atlantic Monthly* 93 (January 1904): 1–5; and R. A. Scott-James, "Popularity in Literature," *North American Review* 197 (May 1913): 677–91.

39. "The Rights of 'Unknown Authors,'" *Century Magazine* 41 (February 1904): 629. See also Edward Bok, "Helps to Literary Success," *Ladies' Home Journal* 7 (June 1890): 12; "About Authors," *Bookman* 21 (March 1905): 10–11; W. Davenport Adams, "How to Make a Living by Literature," *Bookman* 2 (October 1895): 124–27; "The Penalties of Authorship," *Harper's New Monthly Magazine* 73 (August 1886): 457–61; and Jack London, "First Aid to Rising Authors," *Junior Munsey Magazine* (December 9, 1900), reprinted in Dale Walker and Jeanne Campbell Reesman, eds., *No Mentor but Myself: Jack London on Writing and Writers* (Stanford, CA: Stanford University Press, 1999), 23–29. On the rise of self-help culture generally, see Joan Shelley Rubin, *The Making of Middlebrow Culture* (Chapel Hill: University of North Carolina Press, 1992), 1–34; and T. J. Jackson Lears, "From Salvation to Self-Realization," in *The Culture of Consumption: Critical Essays in American History, 1880–1980*, ed. Richard Wightman Fox and T. J. Jackson Lears (New York: Pantheon, 1983), 1–38.

40. Julian Hawthorne, "Inspiration 'Ex Machina,'" *Appleton's Booklovers Magazine* 17, no. 6 (June 1906): 814.

41. Carolyn Wells, "A Ballade of Ambition," *Bookman* 14 (November 1901): 230.

42. On the emergence of the best-seller list, and the term "best seller," during this era, see Frank Luther Mott, *Golden Multitudes: The Story of Best Sellers in the United States* (New York: Macmillan, 1947), 6–11, 204–6.

43. Gelett Burgess, "An Interview with Nobody," *Bookman* 14 (November 1901): 230.

44. Ibid.

45. Ibid., 232.

46. Edith Wharton, "Copy," *Scribner's* 27, no. 6 (June 1900): 657–63 (hereafter cited parenthetically in the text).

47. Kaplan, *Social Construction of American Realism*, 82.

48. Ibid., 81–104.

49. McGill, "The Matter of the Text," 42.

50. Nina Miller, *Making Love Modern: The Intimate Public Worlds of New York's Literary Women* (New York: Oxford University Press, 1999), 49.

51. Ibid., 98.

52. Frank Lentricchia, *Ariel and the Police: Michel Foucault, William James, Wallace Stevens* (Madison: University of Wisconsin Press, 1988), 187.

53. Andreas Huyssen, *After the Great Divide: Modernism, Mass Culture, Postmodernism* (Bloomington: Indiana University Press, 1986), 47.

54. Ibid., 55.

55. Ibid., 52.

56. See, in particular, Michael Kimmel, *Manhood in America: A Cultural History* (New York: Free Press, 1996), 81–188; T. J. Jackson Lears, *No Place of Grace: Antimodernism and the Transformation of American Culture, 1880–1920* (Chicago: University of Chicago Press, 1981), 97–140; Alan Trachtenberg, *The Incorporation of America: Culture and Society in the Gilded Age* (New York: Hill and Wang, 1982), 140–81; and Wilson, *Labor of Words*, 1–16.

57. See Ann Douglass, *The Feminization of American Culture* (New York: Anchor Press, 1977).

58. Michael Newbury, *Figuring Authorship in Antebellum America* (Stanford, CA: Stanford University Press, 1997), 81. See also Richard Brodhead, *The School of Hawthorne* (New York: Oxford University Press, 1986), 48–80; R. Jackson Wilson, *Figures of Speech: American Writers and the Literary Marketplace, from Benjamin Franklin to Emily Dickinson* (Baltimore: Johns Hopkins University Press, 1989); Michael T. Gilmore, *American Romanticism and the Marketplace* (Chicago: University of Chicago Press, 1985); and Thomas Baker, *Sentiment and Celebrity: Nathaniel Parker Willis and the Trials of Literary Fame* (New York: Oxford University Press, 1999).

59. Newbury, *Figuring Authorship*, 117.

60. Lewis Coser, Charles Kadushin, and Walter Powell, *Books: The Culture and Commerce of Publishing* (New York: Basic Books, 1982), 17–20.

61. Ibid., 8.

62. John Tebbel, *A History of Book Publishing in the United States*, vol. 4, *The Great Change, 1940–1980* (New York: R. R. Bowker, 1981), 724.

63. See Henry Holt, "The Commercialization of Literature," *Atlantic Monthly* (November 1905): 578–600, and Charles Madison, *Book Publishing in America* (New York: McGraw Hill, 1966), 157–398.

64. Holt, "Commercialization," 578.

65. John Tebbel, *A History of Book Publishing in the United States*, vol. 2, *The Expansion of an Industry, 1865–1919* (New York: R. R. Bowker, 1975), 147.

66. Richard Ohmann, *Politics of Letters* (Middletown, CT: Wesleyan University Press, 1987), 135–51. See also Frank Luther Mott, "The Magazine Revolution and Popular Ideas in the Nineties," in *American History: Recent Interpretations*, ed. Abraham Eisenstadt (New York: Thomas Y. Crowell, 1969), 218–32; and Wilson, *Labor of Words*, 40–62.

67. John Tebbel, *A History of Book Publishing in the United States*, vol. 3, *The Golden Age between Two Wars, 1920–1940* (New York: R. R. Bowker, 1978).

68. Frederick Hoffman, Charles Allen, and Carolyn F. Ulrich, *The Little Magazine: A History and a Bibliography* (Princeton, NJ: Princeton University Press, 1947), 3. See also Mark S. Morrisson, *The Public Face of Modernism: Little Magazines, Audiences, and Reception, 1905–1920* (Madison: University of Wisconsin Press, 2001).

69. Strychacz, *Modernism, Mass Culture, and Professionalism*, 3.

70. Fredric Jameson, "Reification and Utopia in Mass Culture," in *Signatures of the Visible* (New York: Routledge, 1990), 14.

71. Kimmel, *Manhood in America*, 262. See also Barbara Ehrenreich, *Hearts of Men: American Dreams and the Flight from Commitment* (New York: Anchor Books, 1983), and Susan Faludi, *Stiffed: The Betrayal of the American Man* (New York: HarperCollins, 1999).

NOTES TO CHAPTER I

1. T. S. Eliot, "A Sceptical Patrician," *Athenæum* (May 23, 1919): 361–62; Louis Kronenburger, "The Education of Henry Adams," in *Books That Changed Our Minds*, ed. Malcolm Cowley and Bernard Smith (New York: Doubleday, 1939), 45–61; and John Carlos Rowe, *Henry Adams and Henry James: The Emergence of a Modern Consciousness* (Ithaca, NY: Cornell University Press, 1976), 93–132.

2. Adams is a standard reference for studies of the rise of autobiography in the United States, but Bok is rarely mentioned, even though his autobiography bears striking formal similarities to Adams's, and even though, at the time, it was at least as popular. See, for example, Albert Stone, *Autobiographical Occasions and Original Acts: Versions of American Identity from Henry Adams to Nate Shaw* (Philadelphia: University of Pennsylvania Press, 1982); Thomas Cooley, *Educated Lives: The Rise of Modern Autobiography in America* (Columbus: Ohio State University Press, 1976); Herbert Leibowitz, *Fabricating Lives: Explorations in American Autobiography* (New York: Knopf, 1989); G. Thomas

Couser, *American Autobiography: The Prophetic Mode* (Amherst: University of
Massachusetts Press, 1979); John Paul Eakin, ed., *American Autobiography:
Retrospect and Prospect* (Madison: University of Wisconsin Press, 1991); and
Mutlu Konuk Blasing, *The Art of Life: Studies in American Autobiographical
Literature* (Austin: University of Texas Press, 1977).

3. Philippe Lejeune, *On Autobiography*, trans. Katherine Leary (Minneapolis: University of Minnesota Press, 1989), 20.

4. Ibid., 42.

5. Henry Adams, *The Education of Henry Adams*, ed. Ernest Samuels (1918;
repr., Boston: Houghton Mifflin, 1973), 512–13 (hereafter cited parenthetically
in the text).

6. T. J. Jackson Lears, *No Place of Grace: Antimodernism and the Transformation of American Culture, 1880–1920* (Chicago: University of Chicago Press,
1981), 287.

7. William Decker affirms that *The Education*, insofar as it can be understood as both "the autobiography of Adams's vocation" and "that vocation's
valedictory enactment," must be considered "as text and act, 'act' referring to
the text as published in a particular mode to a particular audience" (*The Literary Vocation of Henry Adams* [Chapel Hill: University of North Carolina Press,
1990], 43). And Joanne Jacobson also emphasizes that the address of *The Education* can only be considered in terms of Adams's vexed relations to the modern
literary marketplace (*Authority and Alliance in the Letters of Henry Adams*
[Madison: University of Wisconsin Press, 1992], 88–114). The tendency in both
these readings, however, has been to stress *The Education*'s resistance to the
logic of the literary marketplace, thereby failing to account for its subsequent
popularity as anything but a felicitous irony. I hope to prove that *The Education*
anticipates the strategies of self-fashioning whereby modern authors could sustain a pose of being above the market while simultaneously being deeply implicated in it.

8. James Cox notes that the term "autobiography" only entered into popular
usage in the early nineteenth century ("Autobiography and America," in *Aspects
of Narrative: Selected Papers from the English Institute*, ed. J. Hillis Miller [New
York: Columbia University Press, 1971], 147).

9. Quoted in Ernest Samuels, J. C. Levenson, Charles Vandersee, and Viola
Hopkins Winner, eds., *The Collected Letters of Henry Adams, Volume II* (Cambridge, MA: Belknap Press, 1982), 32.

10. Edward Bok, *The Americanization of Edward Bok* (New York: Scribner's, 1920), 2 (hereafter cited parenthetically in the text).

11. Richard Henry Stoddard, "A Box of Autographs," *Scribner's* 9, no. 2
(February 1891): 213.

12. Oliver Wendell Holmes, quoted in Bok, *The Americanization*, 207.

13. Michael Taussig, *The Devil and Commodity Fetishism in South America* (Chapel Hill: University of North Carolina Press, 1980), 37.

14. Jacques Derrida, "Signature Event Context," in *Margins of Philosophy*, trans. Alan Bass (Chicago: University of Chicago Press, 1982), 328. See also Peggy Kamuf, *Signature Pieces: On the Institution of Authorship* (Ithaca, NY: Cornell University Press, 1988).

15. Tamara Plakins Thornton, *Handwriting in America: A Cultural History* (New Haven, CT: Yale University Press, 1996), 108–42.

16. Edward Bok, "The Modern Literary King," *Forum* (November 1895): 334 (hereafter cited parenthetically in the text).

17. Salme Steinberg affirms that "Bok edited his own life story with much of the fervor that he used the blue pencil as editor of the *Journal*" (*Reformer in the Marketplace: Edward W. Bok and the Ladies' Home Journal* [Baton Rouge: Louisiana State University Press, 1979], 35).

18. Henry Adams to Charles Scribner, August 1, 1888, in Ernest Samuels, ed., *Henry Adams: Selected Letters* (Cambridge, MA: Belknap Press, 1982), 204.

19. Marcel Mauss, *The Gift: The Form and Reason for Exchange in Archaic Societies*, ed. W. D. Halls (New York: Norton, 1990), 68.

20. Henry Adams, *History of the United States of America during the Administrations of James Madison* (New York: Library of America, 1986), 1335.

21. Andreas Huyssen, *After the Great Divide: Modernism, Mass Culture, Postmodernism* (Bloomington: Indiana University Press, 1986), 44–62.

22. My reading here is indebted to Rowe's claim that *The Education* marks a shift from "design" to "interpretation" in the understanding of the relation between authorship and literary language (*The Emergence of a Modern Consciousness*, 120–23).

23. N. Katherine Hayles, *Chaos Bound: Orderly Disorder in Contemporary Literature and Science* (Ithaca, NY: Cornell University Press, 1990), 64.

24. Edward Bok, "Can a Man Understand a Woman's Wants," *Ladies' Home Journal* (April 1890): 8.

25. Edward Bok, quoted in Joseph C. Goulden, *The Curtis Caper* (New York: Putnam, 1965), 19. J. Walter Thompson, in his *Series of Talks on Advertising* (New York: J. Walter Thompson, 1909), narrates an illuminating anecdote regarding Bok's methods of understanding his readership: "Edward W. Bok says that he has edited *The Ladies' Home Journal* for the last eighteen years for one woman, and the woman isn't a composite of various individuals, as one would naturally think. She is a real, live personality. Mr. Bok says he has never met her" (29). Apparently, while on a tour of small towns in the United States with his publisher, Cyrus Curtis, Bok saw a female who he thought was "a typical American woman." Thompson claims that Bok essentially stalked this woman, learning her name and secretly observing her home, and then used her as a model for

his readership. He was vindicated when she subscribed to the magazine a few years later.

26. Edward Bok, "The Editor and His Readers," *Ladies' Home Journal* (February 1890): 2.

27. Richard Ohmann, *Politics of Letters* (Middletown, CT: Wesleyan University Press, 1987), 146.

28. Edward Bok, *Twice Thirty: Some Short and Simple Annals of the Road* (New York: Scribner's, 1925), 373 (hereafter cited parenthetically in the text).

29. Henry Adams, quoted in *The Education*, appendix A, 509.

30. Ferris Greenslet, *Under the Bridge* (Cambridge, MA: Riverside Press, 1943), 144. See also Charles A. Madison, *Book Publishing in America* (New York: McGraw Hill, 1966), 252–55.

NOTES TO CHAPTER 2

1. Louis Kaplan, *A Bibliography of American Autobiographies* (Madison: University of Wisconsin Press, 1961). The career designations are Kaplan's. For a discussion of this and other bibliographies of U.S. autobiographies, see Robert R. Sayre, "The Proper Study: Autobiographies in American Studies," *American Quarterly* 29, no. 3, bibliography issue (1977): 241–62.

2. Albert Bigelow Paine, *Mark Twain: A Biography* (New York: Harper and Brothers, 1912), 3:732 (hereafter cited in the text as *MT*); and William Dean Howells, "Mark Twain," in *Critical Essays on Mark Twain, 1867–1910*, ed. Louis J. Budd (Boston: G. K. Hall, 1982), 54.

3. Stuart P. Sherman, "A Literary American," in *Critical Essays on Mark Twain, 1910–1980*, ed. Louis J. Budd (Boston: G. K. Hall, 1982), 31.

4. Justin Kaplan, *Mr. Clemens and Mark Twain* (New York: Simon and Schuster, 1966), 9.

5. Richard S. Lowry, *"Littery Man": Mark Twain and Modern Authorship* (New York: Oxford University Press, 1996), 15.

6. Albert Bigelow Paine, ed., *Mark Twain's Autobiography* (New York: Harper and Brothers, 1924), 1:xi (hereafter cited in the text as *MTA*).

7. Bernard DeVoto, ed., *Mark Twain in Eruption: Hitherto Unpublished Pages about Men and Events* (New York: Harper and Brothers, 1940), xiv.

8. Charles Neider, ed., *The Autobiography of Mark Twain* (New York: Harper and Row, 1959), xvii (hereafter cited in the text as *AMT*).

9. Michael J. Kiskis, ed., *Mark Twain's Own Autobiography: The Chapters from the "North American Review"* (Madison: University of Wisconsin Press, 1990), xxiv.

10. Robert Atwan, "The Territory Behind: Mark Twain and His Autobiographies," in *Located Lives: Place and Idea in Southern Autobiography*, ed. J. Bill Berry (Athens: University of Georgia Press, 1990), 39–51. Other critical works

on the autobiography include Delancey Ferguson, "The Uncollected Portions of Mark Twain's Autobiography," *American Literature* 8 (1936): 37–46; Maxwell Geismar, *Mark Twain: The American Prophet* (Boston: Houghton Mifflin, 1970), 392–435; Marilyn Davis DeEulis, "Mark Twain's Experiments in Autobiography," *American Literature* 53, no. 2 (May 1981): 202–13; Alan Gribben, "Autobiography as Property: Mark Twain and His Legend," in *The Mythologizing of Mark Twain*, ed. Sara de Saussure Davis and Philip D. Beidler (Tuscaloosa: University of Alabama Press, 1984), 39–55; and Warren L. Cherniak, "The Ever-Receding Dream: Henry Adams and Mark Twain as Autobiographers," in *First-Person Singular: Studies in American Autobiography*, ed. A. Robert Lee (New York: St. Martin's, 1988). For a useful online project cross-referencing and comparing the various versions of the autobiography, see Hal L. Waller, "Charting the Autobiographies of Mark Twain," http://xroads.virginia .edu/~MA98/waller/Twain Auto_Site/index.htm.

11. From the text of Clara Clemens Samassoud's will, reprinted in Isabelle Budd, "Clara Samassoud's Will," *Mark Twain Journal* 25, no. 1 (Spring 1987): 21.

12. William Dean Howells, "Autobiography, a New Form of Literature," *Harper's Monthly* 119 (October 1909): 798. For further discussion of this article, see Albert Stone, *Autobiographical Occasions and Original Acts: Versions of American Identity from Henry Adams to Nate Shaw* (Philadelphia: University of Pennsylvania Press, 1982), 2–6.

13. Howells, "Autobiography," 798.

14. Ibid., 797.

15. William Dean Howells, "Literary Genius; Grant's Memoirs," in *William Dean Howells: Selected Literary Criticism*, vol. 2, *1886–1897*, ed. Donald Pizer (Bloomington: Indiana University Press, 1993), 14.

16. Mark Twain, "General Grant's Grammar" (speech, Army and Navy Club dinner, New York City, 1886, reprinted in Paine, *Mark Twain*, appendix Q, 1651.

17. On Twain and subscription publishing, see, in particular, Hamlin Hill, "Mark Twain: Audience and Artistry," *American Quarterly* 15, no. 1 (Spring 1963): 25–40. See also Hamlin Hill, *Mark Twain and Elisha Bliss* (Columbia: University of Missouri Press, 1964); and John Tebbel, *A History of Book Publishing in the United States*, vol. 2, *The Expansion of an Industry, 1865–1919* (New York: R. R. Bowker, 1975), 520–26.

18. In his essay "A 'Talent for Posturing': The Achievement of Mark Twain's Public Personality" (in *The Mythologizing of Mark Twain*, ed. Sara de Saussure Davis and Philip D. Beidler [Tuscaloosa: University of Alabama Preess, 1984]), Louis Budd claims that "for academics, [Twain] offers the surest path for crossing the gap between elite and popular audiences" (98). Budd is one of the most eloquent and engaging critics of Twain's enduring democratic appeal, but I would consider "academics" to be too narrow a category in this regard. The

significance of Twain's complex suspension between highbrow and lowbrow extends beyond a purely academic audience.

19. Jay Martin, *Harvests of Change: American Literature, 1865–1914* (Englewood Cliffs, NJ: Prentice Hall, 1967), 200; Atwan, "The Territory Behind," 43; Henry Nash Smith, "Mark Twain, 'Funniest Man in the World,'" in *The Mythologizing of Mark Twain*, ed. Sara de Saussure Davis and Philip D. Beidler (Tuscaloosa: University of Alabama Preess, 1984), 75.

20. Mark Twain, *Collected Tales, Sketches, Speeches, and Essays, 1891–1910*, ed. Louis Budd (New York: Library of America, 1992), 109–17 (hereafter cited parenthetically in the text).

21. Pierre Bourdieu, *The Field of Cultural Production*, ed. Randal Johnson (New York: Columbia University Press, 1993), 101.

22. Ibid., 81.

23. Paine discusses Twain's discovery of the name in *Mark Twain*, 219–22; and Twain's own version appears in DeVoto, *Mark Twain in Eruption*, 228–29; and Mark Twain, *Roughing It* (New York: Signet, 1961), 265–67. Both Everett Emerson and Justin Kaplan have cast doubt on Twain's story since no evidence has been found that Sellers ever used the name. See Everett Emerson, *The Authentic Mark Twain: A Literary Biography of Samuel L. Clemens* (Philadelphia: University of Pennsylvania Press, 1984), 8–10; and Justin Kaplan and Anne Bernays, *The Language of Names* (New York: Simon and Schuster, 1997), 199–203. Kaplan's earlier biography confirmed and thematized the standard critical use of the name Samuel Clemens for the private individual—husband, householder, and family man—and Mark Twain for the public persona—humorist, lecturer, and author. Though this division oversimplifies a considerably more complex and confusing overlap in use and reference, it also serviceably represents the basic categorical poles of private and public that informed the Clemens/Twain relation. Since my principal concern is with the public reputation, I am emphasizing the name Twain throughout. Yet both names have, understandably, persisted as part of the public image, and when necessary or pertinent, I refer to Clemens as the private individual and Twain as not only a public pose but also a problematic form of literary property.

24. Gribben, "Autobiography as Property," 39.

25. Hamlin Hill, *Mark Twain: God's Fool* (New York: Harper and Row, 1973), xxiii.

26. Samuel Clemens to William Dean Howells, January 16, 1904, in Henry Nash Smith and William Gibson, eds., *Mark Twain–Howells Letters* (Cambridge, MA: Harvard University Press, 1960), 778.

27. Henry Nash Smith and William Gibson, eds., *Mark Twain–Howells Letters* (Cambridge, MA: Harvard University Press, 1960), 780.

28. See, in particular, Atwan, "The Territory Beyond," in which Atwan dis-

cusses the autobiographical dictations in terms of their indebtedness to the Southern oral storytelling tradition.

29. Slavoj Zizek, *The Sublime Object of Ideology* (New York: Routledge, 1989), 135.

30. Slavoj Zizek, *Looking Awry: An Introduction to Jacques Lacan through Popular Culture* (New York: Routledge, 1991), 21.

31. Eugene H. Angert, "Is Mark Twain Dead?" *North American Review* 190 (September 1909): 319.

32. Ibid., 321.

33. Louis Budd, *Our Mark Twain: The Making of His Public Personality* (Philadelphia: University of Pennsylvania Press, 1983), 6.

34. According to Budd (*Our Mark Twain*, 43), people began to impersonate Twain as early as 1868. The practice, of course, continues to this day. For an excellent recent consideration of the significance of impostors in Twain's work, see Susan Gillman, *Dark Twins: Imposture and Identity in Mark Twain's America* (Chicago: University of Chicago Press, 1989).

35. Angert, "Is Mark Twain Dead?" 324.

36. Ibid., 322–23.

37. Ibid., 323.

38. Mark Twain, "Is Shakespeare Dead? (From My Autobiography)," in *What Is Man? And Other Essays* (New York: Harper and Brothers, 1917), 297 (hereafter cited parenthetically in the text).

39. "Mark Twain Turns into a Corporation," *New York Times*, December 24, 1908, 2. Surprisingly little is available on the Mark Twain Company. For what has been published, see Hill, *Mark Twain: God's Fool*, 191–92, 212–13, 257–59; and the entry on the Mark Twain Company, in J. R. LeMaster and James D. Wilson, eds., *The Mark Twain Encyclopedia* (New York: Garland, 1993), 493.

40. Samuel Clemens, "My Dear Mr. Ochs," Ashcroft-Lyon Manuscript, Mark Twain Papers, Bancroft Library, University of California, Berkeley (hereafter cited in the notes as MTP).

41. Samuel Clemens, "Preface to the Unborn Reader," Ashcroft-Lyon Manuscript, MTP.

42. Samuel Clemens, "Dear Howells," Ashcroft-Lyon Manuscript, MTP.

43. Ibid., 6–7.

44. Ibid., 230.

45. Ibid., 78.

46. Ibid., 223.

47. Samuel Clemens to Albert Bigelow Paine, March 2, 1910, Ashcroft-Lyon Manuscript, MTP.

48. Samuel Clemens, autobiographical dictation, August 6, 1909, MTP.

49. Harper and Brothers advertisements for the "author's national edition," MTP.

50. Mark Twain, "Remarks on Copyright," in *Mark Twain Speaking*, ed. Paul Fatout (Iowa City: University of Iowa Press, 1976), 535.

51. Mark Twain, "Concerning Copyright," in *Collected Tales, Sketches, Speeches, and Essays, 1891–1910*, ed. Louis Budd (New York: Library of America, 1992), 629.

52. Twain, "Remarks on Copyright," 534.

53. Mark Twain, quoted in Hill, *Mark Twain: God's Fool*, 164.

54. Samuel Clemens to William Dean Howells, January 16, 1904, in Smith and Gibson, eds., *Mark Twain–Howells Letters*, 779.

55. Twain, "Concerning Copyright," 628.

56. Samuel Clemens to Henry Huttleston Rogers, June [17?], 1906, in Lewis Leary, ed., *Mark Twain's Correspondence with Henry Huttleston Rogers, 1893–1909* (Berkeley: University of California Press, 1969), 611. The significance of Twain's relationship with this extremely wealthy Standard Oil executive can hardly be overestimated. Rogers became Twain's financial adviser and social companion during the Paige typesetter debacle as well as the failure of Charles L. Webster and Company, and he was instrumental in forging Twain's eventual exclusive contract with Harper and Brothers. He also advised Twain at the time to sign his copyrights over to his wife so that he would not lose them in the bankruptcy negotiations. It is almost certain that without Rogers, Twain would never have recovered financially from his bankruptcy and, most likely, the autobiography would never have been written. On the significance of "building" as a figure for writing in Twain's work, see Lowry, "Lottery Man," 3–16.

57. Bruce Bugbee, *Genesis of American Patent and Copyright Law* (Washington, DC: Public Affairs Press, 1967), 5.

58. For instance, Phillip Fisher notes that the name Mark Twain "should be seen not so much as a pen name but as a trademark," yet he neglects to mention Twain's actual attempts to register the name as such ("Appearing and Disappearing in Public: Social Space in Late-Nineteenth-Century America," in *Reconstructing American Literary History*, ed. Sacvan Bercovitch [Cambridge, MA: Harvard University Press, 1986], 165). Louis Budd confirms that Twain "thought of his now-revered signature as a logo—a brand name, even—rather than a pen name" ("Talent for Posturing," 78). And Susan Gillman agrees that Twain "hoped that his pen name, converted to a legal trademark, would hold his copyright in perpetuity" (*Dark Twins*, 184).

59. Budd, *Our Mark Twain*, 62.

60. Quoted in *Clemens v. Belford Clark and Co., Copyright Decisions, 1789–1909* (Washington, DC: U.S. Government Printing Office, 1985), 650–51.

61. Ralph Ashcroft to Samuel Clemens, May 14, 1907, MTP.

62. See Hill, *Mark Twain: God's Fool*, 183. See also R. R. Bowker, *Copyright: Its History and Its Law* (Boston: Houghton Mifflin, 1912), 98–99.

63. Rosemary Coombe, *The Cultural Life of Intellectual Properties: Authorship, Appropriation, and the Law* (Durham, NC: Duke University Press, 1998), 169.

64. Ibid., 174.

65. Gillman, *Dark Twins*, 32.

66. Cynthia D. Schrager, "Mark Twain and Mary Baker Eddy: Gendering the Transpersonal Subject," *American Literature* 70, no. 1 (March 1998): 51.

67. Samuel Clemens, autobiographical dictation, May 18, 1907, MTP.

68. Coombe, *Cultural Life of Intellectual Properties*, 89.

NOTES TO CHAPTER 3

1. Jack London to Cloudesly Johns, April 17, 1899, in Earle Labor, Robert C. Leitz III, and I. Milo Shepard, *The Letters of Jack London*, vol. 1, *1896–1905* (Stanford, CA: Stanford University Press, 1988), 62.

2. Jack London to A. L. Babcock, September 21, 1906, in Labor, Leitz, and Shepard, *Letters*, 609–10. Babcock responded, "Your signature does not correspond with that of the gentleman who gave me the draft, yet there is a similarity. The photograph which you enclosed, while it looks very much like the man who imposed upon me, would not, I think, pass inspection if you were both together, as I think there would be quite a difference in the general appearance of the two men" (September 28, 1906), thus confirming the two principal indexes—photo and signature—that would come to authenticate identity in the modern era. Babcock then suggests that London "have a lot of cards printed, possibly 1,000 or more,—at least a sufficient number to cover the country pretty thoroughly,—with your photograph and signature thereon, stating that an imposter is abroad in the land representing you from time to time, and offering a reward of say $500.00 for his apprehension, you would, in a few months, have no trouble landing him" (October 13, 1906). Yet he was compelled to insert "without giving it general publicity," on realizing, most likely, that such a tactic was as likely to multiply, as to diminish, the number of doubles.

3. Jack London to Jack London, December 23, 1910, in Labor, Leitz, and Shepard, *Letters*, 959.

4. Ibid.

5. Jack London to Edgar Sisson, April 11, 1914, in Labor, Leitz, and Shepard, *Letters*, 1327.

6. For a fascinating discussion of "how Jack London wrote to become 'Jack London,'" see Jonathan Auerbach, *Male Call: Becoming Jack London* (Durham, NC: Duke University Press, 1996). Auerbach focuses exclusively on London's early work, arguing that "once he became popular, London possessed an identity,

a life's story, that he then felt compelled to conserve" (20). In concentrating on how London became famous with his early work, however, *Male Call* would seem to reinscribe the literary "success story" that later work like *Martin Eden* so viciously critiques. In fact, I would claim that London's agency and property in his authorial persona was an ongoing problem that required complex negotiation throughout his career.

7. Ibid.

8. *Chicago Times Herald*, May 30, 1900, Jack London Scrapbook Microfilm, volume 1, Huntington Library, San Marino, CA (hereafter cited in the notes as JLSM).

9. In addition to the case discussed below, London was accused of plagiarizing parts of *The Call of the Wild*, which was said to be indebted to Egerton Young's *My Dogs of the Northland*; *Before Adam* said to be indebted to Stanley Waterloo's *The Story of Ab*; and *The Iron Heel* said to be indebted to Frank Harris's "The Bishop of London and Public Morality."

Plagiarism has tended to be relegated by the academic community to the nether regions of either undergraduate ethics or historical anecdote, foregrounding the legal issue of copyright as the field of more rigorous analytic interest. Thus, Susan Stewart claims that "plagiarism . . . is a crime legislated in England and America by the community of scholarship and not by the more general law" (*Crimes of Writing: Problems in the Containment of Representation* [Durham, NC: Duke University Press, 1991], 24). London's case, however, reveals that it is not always the community of scholars that performs the informal legislation of plagiarism accusations. For London, plagiarism operated as part of a more broadly cultural (as opposed to literary *or* legal) negotiation of a public image. In fact, I would argue that London's problems with both plagiarism and imposture indicate a larger crisis of authorial identity and literary value during this period.

10. "Singular Similarity of a Story Written by Jack London and One Printed Four Years before a New Literary Puzzle," *New York World*, March 25, 1906, 1.

11. Jack London to Samuel McClure, April 10, 1906, in Labor, Leitz, and Shepard, *Letters*, 568.

12. Ibid., 568–69.

13. Ibid., 570. The fact that the story was originally published in *McClure's* and not in the newspapers only confirms the confusion surrounding the distinction between journalism and literature in London's day. On the complex relation between journalism and literature during this era, see Shelley Fisher Fishkin, *From Fact to Fiction: Journalism and Imaginative Writing in America* (Baltimore: Johns Hopkins University Press, 1985); and Thomas Strychacz, *Modernism, Mass Culture, and Professionalism* (New York: Cambridge University Press, 1993), 45–116.

14. London to McClure, 570.

15. The letter was eventually published in the *World* on April 29, 1906,

under the title "Jack London's Explanations," and reprinted as "The Old Story" in *Bookman* 23 (June 1906): 369–71. In fact, *Bookman* had made it a pet project to follow London's problems with plagiarism, going so far as to claim that one of the accusations had itself been plagiarized. See "Virtue and Consistency," *Bookman* 25 (May 1907): 228–31.

16. Thus, London himself realized that his fame was enabled by the proprietary and generic confusions between one man's fact and another man's fiction in the new mass cultural public sphere. Nevertheless, criticism of London, until recently, has been mainly concerned with disentangling the facts of his life from the many fictions that derived from his fame. From the time that his widow, Charmian London, addressed her two-volume *The Book of Jack London* (New York: Century, 1921) to "those sincere and open-minded folk who want to know the real and living facts that I can tell" (vi), up through Joan Hedrick's claim in the introduction to *Solitary Comrade: Jack London and His Work* (Chapel Hill: University of North Carolina Press, 1982), that her study is an "attempt to understand the man who hid beneath the celebrated public persona" (xv), London criticism has tended to pose for itself the principally biographical problem of identifying the "real" Jack London. See also Irving Stone's "biographical novel," *Jack London: Sailor on Horseback* (New York: Signet, 1938); Richard O'Connor, *Jack London: A Biography* (Boston: Little, Brown, 1964); Andrew Sinclair, *Jack: A Biography of Jack London* (New York: Harper and Row, 1977); and Robert Barltrop, *Jack London: The Man, the Writer, the Rebel* (London: Pluto Press, 1976). The most interesting and useful biography of London was written by his estranged daughter: Joan London, *Jack London and His Times: An Unconventional Biography* (Seattle: University of Washington Press, 1939). For a discussion of the prejudices and motives behind the construction of London's biography, see Clarice Stasz, "The Social Construction of Biography: The Case of Jack London," *Modern Fiction Studies* 22 (1976): 51–71; and Richard W. Etulain, "The Lives of Jack London," in *Critical Essays on Jack London*, ed. Jacqueline Tavernier-Courbin (Boston: Little, Brown, 1983), 43–57.

17. "What Manner of Man Jack London Is," *New York World*, March 25, 1906, 1.

18. *Book Buyer*, February 19, 1900, JLSM.

19. Houghton Mifflin bulletin, 1990, JLSM.

20. Jack London, letter to the editor, *Post-Express*, March 8, 1990, JLSM.

21. Augustus Bridle and J. K. McDonald, "Lost in the Land of the Midnight Sun," *McClure's Magazine* (December 1901): 153.

22. Jack London, "Love of Life," in *Love of Life and Other Stories of Excitement and Romance* (New York: Scholastic, 1971), 9 (hereafter cited parenthetically in the text). For a more detailed discussion of London's use of Bridle and McDonald's article for this story, see Franklin Walker, *Jack London and the Klondike* (San Marino: Huntington Library, 1966), 245–54.

23. On this tactic of reduction as characteristic of naturalism more generally, see Walter Benn Michaels, *The Gold Standard and the Logic of Naturalism: American Literature at the Turn of the Century* (Berkeley: University of California Press, 1987); and Mark Seltzer, *Bodies and Machines* (New York: Routledge, 1992). It is noteworthy that London does not feature prominently in either book.

24. Jack London, *Martin Eden* (1909; repr., New York: Penguin Books, 1967), 453–54 (hereafter cited parenthetically in the text). It is worth noting that *Bookman*'s review of *Martin Eden* identified London as one of the founders of "modern primordialism" in fiction ("Primordialism and Some Recent Books," *Bookman* 30 [November 1909]: 278–80).

25. Michael Szalay affirms that "Eden's 'relentless logic' points out the inability of the worker Eden to cause, as an effect of his own actions, the popular success enjoyed by capitalist Eden, who, paradoxically, exploits his proletarian half" (*New Deal Modernism: American Literature and the Invention of the Welfare State* [Durham, NC: Duke University Press, 2000], 32). And Jonathan Auerbach shows how London attempts to resolve this problem such that "the author's literary life, turned into legend, stamps the seal of approval on the writing itself." According to Auerbach, "London manages to suggest an alternative source for all his writing, the author's personally brand-named true 'self'" (*Male Call*, 44–45). But it is precisely this "self," as a source of literary inspiration and value, that later work such as *Martin Eden* was invested in critiquing.

26. Joan Hedrick agrees that "Eden's fall into class-consciousness is also a fall into self-consciousness" (*Solitary Comrade*, 203), but she doesn't pursue the degree to which this "fall" functions as an anticipatory allegory for the birth of the author in the new literary marketplace.

27. On the relation between the imaginary and symbolic identification referenced here, see Slavoj Zizek, *The Sublime Object of Ideology* (New York: Routledge, 1989), 85–131.

28. London's relation to the widespread feminization of genteel literature that accompanied the rise of naturalism and modernism in the United States is particularly interesting since he epitomized the new "masculine" ethic of naturalist fiction while simultaneously relying on the most mushy and sentimental literary conventions in his representations of heterosexual romance. For a discussion of naturalism as a specifically masculine response to genteel literary conventions, see Christopher Wilson, *Labor of Words: Literary Professionalism in the Progressive Era* (Athens: University of Georgia Press, 1985), 1–17, 53–59, 141–68; and T. J. Jackson Lears, *No Place of Grace: Antimodernism and the Transformation of American Culture, 1880–1920* (Chicago: University of Chicago Press, 1981), 97–124.

29. Jack London, open letter, *San Francisco Bulletin*, January 17, 1910, in Labor, Leitz, and Shepard, *Letters*, 865.

30. This transition from a masculine working-class world to a feminized

bourgeois one similarly organizes Joan Hedrick's *Solitary Comrade*; however, while Hedrick is looking for the "real" Jack London, my concern is with the public articulation of London's biography.

31. Jack London, *John Barleycorn* (New York: Oxford University Press, 1913), 2 (hereafter cited parenthetically in the text).

32. See Leslie Fiedler, *Love and Death in the American Novel* (New York: Stein and Day, 1966). For a contemporary reappraisal of Fiedler's book, see Robyn Wiegman, *American Anatomies* (Durham, NC: Duke University Press, 1995), 149–62.

33. In this sense, London illustrates Michael Kimmel's claim that "at the turn of the century, *manhood* was replaced gradually by the term *masculinity*, which referred to a set of behavioral traits and attitudes that were contrasted now with a new opposite, *femininity*. Masculinity was something that had to be constantly demonstrated, the attainment of which was forever in question" (*Manhood in America: A Cultural History* [New York: Free Press, 1996], 120). This concept of masculinity as something that must be constantly proved has increasingly dominated studies of modern gender identity, gradually inverting the traditional priority of male over female identity. Thus Elisabeth Badinter succinctly affirms, "Masculinity comes second and must 'be created'" (*XY: On Masculine Identity*, trans. Lydia Davis [New York: Columbia University Press, 1995], 47). As Badinter's text so effectively details, masculinity in these terms figures as a series of "defense maneuvers: fear of women, fear of showing any sort of femininity, including tenderness, passivity, and caregiving to others, and of course fear of being desired by a man" (47). This model of modern masculinity as an ongoing "job to be done" against the constant threat of feminine engulfment powerfully illuminates the careers under consideration here. Badinter's book provides a useful overview of the scholarship on masculinity that has emerged in the wake of second-wave feminism. See also Dennis Altman, *The Homosexualization of America, the Americanization of the Homosexual* (New York: St. Martin's, 1982); Harry Brod, ed., *The Making of Masculinities: The New Men's Studies* (Boston: Unwin Hyman, 1987); David Gilmore, *Manhood in the Making: Cultural Concepts of Masculinity* (New Haven, CT: Yale University Press, 1990); Michael Kimmel, ed., *Changing Men: New Directions in Research on Men and Masculinity* (Newbury Park, CA: Sage, 1987); Ray Raphael, *The Men from the Boys: Rites of Passage in Male America* (Lincoln: University of Nebraska Press, 1988); and Lynne Segal, *Slow Motion: Changing Masculinities, Changing Men* (New Brunswick, NJ: Rutgers University Press, 1990).

34. Auerbach, *Male Call*, 5.

35. Ibid., 20.

36. James Williams, ed., "The Jack London Promotional Booklets," *Jack London Journal* (1998), 136.

37. Ibid.

38. Clarice Stasz alleges that Charmian herself wrote much of the article, though she states no evidence in support of this contention (*Jack London's Women* [Amherst: University of Massachusetts Press, 2001], 50).

39. Jack London to Houghton Mifflin, January 31, 1900, in Labor, Leitz, and Shepard, *Letters*, 148.

40. Ninetta Eames, "Jack London," *Overland Monthly* (May 1900): 418.

41. Macmillan Company, "Jack London: A Sketch of His Life and Work (1905)," reprinted in *Jack London Journal* (1998): 147.

42. Irving Stone, *Irving Stone's Jack London* (New York: Doubleday, 1977), ix (hereafter cited parenthetically in the text). This edition is a reprint of *Sailor on Horseback*, accompanied by a selection of short stories.

43. Charmian London to Irving Stone, August 24, 1936, Irving Stone File, Huntington London Collection, San Marino, CA (hereafter cited in the notes as ISF).

44. Irving Stone to Charmian London, August 27, 1936, ISF.

45. Charmian London to Irving Stone, October 9, 1936, ISF.

46. Irving Stone to Charmian London, October 10, 1936, ISF.

47. Irving Stone to Eliza Shepard, n.d., 1937, ISF.

48. Charmian London to Henry Maule, July 28, 1937, ISF.

49. Joan London, autobiographical essay, Joan London Collection, Huntington Library, 2, San Marino, CA (hereafter cited in the notes as JLC).

50. Joan London, "London Bridge," JLC, 2.

51. Ibid., 4.

52. Clipping from *American Weekly*, 1930, JLC.

53. Henry Maule to Joan London, July 5, 1938, JLC.

54. William Chaney to Jack London, June 4, 1897, Irving Stone Collection, Bancroft Library, Berkeley, CA (hereafter cited in the notes as ISC).

55. Ibid.

56. *San Francisco Chronicle*, June 1875, ISC.

57. William Chaney to Jack London, June 4, 1897, ISC.

58. Charmian London to Irving Stone, August 2, 1938, ISF.

59. "Jack London Rides Again," *Ken* 2, no. 4 (August 25, 1938): 26.

60. Ibid., 27.

61. Ibid., 26.

62. Ibid.

63. Szalay, *New Deal Modernism*, 29.

NOTES TO CHAPTER 4

1. Gertrude Stein, *Everybody's Autobiography* (New York: Vintage, 1937), 3 (hereafter cited parenthetically in the text).

2. Timothy Dow Adams, *Telling Lies in Modern American Autobiography* (Chapel Hill: University of North Carolina Press, 1990), 21. It is worth noting

that reviewers at the time generally adopted the same practice of referring to Stein by her full name.

3. Gertrude Stein, quoted in Carl Van Vechten, ed., *The Selected Writings of Gertrude Stein* (New York: Random House, 1945), vii.

4. "Authors and Books," *Golden Book* 18 (November 1933): 4A; and Frank Baisden, "Review of *ABT*," *Chattanooga Times*, September 10, 1933. For excerpts from the many reviews of *ABT*, see Ray Lewis White, *Gertrude Stein and Alice B. Toklas: A Reference Guide* (Boston: G. K. Hall, 1984), 35–52. More was written about Stein in the popular press during this year than any other year.

5. Gertrude Stein, *The Autobiography of Alice B. Toklas*, in Van Vechten, *Selected Writings*, 66.

6. For an excellent account of Stein's troubles with the U.S. literary marketplace, see Bryce Conrad, "Gertrude Stein in the American Marketplace, *Journal of Modern Literature* 19, no. 2 (Fall 1995): 215–33. Conrad concludes that "the American market would accept Stein only according to the formula she most wanted to avoid—that of the writer valued not for her art but for her sensationalized personality" (81). I intend to argue that there was a closer, more complicated relation between Stein's art and her personality, that Stein helped to determine the contours of her celebrity persona, and that the U.S. marketplace contributed to the logic of her art.

7. Richard Bridgeman affirms that *EA* was originally received "as a casual production, conceived for profit and exhibiting an egotism so inflated that it could not distinguish the line between prattle and ideas meriting public attention." Yet he concludes: "Today, though, it is clear that *EA* is one of her major successes" (*Gertrude Stein in Pieces* [New York: Oxford University Press, 1970], 284). Ironically, then, a text written to be popular ended up instead becoming a "classic" interesting only to Stein scholars.

8. Catherine R. Stimpson, "Gertrude Stein and the Lesbian Lie," in *American Women's Autobiography: Fea(s)ts of Memory*, ed. Margo Culley (Madison: University of Wisconsin Press, 1992), 152.

9. Ibid.

10. Amy Kaplan, *The Social Construction of American Realism* (Chicago: University of Chicago Press, 1988), 114–15.

11. Susan Schultz, "Gertrude Stein's Self-Advertisement," *Raritan* 12, no. 2 (Fall 1992): 86; Bob Perelman, *The Trouble with Genius: Reading Pound, Joyce, Stein, and Zukofsky* (Berkeley: University of California Press, 1994), 168; and Barbara Will, *Gertrude Stein, Modernism, and the Problem of "Genius"* (Edinburgh: Edinburgh University Press, 2000), 14.

12. See Lisa Ruddick, *Reading Gertrude Stein: Body, Text, Gnosis* (Ithaca, NY: Cornell University Press, 1990), 1–12, 55–137.

13. Otto Weininger, *Sex and Character* (New York: G. P. Putnam, 1906), 113. Gertrude Stein, quoted in Will, *Gertrude Stein*, 58.

14. Will, *Gertrude Stein*, 5.

15. Shari Benstock, *Women of the Left Bank: Paris, 1900–1940* (Austin: University of Texas Press, 1986), 166.

16. Gertrude Stein, quoted in Samuel M. Steward, *Dear Sammy: Letters from Gertrude Stein and Alice B. Toklas* (New York: St. Martin's, 1977), 55, 57.

17. Quoted in W. G. Rogers, *When This You See Remember Me* (New York: Avon, 1948), 99–100.

18. F. W. Dupree, quoted in Van Vechten, *Selected Writings*, xi. It is interesting to note that Edna St. Vincent Millay, who was touring the country at the same time as Stein, was also frequently depicted in ambiguously androgynous terms; however, for Millay it would be youth, not age, that would be emphasized. As one recent biographer affirms, "She was always—whether described by a male or female reporter—a lovely, fragile child" (Nancy Milford, *Savage Beauty: The Life of Edna St. Vincent Millay* [New York: Random House, 2001], 333). Neither one, clearly, could be portrayed as a sexually active adult woman. Millay's tour drew more crowds at the time, but Stein's has been remembered for longer, precisely because it was such a crossover act between avant-garde coterie and mass cultural popularity.

19. Stimpson, "Gertrude Stein," 153.

20. As Michael Szalay observes, "Being paid for writing does not produce for Stein a simple mistake, a problem in which market value is incommensurate with aesthetic identity, so much as it precipitates a crisis in which the very terms that initially constitute identity change" (*New Deal Modernism: American Literature and the Invention of the Welfare State* [Durham, NC: Duke University Press, 2000], 117).

21. Gertrude Stein, "And Now," in *How Writing Is Written: Volume II of the Previously Uncollected Writings of Gertrude Stein*, ed. Robert Bartlett Haas (Los Angeles: Black Sparrow Press, 1974), 63 (hereafter cited parenthetically in the text).

22. In a recent article that details Stein's "career-long project of representing the whole in and as writing," Jennifer Ashton argues that in her lectures in the United States, "Stein finally turns from a phenomenological model of wholes to a logical one, where the whole, instead of being attained through a cumulative experience of its parts, exists in an abstract form prior to any experience of its parts" ("Gertrude Stein for Anyone," *English Literary History* 64 [1997]: 289, 312). Rereading Stein in terms of her conceptual debts to William James and Alfred North Whitehead, Ashton convincingly shows how the apparent failure of *The Making of Americans* to really tell the whole story of everyone led Stein to reconsider the philosophical theory that might make such a project possible. What Ashton neglects to mention is that this reconsideration coincided with Stein's sudden celebrity. For Ashton, the shift seems to depend purely on the internal dynamic development of Stein's writing, and on her developing sense that

The Making of Americans was, to some degree, a failure. I would claim, however, that a close relation can be established between Stein's philosophical turn to a principle of "abstract form prior to any experience of its parts" and her brief, though dramatic immersion in the U.S. culture industries during the Depression era.

23. Bryce Conrad argues that Stein's belief that her popularity might derive from "having a small audience" is "confounding," and claims that such statements prove that Stein fundamentally misunderstood the nature of her U.S. popularity ("Stein in the American Marketplace," 231). Conrad, I believe, underestimates Stein's astuteness in this regard. Modernism in general achieved a certain mainstream cachet through advertising itself as obscure.

24. Catherine Parke, "'Simple Through Complication': Gertrude Stein Thinking," *American Literature* 60, no. 4 (December 1988): 555.

25. See Diana Souhami, *Gertrude and Alice* (San Francisco: Pandora, 1991), 195. Bob Perelman confirms that as a genius, Stein was "an ideal consumer as well as an ideal commodity" (*Trouble with Genius*, 167).

26. Gertrude Stein, quoted in Steward, *Dear Sammy*, 26.

27. Shultz, "Stein's Self-Advertisement," 86; and Parke, 559.

28. Donald Sutherland, in his influential early study, *Gertrude Stein: A Biography of Her Work* (New Haven, CT: Yale University Press, 1951), claims that "the idea that present thinking is the final reality was to be the axis or pole of Gertrude Stein's universe" (7). Allegra Stewart, in *Gertrude Stein and the Present* (Cambridge, MA: Harvard University Press, 1967), agrees that Stein's writing is centrally an expression of "the psychological experience of deep concentration, self-realization, and 'ingatheredness'" (vii).

29. Gertrude Stein, *The Geographical History of America, or The Relation of Human Nature to the Human Mind*, in *Gertrude Stein: Writings, 1932–1946*, ed. Catherine R. Stimpson and Harriet Chessman (New York: Library of America, 1998), 403 (hereafter cited parenthetically in the text).

30. Conrad, "Stein in the American Marketplace," 229–30.

31. Gertrude Stein, "Money," in *How Writing Is Written: Volume II of the Previously Uncollected Writings of Gertrude Stein*, ed. Robert Bartlett Haas (Los Angeles: Black Sparrow Press, 1974), 106.

32. Michael Szalay affirms that Stein's "interest in money has as much to do with literary form as with conservative politics" (*New Deal Modernism*, 89).

33. James Agee, "Stein's Way," *Time*, September 11, 1933, 57–60, quoted in White, *A Reference Guide*, 36.

34. Pierre Bourdieu, *The Field of Cultural Production: Essays on Art and Literature*, ed. Randal Johnson (New York: Columbia University Press, 1993), 40.

35. Ibid., 104.

36. On Cerf's amusing relationship with Stein, see *At Random: The Reminis-*

cences of Bennett Cerf (New York: Random House, 1977), 101–8. Cerf would be instrumental in cementing both Stein's critical reputation and popular reception in the United States. He stayed true to his promise, publishing whatever Stein wanted, even when he himself didn't understand it, culminating in the *Selected Writings*, which remains the standard introduction to Stein's work.

37. Bourdieu, *Field of Cultural Production*, 60.

38. "Testimony against Gertrude Stein," supplement to *transition* (February 1935): 2.

39. Gertrude Stein, "How Writing Is Written," in *How Writing Is Written: Volume II of the Previously Uncollected Writings of Gertrude Stein*, ed. Robert Bartlett Haas (Los Angeles: Black Sparrow Press, 1974), 151 (hereafter cited parenthetically in the text).

40. Significantly, of the nineteen books that sold over 1.2 million copies in the 1930s, more than half were mysteries (see Frank Luther Mott, *Golden Multitudes: The Story of Best Sellers in the United States* [New York: Macmillan, 1947], 313–14). Stein correspondingly changed her reading habits in this decade, claiming in *EA* that "now I buy only the cheapest detective and adventure stories and then I bought the most expensive history and poetry and literature" (146). She apparently calibrated her reading habits to her reputation by shifting from literary highbrow to popular middlebrow. As a member of modernist bohemia in Paris, her book purchases were not only literary, they were "expensive." If no one was buying her writing, its value might still be confirmed by the money she spent on her reading. As a U.S. celebrity, Stein now only buys the "cheapest" and most popular books. Significantly, people are now also paying money for her writing.

41. Gertrude Stein, "American Crimes and How They Matter," in *How Writing Is Written: Volume II of the Previously Uncollected Writings of Gertrude Stein*, ed. Robert Bartlett Haas (Los Angeles: Black Sparrow Press, 1974), 104.

42. Gertrude Stein, "American Newspapers," in *How Writing Is Written: Volume II of the Previously Uncollected Writings of Gertrude Stein*, ed. Robert Bartlett Haas (Los Angeles: Black Sparrow Press, 1974), 89.

NOTES TO CHAPTER 5

1. Edmund Wilson, "Ernest Hemingway: Gauge of Morale," in *Hemingway: The Critical Heritage*, ed. Jeffrey Meyers (London: Routledge, 1982), 304.

2. Ibid., 305.

3. John Raeburn, *Fame Became of Him: Hemingway as a Public Writer* (Bloomington: Indiana University Press, 1984), 13.

4. Ibid., 1, 201.

5. Leonard J. Leff, *Hemingway and His Conspirators: Hollywood, Scrib-*

ner's, and the Making of American Celebrity Culture (Lanham, MD: Rowman and Littlefield, 1997), 199.

6. Philip Young, *Ernest Hemingway: A Reconsideration* (University Park: Penn State University Press, 1966), 170 (hereafter cited parenthetically in the text).

7. Carl P. Eby, *Hemingway's Fetishism: Psychoanalysis and the Mirror of Manhood* (Albany: State University of New York Press, 1999), 206, 239.

8. Ibid., 2.

9. Debra A. Moddelmog, *Reading Desire: In Pursuit of Ernest Hemingway* (Ithaca, NY: Cornell University Press, 1999), 59.

10. Leff, *Hemingway and His Conspirators*, xvii.

11. Granville Hicks, *Nation*, reprinted in Jeffrey Meyers, ed., *Hemingway: The Criticial Heritage* (London: Routledge, 1982), 162–63.

12. Robert Coates, *New Yorker*, reprinted in Meyers, *Criticial Heritage*, 161.

13. Max Eastman, *New Republic*, reprinted in Meyers, *Criticial Heritage*, 176.

14. H. L. Mencken, *American Mercury*, reprinted in Meyers, *Criticial Heritage*, 170.

15. Coates, reprinted in Meyers, 161, 162.

16. Leff, *Hemingway and His Conspirators*, 165.

17. Raeburn, *Fame Became of Him*, 8.

18. F. Scott Fitzgerald to Maxwell Perkins, quoted in A. Scott Berg, *Maxwell Perkins: Editor of Genius* (New York: Pocket Books, 1978), 116–17.

19. Ernest Hemingway, quoted in Leff, *Hemingway and His Conspirators*, 102.

20. Andreas Huyssen, *After the Great Divide: Modernism, Mass Culture, Postmodernism* (Bloomington: Indiana University Press, 1986), 46, 55.

21. Ernest Hemingway, *Death in the Afternoon* (1982; repr., New York: Simon and Schuster, 1960), 120 (hereafter cited parenthetically in the text).

22. One exception is Leslie Fiedler, who affirms that Hemingway "became, in the course of time, the *persona* he had invented to preserve himself . . . in short, the Bull" (*Waiting for the End: A Portrait of Twentieth-Century American Literature and Its Writers* [New York: Stein and Day, 1964], 15).

23. Virginia Woolf, *New York Herald Tribune Books*, reprinted in Meyers, *Cultural Heritage*, 105.

24. Ernest Hemingway to Maxwell Perkins, July 24, 1926, in Carlos Baker, ed., *Ernest Hemingway: Selected Letters, 1917–1961* (New York: Scribner's, 1981), 211.

25. Ibid., August 26, 1926, 215.

26. Ibid., November 16, 1926, 223.

27. Ibid., July 24, 1926, 211.

28. Ibid., September 7, 1935, 421.

29. Gertrude Stein, *The Autobiography of Alice B. Toklas*, in *Selected Writings of Gertrude Stein*, ed. Carl Van Vechten (New York: Vintage, 1945), 204.

30. Ernest Hemingway to Sherwood Anderson, March 9, 1922, in Baker, *Selected Letters*, 62.

31. Ernest Hemingway to Janet Flanner, April 8, 1933, in Baker, *Selected Letters*, 387–88.

32. Ernest Hemingway, introduction to *This Must Be the Place: Memoirs of Montparnasse by Jimmie "the Barman" Charters*, as told to Morrill Cody, ed. Hugh Ford (New York: Collier Books, 1937), 1 (hereafter cited parenthetically in the text).

33. James R. Mellow, *Hemingway: A Life without Consequences* (Reading, PA: Addison-Wesley, 1992), 397.

34. Raeburn, *Fame Became of Him*, 141.

35. Ibid., 38, 43.

36. Ernest Hemingway, *The Sun Also Rises* (New York: Scribner's, 1926), 172.

37. Nancy R. Comley and Robert Scholes, *Hemingway's Genders: Rereading the Hemingway Text* (New Haven, CT: Yale University Press, 1994), 107.

38. Ernest Hemingway, quoted in Matthew Bruccoli, *Fitzgerald and Hemingway: A Dangerous Friendship* (New York: Carroll and Graf, 1994), 160.

39. F. Scott Fitzgerald, quoted in Bruccoli, *A Dangerous Friendship*, 175; and F. Scott Fitzgerald, *The Crack Up*, ed. Edmund Wilson (New York: New Directions, 1956), 99.

40. See Scott Donaldson, *Hemingway vs. Fitzgerald: The Rise and Fall of a Literary Friendship* (New York: Overlook, 1999), 303.

41. Ibid., 219.

42. Arnold Gingrich, *Nothing but People: The Early Days at Esquire, a Personal History, 1928–1958* (New York: Crown, 1971), 81.

43. Ibid., 10. See also Theodore Peterson, *Magazines in the Twentieth Century* (Urbana: University of Illinois Press, 1964), 273–81. Using Hemingway's name as bait, Gingrich initially offered one hundred dollars an article, but also promised immediate payment (Hemingway himself required that he get twice as much as Gingrich's going rate). This was far less than most authors (especially Hemingway and Fitzgerald) received from the mainstream "slicks," but considerably more than little magazines offered.

44. Ernest Hemingway, "The Snows of Kilimanjaro," *Esquire* (August 1936), 41.

45. Ernest Hemingway, quoted in Bruccoli, *A Dangerous Friendship*, 190.

46. Ibid., 132.

47. See Bruccoli, *A Dangerous Friendship*, 208.

48. Ibid., 1.

49. See Arnold Gingrich, "Scott, Ernest, and Whoever," *Esquire*, December

1966, 188; and Sheila Graham, *The Real F. Scott Fitzgerald* (New York: Grosset and Dunlap, 1976), 120. Matthew Bruccoli affirms, "This controversy is unprecedented in American literary history" (*A Dangerous Friendship*, 109 n. 3).

50. Ernest Hemingway, *A Moveable Feast* (New York: Scribner's, 1964), 190 (hereafter cited parenthetically in the text).

51. Ernest Hemingway to Charles Scribner, September 6–7, 1949, in Baker, *Selected Letters*, 673.

52. Leff, *Hemingway and His Conspirators*, 79.

53. Michael Szalay, *New Deal Modernism: American Literature and the Invention of the Welfare State* (Durham, NC: Duke University Press, 2000), 95.

54. Ernest Hemingway, quoted in Leff, *Hemingway and His Conspirators*, 3.

55. Ernest Hemingway to James Gamble, March 3, 1919, in Baker, *Selected Letters*, 21.

56. Hemingway to Perkins, June 5, 1926, in Baker, *Selected Letters*, 209.

57. Carlos Baker, *Hemingway: The Writer as Artist* (1952; repr., Princeton, NJ: Princeton University Press, 1972), 78, 79.

58. Hemingway to Perkins, February 14, 1927, in Baker, *Selected Letters*, 245.

59. Ibid., February 19, 1927, 247.

60. Ibid., December 7, 1932, 379. On Hollywood's use of Hemingway's image to promote films based on his books, see Frank M. Laurence, *Hemingway and the Movies* (Jackson: University of Mississippi Press, 1981).

61. Raeburn, *Fame Became of Him*, 141, 38, 43.

62. Hemingway to Perkins, June 28, 1932, in Baker, *Selected Letters*, 361.

63. Mellow, *A Life without Consequences*, 566, 573, 577.

64. Ernest Hemingway to Thomas Bledsoe, January 17 and 31, 1952, in Baker, *Selected Letters*, 748.

65. Ernest Hemingway to Wallace Meyer, February 21, 1952, in Baker, *Selected Letters*, 751.

66. Ernest Hemingway to Philip Young, March 6, 1952, in Baker, *Selected Letters*, 761. None of the correspondence concerning Young's study is quoted in his preface since, as he notes, "Hemingway wrote out an edict, with his wife as witness to it, to the effect that his letters, or even parts of them, were never to be published." Nevertheless, he realizes that "no one knows what 'never' to be published, in this case, means. One thing it almost surely does not mean is 'never.' It certainly, however, does not mean 'now'" (9).

67. Hemingway to Young, May 27, 1952, in Baker, *Selected Letters*, 761–62.

68. Philip Young, "Hemingway's Manuscripts: The Vault Reconsidered," *Studies in American Fiction* 2, no. 1 (Spring 1974): 8.

69. Kenneth S. Lynn, *Hemingway* (New York: Fawcett Columbine, 1987), 10.

70. Comley and Scholes, *Hemingway's Genders*, ix.

71. Eby, *Hemingway's Fetishism*, 206.

72. Mark Spilka, *Hemingway's Quarrel with Androgyny* (Lincoln: University of Nebraska Press, 1990), 3, 334.

73. Lance Morrow, "A Quarter-Century Later, the Myth Endures," *Time*, August 25, 1986, 70.

74. Indeed, the publication of *The Garden of Eden* coincided with a veritable avalanche of Hemingway biographies, including Lynn's *Hemingway* (1987), Mellow's *A Life without Consequences* (1992), Peter Griffin's *Along with Youth* (1985), and Michael Reynolds's five-volume biography (1986–99).

75. Ernest Hemingway, *The Garden of Eden* (New York: Scribner's, 1986), 10 (hereafter cited parenthetically in the text).

76. Actually, in the unedited manuscript version, Catherine suggests publishing only five copies, for themselves and their friends Nick and Barbara, who editor Tom Jenks excised from the published text. David then reminds her that you have to sell a book to obtain copyright. This conversation underlines the tension in modernist authorship between writing as the discourse of an exclusive social coterie and writing as the expression of the individual authorial consciousness.

77. J. Gerald Kennedy, "Hemingway's Gender Trouble," *American Literature* 63, no. 2 (June 1991): 205.

78. Robert E. Fleming, "The Endings of Hemingway's *Garden of Eden*," in *Ernest Hemingway: Seven Decades of Criticism*, ed. Linda Wagner-Martin (East Lansing: Michigan State University Press, 1998), 290. Rose Marie Burwell agrees that "the narrative innovation of *Eden* was significantly obscured in its editing for publication" (*Hemingway: The Postwar Years and the Posthumous Novels* [New York: Cambridge University Press, 1996], 5). Fleming's article, originally published in *American Literature* in 1989, and Burwell's book-length study, confirmed that the academic community was unhappy with Jenks's work on the manuscript. Jenks himself, in a talk at the 1986 Modern Language Association Convention, later published in the *Hemingway Review*, claimed that he edited it "not for any special audience, but for general readers" ("Editing Hemingway: *The Garden of Eden*," *Hemingway Review* [Fall 1987]: 30).

NOTES TO CHAPTER 6

Epigraph. The epigraph to this chapter is drawn from Norman Mailer, *Of a Fire on the Moon* (New York: New American Library, 1969), 101.

1. Norman Mailer, *The Time of Our Time* (New York: Modern Library, 1998), 3–4. On the boxing match with Morley Callaghan, see James R. Mellow, *Hemingway: A Life without Consequences* (Reading, PA: Addison-Wesley, 1992), 386–88. See also Morley Callaghan, *That Summer in Paris* (New York: Dell, 1963).

2. Norman Mailer, *Advertisements for Myself* (New York: Perigree Books, 1959), 3 (hereafter cited parenthetically in the text).

3. Leo Braudy, ed., *Norman Mailer: A Collection of Critical Essays* (Englewood Cliffs, NJ: Prentice Hall, 1972), 1.

4. Mary Dearborn, *Mailer: A Biography* (New York: Houghton Mifflin, 1999), 26.

5. On the sense of historical belatedness that plagued post–World War II novelists, see John Aldridge, *After the Lost Generation* (New York: Noonday, 1958).

6. This is not to say that there aren't still celebrity authors. There are many, and many of them continue to ballast their fame with an allure of high cultural cachet. Nevertheless, the postmodern fragmentation of the cultural marketplace and the postfeminist dismantling of traditional U.S. masculinity have greatly diminished the scale and scope of authorial celebrity as I define it here. For an analysis of postmodern authorial stars, see Joe Moran, *Star Authors: Literary Celebrity in America* (London: Pluto Press, 2000).

7. Norman Mailer, interview in "Rugged Times," *New Yorker* 24 (October 23, 1948): 25.

8. Norman Podhoretz, quoted in Peter Manso, *Mailer: His Life and Times* (New York: Penguin Books, 1985), 266. Manso's biography is composed of quotes from Mailer and his contemporaries—a form that as with Denis Brian's *The True Gen: An Intimate Portrait of Hemingway by Those Who Knew Him* (New York: Delta, 1981), highlights the dialectical composition of the celebrity author's persona. As Mailer's second wife, Adele, notes in Manso's book, "You have to understand who all the people are who are talking about Norman. Norman responds to that, it's part of his persona" (236).

9. *The Deer Park* was rejected by Rinehart, Random House, Knopf, Scribner's, Harper and Row, Simon and Schuster, and Harcourt, Brace before finally being accepted by Putnam's. See Hillary Mills, *Mailer: A Biography* (New York: Empire, 1982), 141–61.

10. Richard Poirier, who remains Mailer's most astute critic, claims that "the time of his time probably has no historical equivalent, only a literary one" (*Norman Mailer* [New York: Viking, 1972], 94), confirming that Mailer's sense of being historically out of synch is precisely a strategy of being literary in the modernist sense.

11. Norman Mailer, quoted in Manso, *Mailer*, 167.

12. According to Mary Dearborn, Mailer developed five major accents: "a British, upper-crust one . . . , a black jazz player's, a kind of gangster one, an Irish brogue, and, most notably, his Texas voice. He'd often use one accent at one party and then, moving on to another venue, adopt a different one" (*A Biography*, 109). Critics have made much of Mailer's protean abilities in this regard;

nevertheless, it is worth indicating at this point that a fundamentally masculine ethos ballasts them all.

13. Mills, *A Biography*, 157.

14. John Tebbel, *A History of Book Publishing in the United States*, vol. 4, *The Great Change, 1940–1980* (New York: R. R. Bowker, 1981), 724.

15. Poirier, *Norman Mailer*, 108.

16. On post–World War II transformations in gender roles and sexuality, see Barbara Ehrenreich, *The Hearts of Men: American Dreams and the Flight from Commitment* (Garden City, NJ: Anchor Books, 1983); Kaja Silverman, *Male Subjectivity at the Margins* (New York: Routledge, 1992); David Savran, *Taking It Like a Man* (Princeton, NJ: Princeton University Press, 1998); and Naomi Wolf, *Stiffed: The Betrayal of the American Man* (New York: Perennial, 1999).

17. For a discussion of Mailer's relationship with the Beats in terms of U.S. models of masculinity, see Savran, *Taking It Like a Man*, 3–103.

18. Norman Mailer, *The Presidential Papers* (New York: Bantam, 1964), 103, 104 (hereafter cited parenthetically in the text).

19. Richard Poirier agrees that Mailer's work exhibits "a violent and unsuccessful magnification of the self through language in the effort to meet and overwhelm the phenomenon of death. Mailer, who is surely one of our most astute literary critics, shows his awareness of these issues whenever he talks of Hemingway" (*The Performing Self: Compositions and Decompositions in the Language of Contemporary Life* [New Brunswick, NJ: Rutgers University Press, 1992], 102).

20. Norman Mailer, *The Armies of the Night: History as a Novel, the Novel as History* (New York: Penguin, 1968), 200 (hereafter abbreviated *AN*. All further citations are from this edition).

21. Philip D. Beidler, *Scriptures for a Generation: What We Were Reading in the Sixties* (Athens: University of Georgia Press, 1994), 134.

22. Alan Trachtenberg, "Mailer on the Steps of the Pentagon," *Nation*, May 27, 1968, 702.

23. Henry Resnick, "Hand on the Pulse of America," *Saturday Review*, May 4, 1968, 25.

24. Beidler, *Scriptures for a Generation*, 134.

25. Norman Mailer, *Pieces and Pontifications* (Boston: Little, Brown, 1982), 186, 187. Mailer apparently had read *The Education* while at Harvard. It is also worth noting that *The Americanization of Edward Bok* appears on a list Mailer provided for Harvard of books he was reading. See Mills, *A Biography*, 43.

26. Barbara Probst Solomon, quoted in Mailer, *Pieces and Pontifications*, 187.

27. Norman Mailer, *Of a Fire on the Moon* (New York: New American Library, 1969), 9 (hereafter cited parenthetically in the text).

28. Gordon Taylor, "Of Adams and Aquarius," *American Literature* 46 (March 1974): 68–82. See also Robert Solataroff, *Down Mailer's Way* (Urbana: University of Illinois Press, 1974), 218–19.

29. Norman Mailer, quoted in Mills, *A Biography*, 276.

30. Gloria Steinem, quoted in Manso, *Mailer*, 588.

31. Kate Millett, *Sexual Politics* (New York: Equinox, 1969), 314.

32. Norman Mailer, *The Prisoner of Sex* (New York: Signet, 1971), 11 (hereafter cited parenthetically in the text).

33. Michael K. Glenday, *Norman Mailer* (New York: St. Martin's, 1995), 40.

34. Norman Mailer, quoted in Mills, *A Biography*, 400.

35. Norman Mailer, *Cannibals and Christians* (New York: Dell, 1966), 7.

36. *Marilyn: A Biography by Norman Mailer* (New York: Alskog, 1972), 15 (hereafter cited parenthetically in the text).

37. Pauline Kael, quoted in Mills, *A Biography*, 406.

38. Norman Mailer, *Of Women and Their Elegance* (New York: Tor, 1980), 130.

39. Norman Mailer, quoted in "Two Myths Converge: NM discovers MM," *Time*, July 16, 1973, 64.

40. "Two Myths Converge," 63.

41. See Dearborn, *A Biography*, 314.

42. Glenday, *Norman Mailer*, 13.

43. Norman Mailer, *St. George and the Godfather* (New York: Signet, 1972), 56.

44. Norman Mailer, *The Fight* (New York: Vintage, 1975), 31(hereafter cited parenthetically in the text).

45. Richard Stern, "Where Is That Self-Mocking Literary Imp?" *Chicago* 29 (January 1980): 108.

46. Sean McCann, "The Imperiled Republic: Normal Mailer and the Poetics of Anti-Liberalism," *English Literary History* 67 (2000): 295.

NOTES TO THE CODA

1. Joe Moran, *Star Authors: Literary Celebrity in America* (London: Pluto Press, 2000), 116. Moran's other examples are John Updike, Phillip Roth, and Cathy Acker. It is interesting to note in this regard that both Updike and Roth achieved their most prominent celebrity in the 1960s. None of these authors has been able to command either the high cultural cachet or mainstream popularity of celebrity authors in the modern era. It is also worth mentioning that DeLillo's earlier novel about celebrity, *Great Jones Street*, deals with a rock musician, and that one of his first major interviews was with Anthony DeCurtis for *Rolling Stone*. One could argue that musical celebrities, from Bob Dylan to Kurt Cobain,

have taken up the modernist model of authorial celebrity, posing as both solitary geniuses and pop icons, and migrating from autonomous artistic milieus to mainstream acclaim. But that's material for another book.

2. Moran, *Star Authors*, 129. See also Mark Osteen, "Becoming Incorporated: Spectacular Authorship and Delillo's *Mao II*," *Modern Fiction Studies* 45, no. 3 (Fall 1999), which confirms that Bill Gray, the protagonist of *Mao II*, "exemplifies the Romantic or Dedalian model of authorship in its death throes" (643).

3. Moran, *Star Authors*, 117.

4. Don Delillo, quoted in Osteen, "Becoming Incorporated," 664.

5. Moran, *Star Authors*, 120, 54.

6. J. D. Salinger, quoted in Paul Alexander, *Salinger: A Biography* (Los Angeles: Renaissance Books, 1999), 250. Like other critics, Alexander makes much of the fact that "Salinger has stayed in the public eye by *withdrawing* from it" (26), but such a paradox only affirms that the Hemingway model is no longer available.

7. Charles Newman, *The Post-Modern Aura: The Act of Fiction in the Age of Inflation* (Evanston, IL: Northwestern University Press, 1985), 172.

8. J. D. Salinger, *Raise High the Roof Beam, Carpenter, and Seymour: An Introduction* (New York: Bantam, 1959), 105.

9. Ian Hamilton, *In Search of J. D. Salinger* (New York: Random House, 1988), 7.

10. Joyce Maynard, *At Home in the World* (New York: Picador, 1998), 302.

11. Margaret Salinger, *Dream Catcher* (New York: Washington Square Press, 2000), 424.

12. André Schiffrin, *The Business of Books: How International Conglomerates Took Over Publishing and Changed the Way We Read* (New York: Verso, 2000), 70, 152.

13. Ibid., 7. See also Lewis Coser, Charles Kadushin, and Walter Powell, *Books: The Culture and Commerce of Publishing* (New York: Basic Books, 1982); John Tebbel, *A History of Book Publishing in the United States*, vol. 4, *The Great Change, 1940–1980* (New York: R. R. Bowker, 1981); and Lynn Hirschberg, "Nothing Random," *New York Times Magazine*, July 20, 2003, 28–66.

Index

Abbott, Lyman, 53
Adams, Charles Francis, 33–34, 36
Adams Henry, 23–24, 29–41, 44,
47–52, 54–57, 115–16, 177,
185–87, 189; *Education of Henry
Adams,* 23–24, 29–40, 43, 49–51,
54–56, 115–16, 185–86, 230n. 25;
and father, relationship to, 33–34;
as Harvard student, 35–36; *History of the United States Under the
Administrations of Thomas Jefferson and James Madison,* 39, 47; as
journalist, 34, 37–39; on literary
form, 36–37; as modernist, 29–30,
54–56; "The New York Gold Conspiracy," 38; "The Session," 38
Adams, John, 44
Adams, John Quincy, 44
Addams, Jane, 53
Agee, James, 131
Alcott, Louisa May, 57; *Little
Women,* 57
Ali Muhammad, 194–95
Allen, Helen, 76
American Publishing Co., 77
Anderson, Sherwood, 152
Angert, Eugene, 72–73; "Is Mark
Twain Dead?" 72–73
Apparel Arts, 155
Arnold, Matthew, 61
Ashcroft, Ralph, 74–76, 80
Ashton, Jennifer, 222n. 22

Athenaeum, The, 29
Atkins, Susan, 196
Atlantic Monthly, 55, 132, 140
Atwan, Robert, 58, 64
Audience, 2, 4, 8, 23, 29, 46, 185;
agency of, 51–53, 64, 81, 91,
97–98; elite vs. mainstream, 6, 17,
131–32, 181; expectations of, 65;
as feminine, 51–53, 64, 81, 91,
97–98; as potential authors,
11–12, 14–15; and subscription
publishing, 61–62
Auerbach, Jonathan, 103, 215n. 6,
218n. 23
Authorship, 4–8, 11–17, 19–22,
36–38, 45–49, 57–65, 117, 20,
140–65, 175–87, 193, 196,
199–200; and audience, 45–46,
64–65, 143–51, 180–81; authorrecluse, 197–99; and autobiography, 7–8, 36–37, 47, 57–61,
63–65, 78–82, 125–27; and
bullfighting, 144, 163–64; and
celebrity, 4–7, 12–17, 19, 62, 64,
90–92, 97–98, 117, 140, 144,
156–57, 162–64, 168, 175–80; as
corporate, 59, 78–82; "Death of
the Author," 4–5; democratization
of, 11–12; and genius, 4–6, 120,
127, 177–78, 187, 196–99; as homoerotic, 143, 151–58; and masculinity, 139, 140–43, 146–51,

233

Authorship (*Continued*)
175–77, 193; modernist ideas of,
64–65, 118, 120, 127–28, 134,
139, 141, 155–58, 173, 175–80,
184–86, 196–98; and personality,
6, 13, 84–85, 117, 175–80,
199–200; "What is an Author?"
4–5
Autobiography, 3, 57–65, 68–82,
115–19, 203n. 19, 208n. 8; "autobiographical pact" (Lejeuene), 7–8,
115; as democratic, 59–65,
125–29; Howells on, 60–61; intellectual property, relationship to,
72–82; origin as term, 208n. 8; rise
of, 57; in third person, 29–32,
44–47, 51–54
Autograph, 13–14, 42–54; collecting
of, 42–45. *See also* Signature

Babcock, A. L., 215n. 2
Badinter, Elisabeth, 219n. 33
Baker, Carlos, 161, 165, 168
Barthes, Roland, 4–6, 8, 202n. 11;
"Death of the Author," 4
Baudrillard, Jean, 202n. 11
Beats, the, 182–83, 184, 200
Beckett, Samuel, 188
Beecher, Henry Ward, 44–45
Beidler, Philip, 184–85
Benstock, Shari, 120
Bertelsmann, 200
Bestsellers, 12, 205n. 42
Biography, 158–62, 164
Bird, Bill, 145
Blasing, Mutlu Konuk, 7
Bledsoe, Thomas, 165–67
Blodgett, D. J., 79–80
Bok, Edward, 23–24, 29–31, 39–49,
51–57, 115–16, 187, 199, 209n.
25; *Americanization of Edward
Bok*, 23–24, 29–31, 39–47, 52–53,
55–56, 115–16, 230n. 25; as auto-
graph collector, 23–24, 29, 40,

44–49, 51–53; as editor of *Ladies'
Home Journal*, 23–24, 29, 40,
44–49, 51–53; "Modern Literary
King," 45–46; *Twice Thirty*, 53–54
Bookman, 12, 217n. 15
Books That Changed Our Minds, 29
Booth, William Stone, 73; *Some Char-
acteristic Signatures of Francis
Bacon*, 73
Borus, Daniel, 2
Bourdieu, Pierre, 6, 66, 131–33; *The
Field of Cultural Production*, 6,
66, 131–33
Brandeis, Louis, 9–11, 13
Braques, Georges, 133
Braudy, Leo, 176
Breit, Harvey, 157
Bridgeman, Richard, 221n. 7
Bridle, Augustus, 86–87, 89–90
Bronte, Charlotte, 119
Brooklyn Eagle, 40
Brooks, Phillips, 43
Brooks, Van Wyck, 181
Broom, 132
Bruccoli, Matthew, 156
Budd, Louis, 79, 211n. 18, 214n. 58
Bugbee, Bruce, 79
Burke, Séan, 5
Burwell, Rose Marie, 228n. 78

Callaghan, Morley, 175–76
Cawelti, John, 201n. 3
Celebrity: and autobiography, 7–8,
57, 63, 68, 78–82, 117, 125–28;
cinematic, 191–94; and death,
65–74, 131–37, 158–67, 184–95;
Dyer on, 3; and genius, 83–84,
118–21, 131–37; and identity crisis, 1–2, 122–27; as intellectual
property, 12–13, 15–16, 59,
74–82; literary, 1, 4–6, 13–17, 19,
41–47, 57–89, 97–98, 103–9,
115–18, 121–23, 126–28, 131–37,
139–41, 143–46, 152–58, 162–66,

168, 170–73, 175–80, 183–85,
193–200; Marshall on, 3–4; musi-
cal, 231n. 1; theories of, 3–4. *See
also* Personality; Publicity
Censorship, 150
Century Magazine, 57
Cerf, Bennett, 21, 132, 145, 223n. 36;
relationship to Gertrude Stein, 132,
223n. 36
Cézanne, Paul, 123
Chaney, William, 109–11
Charles L. Webster and Co., 60
Christian Science, 81
Claire Marie Press, 132
Clemens, Clara (Samassoud), 59,
74–75
Clemens, Jean, 74
Clemens, Samuel. *See* Twain, Mark
Clemens, Susy, 68
Clemens v. Belford Clark and Co.,
79–80
Coates, Robert, 144
Cobain, Kurt, 231n. 1
Colliers, 84
Collins, Jackie, 199
Comley, Nancy, 154, 169
Conrad, Bryce, 129, 221n. 6, 223n. 23
Contact Editions, 145
Coombe, Rosemary, 80, 82
Cooper, Gary, 162
Copyright, 9–10, 16, 73–74, 139,
193; international, 38, 59; Twain
on, 24, 59, 76–82. *See also* Intel-
lectual property
Coser, Lewis, 19
Cosmopolitan Magazine, 65
Cowley, Malcolm, 29, 156, 165
Cox, James, 208n. 8
Cultural studies, 3, 30
Curtis, Cyrus, 209n. 25

Dearborn, Mary, 176, 229n. 12
Decker, William, 208n. 7
DeCurtis, Anthony, 231n. 1

Delillo, Don, 197–98, 231n. 1; *Great
Jones Street,* 231n. 1; *Mao II,* 197
Derrida, Jacques, 4–5, 42, 44, 202n.
11
DeVoto, Bernard, 58, 67, 69
Dillinger, John, 135–36
Doubleday and Doran, 107
Double Dealer, 145
Douglass, Ann, 19; *The Feminization
of American Culture,* 19
Dreiser, Theodore, 118
Dupree, F. W., 121
Dyer, Richard, 3, 201n. 6; *Stars,* 3,
201n. 6
Dylan, Bob, 231n. 1

Eakin, John Paul, 7–8
Eames, Ninetta, 103–4, 111
Eastman, Max, 144
Eby, Carl, 142, 169; *Hemingway's
Fetishism,* 142, 169
Eddy, Mary Baker, 81
Edinburgh Review, 38
El Greco, 154
Eliot, George, 119
Eliot, T.S., 5–6, 29, 158; "Tradition
and the Individual Talent," 5–6,
158
Emerson, Ralph Waldo, 43–44
Esquire, 155
Exley, Frederick, 182

Fame. *See* Celebrity
Faulkner, William, 178
Feminism, 22–23, 27, 177–78,
187–94, 199
Fenton, Charles, 165; *The Apprentice-
ship of Ernest Hemingway,* 165
Fetishism, 42
Fiedler, Leslie, 100, 225n. 22
Field of cultural production, 6, 26,
29–30, 59, 77, 82, 131–34, 139,
143–45, 167–68, 178–81,
198–200. *See also* Bourdieu, Pierre

London, Jack, 2, 18, 21, 24–25, 57, 83–114, 122, 139, 197, 216n. 9, 218n. 25; *Before Adam*, 216n. 9; *Call of the Wild*, 104, 216n. 9; illegitimacy of, 25, 103, 105–7, 110; impersonations of, 83–87; *Iron Heel*, 216n. 9; *John Barleycorn*, 98–103, 112; "Love of Life," 86–87, 89–90, 92; "Man on Trail," 103; *Martin Eden*, 25, 57, 85, 90–98, 101–3, 105, 114, 122, 216n. 9, 218n. 25; and masculinity, 85, 99–102, 105; plagiarism accusations, 86–90, 216n. 9; as pseudonym, 89, 104; *Son of the Wolf*, 89, 103
London, Joan, 105, 107–9, 217n. 16; *Jack London and His Times*, 109, 217n. 16
Longfellow, Henry Wadsworth, 41, 43
Loos, Anita, 2
"Lost in the Land of the Midnight Sun," 86–87, 89–90
Lowell, James Russell, 41
Lowry, Richard, 58
Lynn, Kenneth, 169
Lyon, Isabel, 74–76

Macmillan, 103–4
Madison, Charles, 20
Mailer, Norman, 18, 22, 27, 85, 175–97; and Adams, relationship to, 177, 186; *Advertisements for Myself*, 27, 175–77, 179–83, 194; *American Dream*, 187; *Ancient Evenings*, 195–96; *Armies of the Night*, 183–86, 189; *Barbary Shore*, 27, 175, 178, 181; *Cannibals and Christians*, 192; *Deer Park*, 27, 175, 178, 181–82; *Executioner's Song*, 195–96; and feminism, 22, 27, 177–78, 187–94; *The Fight*, 183, 194–95; *Harlot's Ghost*, 196; and Hemingway, rela-

tionship to, 27, 175–77, 183–86, 195; *Marilyn: A Biography*, 191–94; and masculinity, 18, 22, 27, 176–78, 182–83, 185–94; *Miami and the Siege of Chicago*, 183; *Naked and the Dead*, 27, 177–78; *Of a Fire on the Moon*, 183, 186–87; *Presidential Papers*, 183, 192; *Prisoner of Sex*, 27, 183, 188–91; *St. George and the Godfather*, 183, 194; *Time of Our Time*, 175
Mallarmé, Stéphane, 4
Manso, Peter, 229n. 8
Mark Twain Company, 24, 59, 73–76, 79–82, 213n. 39
Mark Twain Papers and Project, 70, 75, 79
Marshall, P. David, 3–5; *Celebrity and Power*, 3–5
Martin, Jay, 64
Masculinity, 22–27, 49–54, 85, 98–102, 104–6, 139–58, 172, 176–78, 182–94, 199, 218n. 28; crisis of, 17–19, 22–23; and genius, 120; and homophobia, 151–58; as performative, 100–101, 182, 190–91, 219n. 33
Mass culture, 2–4, 11–13, 18–27, 29–31, 40, 118, 148, 188; as feminine, 18, 49–51, 122, 146; and modernism, 17–18, 24, 26, 49–51, 122, 139–41, 143–51, 155–58, 161, 167–68, 172–73, 175–78, 184–96; and publishing, 19–22, 180–81, 199–200
Matisse, Henri, 120, 123, 133
Maule, Henry, 107–9
Mauss, Marcel, 48; *The Gift*, 48
Maynard, Joyce, 199; *At Home in the World*, 199
McCalmon, Robert, 145, 154–55
McCann, Sean, 196
McClure, Samuel, 86–89

About the Author

Loren Glass is Assistant Professor of English and Cultural Studies at the University of Iowa.